Language, Schooling, and Cultural Conflict

Language, Schooling, and Cultural Conflict

The Origins of the French-Language Controversy in Ontario

CHAD GAFFIELD

McGill-Queen's University Press
Kingston and Montreal

©McGill-Queen's University Press 1987
ISBN 0-7735-0602-0

Legal deposit 2d quarter 1987
Bibliothèque nationale du Québec

Printed in Canada

This book has been published with the help of a grant
from the Social Science Federation of Canada, using
funds provided by the Social Sciences and Humanities
Research Council of Canada.

Printed on acid-free paper

Canadian Cataloguing in Publication Data

Gaffield, Chad, 1951-
Language, schooling, and cultural conflict
Includes index.
ISBN 0-7735-0602-0
1. Language and education – Ontario – Prescott
(County) – History – 19th century. 2. Canada –
English–French relations. I. Title.
FC3095.P74Z58 1987   971.3'86   c87-093276-4
F1059.P74G33 1987

To my family

Contents

Tables

Figures

Preface

The central drama of Canadian history, the one which distinguishes Canada from other Western countries, involves the ways in which two founding peoples have fought, cooperated, remained apart, come together, and along the way created a political state. Scholars usually examine this historical drama as the intellectual history of a small number of urban-based leaders. However, the actual protagonists of Canadian history also include the rest of the population, most of them, until quite recently, living in rural villages and settlements. How do the thoughts and behaviour of such historically anonymous individuals relate to the established record of Canada's past? The answers to this question will, like most of the historical process, never be completely understood. Perhaps they were not fully grasped at the time, even by the participants. But such a question must be pursued since it probes to the heart of Canadian history.

The drama of our past is not a series of unique events, but rather the continuous history of men and women coming to grips with their own changing circumstances. A most contentious articulation of this process has concerned schooling for francophones outside Quebec. From the mid-nineteenth century, when public school systems were first established in Canada, controversies have erupted in every province where francophones have formed sizeable communities. These controversies have been the focus of a vast literature which treats the language-of-instruction issue as a struggle of ideas and ambitions involving politicians, bishops, and various social leaders.[1]

In contrast, this book attempts to explore the language question in terms of the social history and cultural identity of a particular region. Specifically, the following chapters examine Prescott County, which became the centre of the language-of-instruction controversy in Ontario during the late nineteenth century. From the 1850s, Prescott County has been the geographic interface of English and French Canada, the buckle of the bilingual belt. The county became the object of provincial attention in the 1880s after immigration from Quebec had transformed the region from a frontier zone sparsely settled by anglophones to a populated area with a francophone majority. After 1885, controversy grew in intensity as the Ontario government began adopting a series of measures to curtail French-language instruction in all provincial schools.

The accepted historical record of the Ontario language-of-instruction question emphasizes the years of the early twentieth century, especially the events surrounding the circulation of Regulation 17 in 1912. This official circular of instructions was sent to all public and Roman Catholic separate schools in the province, informing them that the use of French as a language of instruction "shall not be continued beyond Form 1."[2] Historians trace the origins of Regulation 17 to the 1880s, when important anglophone politicians and newspaper editors came to believe that francophone immigration to eastern Ontario was jeopardizing the cultural balance of Confederation. These spokesmen claimed that a francophone "invasion" was now challenging anglophone hegemony in Ontario and argued that this challenge had to be answered by educational policies designed to ensure the cultural character of the public school system. Historians have suggested that the alienation produced by events such as Louis Riel's hanging and the Jesuit Estates Act help explain why this argument came to be increasingly supported by anglophones during the late nineteenth century.[3]

This study reinterprets the origins of the Ontario language-of-instruction controversy in three ways. First, evidence is presented to suggest that the coercive language policies of the end of the century were directly connected to the educational history of eastern Ontario, especially of Prescott County. This analysis emphasizes the interaction of local school development and official language policy throughout the second half of the nineteenth century. The new language policies of 1885 and thereafter are seen to be more than the result of a surge of anglo-Protestant nativism. Rather, local circumstances in Prescott County affected provincial educational policy; from both provincial and local perspectives, there was a logical continuity behind the late-century policy shifts.

This study also examines the importance of local demographic and economic developments to the history of minority-language education in Ontario. Behind the language controversy were complex population patterns and economic trends, which engendered a changing material context for educational considerations. This context cannot be properly described in the traditional terms of "invasion." Indeed, the experience of Prescott County suggests a quite different chronology and character for the history of francophone settlement in eastern Ontario. In turn, this history relates directly to the question of schooling and especially to the language-of-instruction controversy.

The reconsideration of official policies and the analysis of Prescott County's social history leads to the crucial third element in the reinterpretation of the language question: the birth of Franco-Ontarian identity in the 1880s. (Evidence of this birth in Prescott County does not undermine the valuable work of scholars who have shown that the term "Franco-Ontarian" was not used before the 1960s. Indeed, the Prescott County example supports the conclusion that the phrase "French Canadians in Ontario" was consistently employed throughout the nineteenth century.)[4] The decades before the 1880s can be seen as a period of gestation leading to the birth of an offspring, unnamed and not fully formed but possessing the potential necessary for later development. In the 1880s, the francophones of Prescott County articulated a sense of themselves rooted in the past but born in their contemporary circumstances. Their words and actions suggest that the language-of-instruction controversy reflected a conjuncture of this development with provincial and national trends.

Taken together, these arguments reinterpret the language controversy by examining the interplay of cultural groups in the context of social change. This examination is informed by recent research on the nature and historical meaning of culture, ethnicity, and group identity. Such research is especially important in two ways.

First, scholars have shown that systematic studies often do not support established assumptions about the relationship between certain groups and certain historical experiences. For example, Gordon Darroch and Michael Ornstein have used a national sample from the 1871 manuscript census to challenge the traditional shape of the relationship between ethnicity and occupational structure in Canada. At the national level, they find, "The occupational structure of the French-Catholic population closely resembled the occupational structure of the nation as a whole." Darroch and Ornstein show that this surprising pattern in 1871 included important regional differences which, they suggest, should be pursued in community studies.[5] Similarly, Frank Lewis and Marvin McInnis use 1851 census district data to compare the agricultural efficiency of anglophone and francophone farmers in Quebec. They too conclude that the established images are unfounded; there was no major productivity differential between anglophone and francophone farmers.[6] Their research builds upon the recent rethinking of Quebec's history which, for the second half of the nineteenth century, has been so effectively synthesized by Paul-André Linteau, René Durocher, and Jean-Claude Robert in *Histoire du Québec contemporain: de la Confédération à la crise* (1867–1929).[7]

Such work is by no means conclusive, but the implications for further research are clear.[8] Canadian historians must be very cautious in considering any established assumptions about the historical experience of groups such as French Canadians in the nineteenth century. Similarly, scholars must examine critically the observations and claims of contemporary writers whose views have been the traditional basis of historical research. For this purpose, routinely generated sources, such as the manuscript census, are particularly valuable. Such data need not be treated as empirical facts but rather can be used as indicators of behavioural patterns and trends.[9] This study, for example, so uses the manuscript census enumerations of the 1851–81 period for two townships in Prescott County. Their evidence is added to an array of local documentary sources to provide a critical perspective on nineteenth-century perceptions and assumptions.

This study also draws upon recent research which emphasizes that culture, ethnicity, and identity are not static categories but rather dynamic processes occurring in changing historical contexts. In such research, the ideas and actions of a particular group are not assumed to be reflective of immutable characteristics which transcend time and place. Rather, the ways in which individuals think, behave, and see themselves are viewed as interactions of previous experience and contemporary circumstances.[10] Historians have only begun to explore such interactions, and, as a result, unexamined and ahistorical generalizations about various groups still are evident even in the most scholarly works. Indeed, the monumental *Harvard Encyclopedia of American Ethnic Groups* uses French Canadians to illustrate the unusual case of a "sharply" defined ethnicity. In this case, three "indexes overlap": a residence "mostly" in Quebec; a Catholic religion "rather than Protestant like most other Canadians"; and an historic concentration "in the lower and lower-middle classes in contrast with the English-speaking employers and professionals in the province [of Quebec]."[11] The maintenance of such misleading, timeless generalizations encourages continued research, which can contribute better definitions and understandings of groups whose members share historical experiences and who come to see themselves and to be seen as distinctive.

In this sense, the following study offers a direct comparison of the writings of school officials in nineteenth-century Ontario with the actual thoughts and experience of residents in Prescott County. The study begins with an analysis of official attitudes toward French-language schooling, which provides an overall framework for exploring the chronology and demography of settlement, the economic structure, and the role of schooling within Prescott County's social organization. The changing cultural relations of the 1880s are then examined with respect to both local politics and the history of Catholic separate schools.

My most important conclusion is that the behaviour, attitudes, and perceptions of anglophones and francophones must be examined in the context of their own material lives. In particular, the history of the language question must be analysed as part of the larger social evolution of specific communities.

My research has been made possible by the support and computer facilities of the Ontario Institute for Studies in Education and the University of Victoria. I thank Ian Winchester for first introducing me to the Canadian Social History Project and for having given me subtle guidance and perceptive criticism since we first met in 1974. I am also grateful for David Levine's friendship and scholarly advice and Alison Prentice's consistent support and helpful suggestions. My research is further indebted to Michael Katz, whose ideas stimulated me and whose informal support was always a source of encouragement. Parts of earlier versions of this study received valuable criticism from Susan Houston, Robert Harney, Raymond Mougeon, Donald Cartwright, John Willis, Marvin Lazerson, Brian Young, Stan Mealing, Harvey Graff, Normand Séguin, Marvin McInnis, and Peter Baskerville. I also thank Don Akenson for his faithful support and Lenore d'Anjou for her substantial assistance. I doubt that this book will fully satisfy the excellent students I have had the good fortune to know, but without their stimulation it would be even less satisfactory.

Members of the Prescott County Historical Society, especially James Donaldson and William Byers, have been exceedingly generous and supportive. I am grateful for the opportunity to research in repositories such as those at St-Victor-d'Alfred, the Archdiocese of Ottawa, the Thomas Fisher Rare Book Library, the Provincial Archives of Ontario, and the Public Archives of Canada.

Parts of Chapters 2, 3, and 4 have been published in different form in "Canadian Families in Cultural Context," Canadian Historical Association *Historical Papers* (1979), "Boom and Bust," Canadian Historical Association *Historical Papers* (1982); and "Schooling, the Economy, and Rural Society," in Joy Parr, ed., *Childhood and Family in Canadian History* (Toronto: McClelland and Stewart 1982). I am grateful to the editors and publishers for permission to make use of this material.

Finally and most important, thanks, Pam, for being you.

Language, Schooling, and Cultural Conflict

Prologue

The Prescott and Russell schools are the nurseries not merely of an alien tongue but of alien customs, of alien sentiments, and, we say it without offence, of a wholly alien people ... The system in vogue in the schools renders it quite impossible for the young generation to rise above the intellectual level of the average Lower Canadian *habitant*; and if it be allowed to continue, the Eastern part of Ontario, into which the French are steadily marching, is doomed before many years to be as dark a spot on the map of intelligence, as any portion of Quebec.

Toronto *Mail*, 24 November 1886

Tout Canadien, quelque soit son origine anglaise, française, irlandaise ou écossaise, est naturellement et parfaitement dans son pays en n'importe quelle partie du Canada, en Ontario tout comme ailleurs.
    Sa province est celle où il préfère élire domicile.
    Cette mille fois vraie vérité semble s'appliquer particulièrement au Canadien-Français, lui qui est arrivé six quarts de siècle avant tous les autres, et qui de son sang leur a tracé le chemin.

La Nation (Plantagenet,
Prescott County, Ontario)
12 September 1885

It was absurd for the leader of the Opposition to say that the Government did not desire the French population to learn English. If his hon. friend really seriously meant any such statement as that he must be pretty nearly approaching absolute idiocy. (Cheers and laughter) ... The government were as anxious as he was to see their French fellow-subjects speak the English language; but the difficulty was how to bring about that result.

Speech by Oliver Mowat,
Premier of Ontario, in the
Legislative Assembly,
3 April 1890

FIGURE 1
Prescott County, Ontario

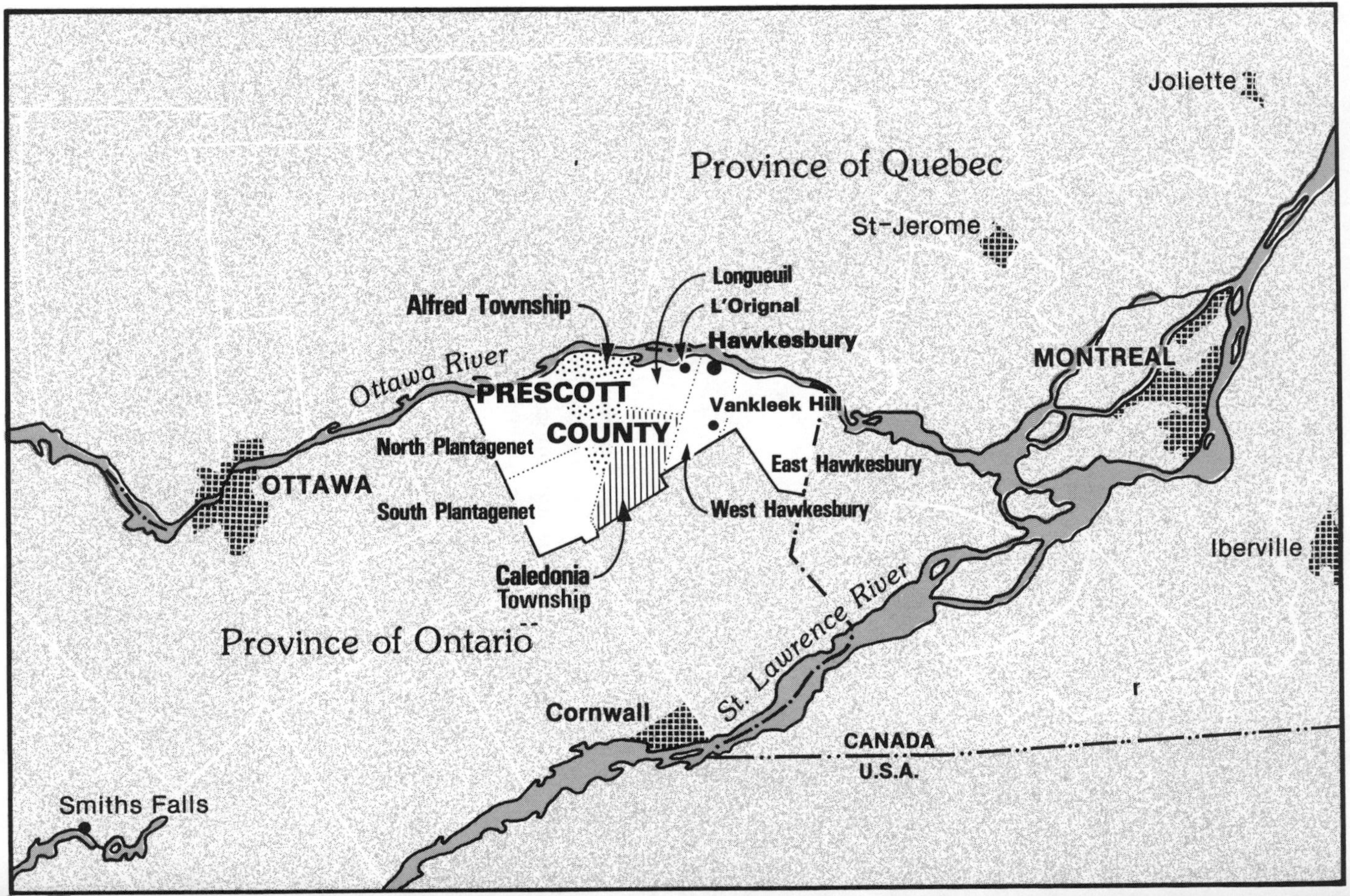

CHAPTER ONE

Ryerson, Ross, and the Concept of Voluntary Assimilation

In the past fifteen years, the history of education in Ontario has attracted enormous interest among historians. The result has been a great number of journal articles and books involving heated theoretical and methodological debates. Surprisingly, however, social historians have given the history of non-English-language schooling very little attention. This neglect is the result of several factors. Social historians have focused on cities;[1] almost all non-English-language schools were in small towns and rural areas. Moreover, recent historians of education have stressed that the Ontario school system, as it was established in the nineteenth century, adopted the cultural character of generalized Western society. Researchers have emphasized that Ontario schools integrated textbooks from Ireland, teaching methods from Prussia, and educational administration from New York and Massachusetts. The result is considered an educational system with great similarities to the systems of a variety of other Western countries.[2] The interaction between specific groups, such as francophones, and the nineteenth-century Ontario schools has not, in itself, been the object of much research.[3]

Quite recently, however, historians of education have begun to discover the value of studying the small towns and rural areas of nineteenth-century Ontario and of reconsidering the cultural character of the province's developing school system. Two aspects of this research are especially relevant to the history of French-language schooling. The first involves questions of school establishment and control: who built the educational system? who determined the structure and character of local schools? Some decades ago, historians answered these questions by pointing to an educated, enlightened elite determined to share the benefits of education with those less fortunate.[4] In the 1970s, researchers often still held this elite responsible for public schooling but depicted them as self-serving, rather than as humanitarian, and as interested in social control more than educational "progress."[5] Both interpretations stressed agency at the top with beneficiaries – or victims – at the bottom.

These perspectives have now been challenged by historians who have found significant local initiative and a certain autonomy in rural areas, especially during the formative decades of the school system.[6] Their work puts in question the established emphasis on the ideas and actions of certain urban leaders and encourages further research on the extent of agency in specific communities. These findings suggest that the language-of-instruction policies must be examined from the perspectives of both local and provincial school officials. The development of these policies may have involved more than the view from Toronto.

The second aspect of recent research which relates directly to the history of French-language schooling in Ontario involves a reconsideration of the cultural character of the nineteenth-century school system. Was it a distillation of features from other Western, especially anglophone, countries? Were the schools really "common"? The traditional answers to these questions emphasized the anti-American, pro-British ambition of educational leaders.[7] Revisionist historians of the 1970s rejected this emphasis, stressing instead the class-based perspectives of leading school promoters in all Western countries.[8] Current research is now questioning both views by revealing the specifically Irish character of the school system established in the 1840s and 1850s. Studies suggest that the use of Irish textbooks was only one aspect of Ontario's substantial re-creation of the Irish educational structure.[9]

The implications of such research extend to the question of French-language schooling since Irish immigrants and their descendents were frequently neighbours of francophones in nineteenth-century rural Ontario, especially in Prescott County. Did Irish settlers have an important comparative advantage over francophone settlers with respect to the nature and structure of the developing school system in Ontario? Was the question of language only part of a much larger cultural context in Ontario schooling?

THE RYERSONIAN YEARS

Questions of control and of cultural character provide points of departure for reconsidering the evolution of official policies on French-language schooling in nineteenth-century Ontario. From the 1840s to 1876, the central figure was Egerton Ryerson, a Methodist minister who began a long career of educational leadership when he took up the cause of nondenominational schooling in the late 1820s. Twenty years later, Ryerson had the opportunity to set out a comprehensive framework for public education, having become superintendent of education for Upper Canada. This position had been created by the School Act of 1841, legislation intended to encourage a uniform school system for the united Province of Canada. The act did not, however, effectively resolve the complicated issues of control, administration, and finance. In his report for 1846, Ryerson made extensive recommendations for legislative change, which led to the Common School acts of 1846 and 1850. This legislation provided the foundation for a universal, tax-supported, elementary school system.[10]

During these formative years of the Ontario school system, francophone settlement was spreading steadily, especially in rural areas. At the outset of the century, the heaviest concentration of francophones was in the southwestern corner of Upper Canada, in the counties of Essex and Kent. After the 1830s, this settlement was increasingly balanced by immigration from Quebec to the eastern counties of Prescott and Russell and to the city of Ottawa. By 1871, the two corners of Ontario included some 30,000 francophones. Additional settlement in other parts of the province brought the total to 75,383. (See Figure 2.)

Early Rulings on Language Questions

The legislation founding the Ontario educational system did not address the question of language. Presumably, the lawmakers assumed that English would be the language-of-instruction, and they made no provision for other possibilities. Immediately, however, educational officials had to respond to inquiries from communities in which language diversity posed administrative questions. These responses established policies on the question of language during the Ryersonian period, and, not surprisingly, historians have used them to interpret the educational implications of francophone settlement in Ontario. The uncontested conclusion is that official policy between the 1840s and 1876 permitted language diversity with respect to both teachers and textbooks. Official responses to the questions of local communities indicate consistent toleration of not only French- but also German-language schools. As a result, historians have drawn a sharp contrast between the tolerant Ryersonian period and the anti-French policies of the later nineteenth century.[11]

The official rulings before 1876 can, however, be seen quite differently if they are placed in the broader context of Ryerson's general

FIGURE 2
Francophone Settlement in Ontario, 1871

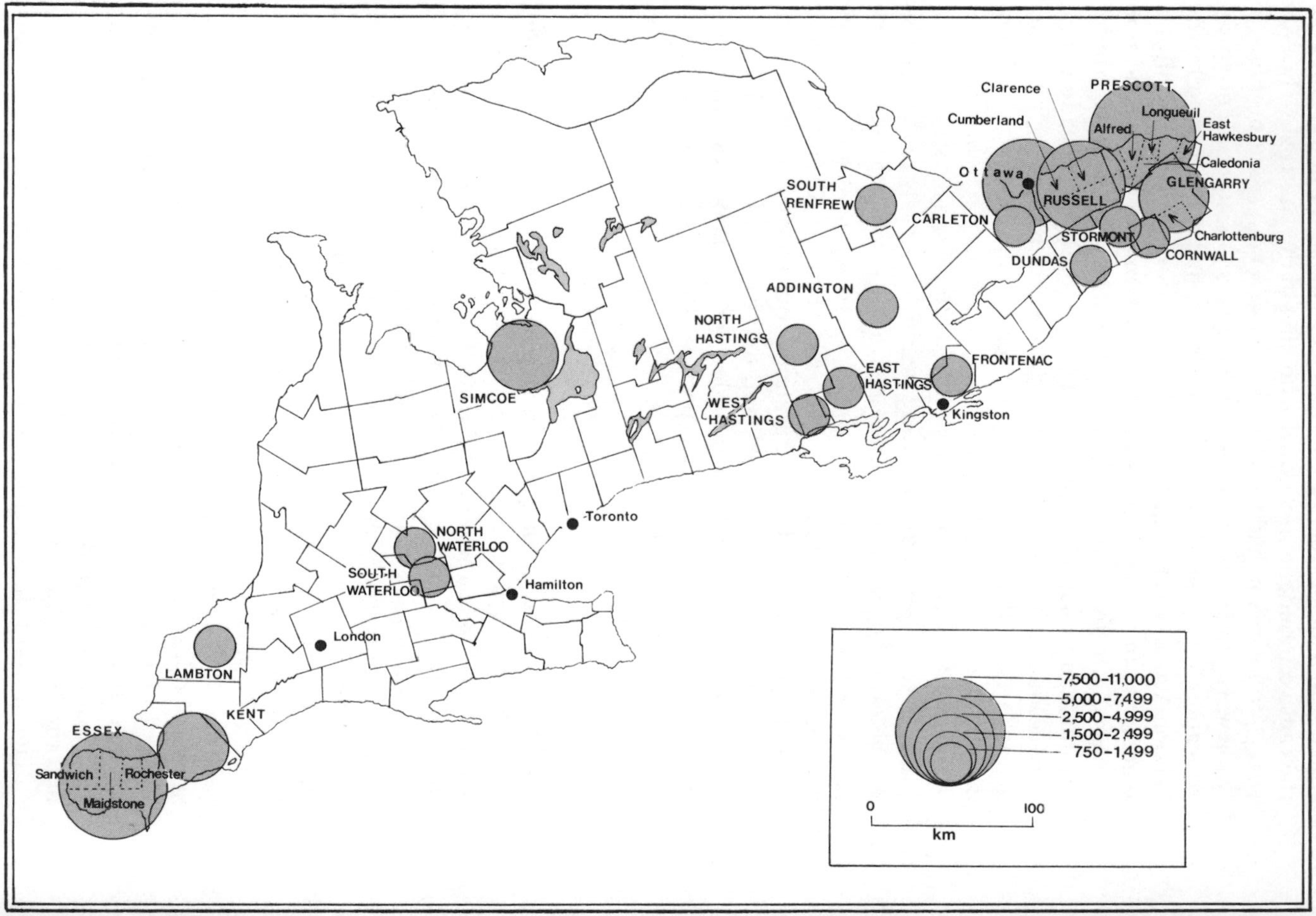

Legend:
7,500–11,000
5,000–7,499
2,500–4,999
1,500–2,499
750–1,499

km
0   100

PRESCOT
Longueuil
East Hawkesbury
Caledonia
Charlottenburg
GLENGARRY
CORNWALL
Alfred
RUSSELL
STORMONT
Clarence
Cumberland
Ottawa
CARLETON
DUNDAS
FRONTENAC
Kingston
SOUTH RENFREW
ADDINGTON
EAST HASTINGS
NORTH HASTINGS
WEST HASTINGS
SIMCOE
Toronto
Hamilton
NORTH WATERLOO
SOUTH WATERLOO
London
KENT
LAMBTON
ESSEX
Sandwich
Rochester
Maidstone

educational perspective and of the writings of local school officials at the time. Correspondence from Prescott County, for example, suggests a quite different understanding of the language policy during the Ryersonian period. Moreover, both local and provincial evidence from later in the nineteenth century supports this revised interpretation.

Teachers. Many of the formal statements on questions of language are familiar from previous studies, and they need only be summarized here to illustrate their flexibility and acceptance of local diversity. On 25 April 1851, for example, the Council of Public Instruction, which set policy for the Department of Education, met to respond to requests for clarification of the language requirements for teacher certification. The immediate cause of this meeting was a controversy over French-language instruction in the southwestern Township of Sandwich, but the question also arose for German-language schools in counties such as Waterloo, Perth, and Bruce. Egerton Ryerson, the member with greatest influence on the decisions of the council, was in England at the time, but his absence did not prevent decisive action. After reviewing various letters and petitions, the council confirmed that the School Act had no specific requirement of English-language ability for teacher certification. However, the council pointed out that the program of examination obviously did not anticipate non-English-language instruction; in fact, several references implied English comprehension. To clarify this ambiguity, the council formally ruled that, in teacher examinations, "a knowledge of French or German may be substituted for a knowledge of the English grammar, and the certificate ... [should] be expressly limited accordingly."[12]

Subsequent official rulings attempted to refine this policy. On 17 December 1858, the council made explicit that the equation of French and English grammar in teacher examinations pertained specifically to qualifications for third-class certificates.[13] However, the group did not comment on language requirements for first- and second-class certificates, and, in practice, Ryerson does not appear to have made this distinction. For example, on 19 December 1859, the illiterate trustees of East Hawkesbury, a heavily francophone township in Prescott County, had an inquiry written on their behalf to James Gamble, the local superintendent. The trustees, who were francophones, explained that they had engaged two teachers in order to accommodate the two linguistic groups of the district. One teacher was a unilingual francophone, who had been awarded a second-class certificate in Quebec, and the other was an uncertified anglophone.

This arrangement was said to have been working well until the trustees discovered that they could not receive the provincial government grant awarded each public school unless both teachers held certificates from Canada West. The trustees pointed out, "This we were unaware of ... and we are at a loss how to act."[14] The local superintendent, similarly at a loss, wrote to Ryerson requesting an exemption from having to employ only Canada-West-certified teachers in light of the "peculiar difficulties" of the school section; in response, Ryerson, supporting the local trustees, ordered the county board to award an equivalent certificate to the teacher with a second-class certificate from Canada East and to grant a temporary certificate to the English-speaking assistant.[15]

Ryerson did not deal with many of the other practical implications of the acceptance of French-language instruction, but certain difficulties could not be overlooked. The potential substitution of French grammar in examinations for teacher certification obviously implied that officials were prepared to test candidates in that language. This was not always the case. The 1859 letter from the trustees of East Hawkesbury also claimed that the school grant had been withheld after they had hired a teacher whom the local superintendent "could not examine ... in French." In this instance, as we have seen, Ryerson simply told the superintendent to award a certificate without examination and to allot the school fund.[16] However, the general difficulty of examining francophone candidates remained. Finally, on 9 February 1872, the Council of Public Instruction authorized county councils "to appoint one or more persons (who in their judgement may be competent) to examine candidates" in the French language.[17]

Bilingual Teaching. In the years after 1851, official sanction was also given to the teaching of French as part of the curriculum, rather than as the sole means of communication in the classroom. Although the distinction between coexistent French-language and English-language classes and bilingual classes often confused educational leaders, it was clear and important at the local level. In 1857, the trustees of the linguistically mixed Township of Charlottenburgh in Glengarry County wrote to Ryerson that "four or five years ago ... an intelligent and qualified teacher" had been hired to teach both the English and French languages "to those who were desirous of it, without infringing on the time of the other respective classes." Now a local resident had objected to the teaching of "French studies," and the trustees feared that this person might be able to "prevent us from getting our legislative school grant" if bilingual teachers were, in fact, not lawful. Ryerson's response to this inquiry extended his earlier pronouncement on French-language instruction. He asserted:

As the French is the recognized language in the country as well as the English, it is quite proper and lawful for the trustees to allow both languages to be taught in their school to children whose parents may desire them to learn both.[18]

Bilingual instruction was thereby given official sanction in Canada West.

Textbooks. Similarly, local inquiries led to official approval of the use of French-language textbooks. On 25 September 1856, the local superintendent of Kent County wrote to Ryerson to ascertain "what series of books" were recommended "when it is necessary to use books in the French language." For once, Ryerson was without an opinion. He admitted the lack of a "prescribed or recommended" list of books for French-language schools and, consequently, "I do not see that we can do anything in regard to the kind of books which are used in the few schools of French people in Upper Canada."[19] On 21 December 1865, the Kent County superintendent asked whether the Council of Public Instruction had yet approved any books in the French language; if not, he continued, could Lower Canada's list be used as a substitute? Ryerson responded that no list had yet been compiled for Upper Canada, but that the common schools could use "the French text-books authorized in Lower Canada, or any other which the trustees and teachers may prefer."[20]

It is interesting to note that Ryerson gave this ruling in the knowledge that textbooks from Canada East sometimes introduced an unabashedly denominational religious element into the common schools of Canada West. For example, the Kent County report revealed that two French schools "use a series of French books ... which are exclusively devoted to the teaching of the peculiar dogmas of the Catholic Church." Nonetheless, Ryerson wrote that as long as the pupils attending these schools were "for the most part or altogether Roman Catholic," use of that series of books had to be accepted.[21]

During 1866, however, charges against religious instruction and the observance of holy days in the common schools of Rochester and Maidstone in Essex County were brought to Ryerson's attention. In addressing the local superintendent on these charges, Ryerson explained that regulations now forbade denominational religious instruction in public schools, and that if Catholic teaching were to continue in Rochester and Maidstone, a separate school would have to be formed to avoid loss of the school grant. Ryerson's explanation was questioned by the bishop of Sandwich, who argued that since the parents, children, teachers, and trustees were all French-Canadian Catholics, there was no need for the Maidstone and Rochester residents to form a separate school nor was there justification for withholding the educational grant. The bishop blamed the dispute on one local troublemaker.[22] Somewhat surprisingly, the Education Department reversed its earlier decision and gave permission for the schools to remain within the public system despite continued religious instruction. J. George Hodgins, Ryerson's assistant, explained that this permission depended upon the continued francophone character of the community, and that should any "English-speaking Protestant ratepayers" object to the religiously oriented textbooks, a separate school would have to be formed.[23]

Finally, in 1868 the Council of Public Instruction, seeking to prevent religious influence from infiltrating the public system through textbooks, compiled a list of nine books – dealing with arithmetic, geography, and grammar, both French and English – for use in French-language schools.[24] Denominationally slanted books long remained familiar in French-language public schools, however; in 1875, the Prescott County school inspector was informed that the Education Department could supply "Roman Catholic and some Protestant books in the French language suitable for prizes and libraries" for the public schools of his area.[25]

A Culture-Free School System?

Taken together, these rulings on teachers and textbooks suggest that official policy accepted language diversity as a necessary part of the emerging educational system. One can infer that regulations were flexible and that the central authorities were sensitive to the diverse needs of various communities. But are such conclusions warranted? Was a relatively culture-free school system really under construction? Was the Ryersonian period the golden age of French-language schooling in Ontario?

The need to examine these questions is suggested by a variety of sources that disprove the image of Ryerson as a tolerant man with a bicultural flair. They indicate that a dominant theme in his promotion of formal education was the importance of the British heritage to the development of Canadian society. "The youthful mind of Canada," he insisted, must "be matured and moulded" according to English tradition "if this Country is long to remain an appendage of the British Crown." A universal and free common school system was central to this ambition. The schools would, over time, "direct the public mind into new channels of thinking, and furnish ... instruction and material ... that would render this country British in Domestic feeling."[26] Ryerson frequently expressed hope that students would be "moulded" by British influence, including an understanding of British history and literature. In his mind, the "wealth and glory of our father land" included the "proudest achievements of human genius and industry," and he predicted that familiarity with these achievements would lead the student in Canada to "an acquaintance with the civil and social institutions, and society, and essential interests of his country."[27]

Similarly, Ryerson did not seem to envision a common school system in Canada West in which francophone identity could be supported. In fact, he contrasted the school system of Canada East with the ideal of uniform schooling in Canada West, explaining, in 1847, that the "school system of Lower Canada ... is very different from ours. It is expressly designed both for two races and for two classes of the population."[28] Ryerson's perception that Canada East was a two-race, two-class society requiring two school systems was consistent with his desire that Canada West have a single system united by adherence to British tradition.

The Meaning of "British." What did Ryerson mean by "British" tradition? Was he referring to all groups from the British Isles, or did he see important distinctions between, for example, the Irish and their Scottish and English counterparts? This consideration is crucial to understanding what Ryerson meant when he wrote about the need to "render this country British in Domestic feeling."[29] There is no evidence in this statement or similar ones that Ryerson was thinking specifically about francophones in Ontario. Nonetheless, his general perspective may be quite relevant to consideration of his attitude toward French-language schooling. The key aspect of the question is whether he included the Irish in his use of "British." If one assumes a literal definition of the term, Ryerson appears to have been directing the school system toward transformation of the Irish immigrants. If, however, his reference was to all groups of British Isles origin, Ryerson's statements seem quite inconsistent with tolerant language policies.

Revisionist historical writing during the 1970s claimed that Ryerson distinguished clearly between the Irish and other anglophone groups in mid-nineteenth-century Ontario. Indeed, a series of studies argued that the Irish immigration of the 1840s' famine was a major stimulus for the school promotion activities of that decade. According to this argument, the schools were designed to transform the "poverty stricken and diseased"immigrants who, if not properly educated, would establish "social insubordination and disorder," especially in growing cities such as Toronto and Hamilton.[30] These historians see the Irish immigrants as epitomizing in the minds of Ryerson and his like, all that was dangerous about the rapid social changes of the mid-nineteenth century. Consequently, they believe, the schools were particularly focused on "improving" the Irish, even to the point of "ridding immigrant children of their Irish brogue."[31] This revisionist interpretation suggests that Ryerson meant "British" literally in his statements on the cultural goals of the school system, and that, by implication, he was directing his comments toward the Irish.

A quite different view has emerged in the recent research which demonstrates an uncanny similarity between the Ryersonian school system of early Ontario and the school system of Ireland. Not only did the two use the same textbooks; they were also organized and administered within strikingly similar structures. This connection has been pursued by Donald Harman Akenson, who depicts Egerton Ryerson as "the active agent in one of the major transatlantic cultural transplantations of the nineteenth century."[32] Akenson argues that Ryerson, especially in his writing on educational matters, became the intellectual understudy of Richard Whateley, who was appointed archbishop of Dublin in 1831 and became one of the founding commissioners of national education in Ireland. Ryerson not only read and greatly admired Whateley's books but also wrote similar material for consumption in Canada, transplanting cultural material directly from Ireland to Ontario. Akenson also shows how the two school systems were fundamentally similar in matters ranging from the modes of teacher training and certification to the employment of school inspectors. Although Ryerson visited many countries to discuss educational matters, he concluded that the Ontario system should be modelled on the Irish system.[33]

Akenson makes clear, however, that Ryerson and other school officials did not implant the Irish system in Ontario. Rather, it grew quite naturally since the Irish were the dominant anglophone group in Ontario during the Ryersonian period. Akenson points out that the 1871 census found that people of Irish origin were more than a third (34.5 per cent) of the total Ontario population, followed at a distance by the Scots (20.3 per cent) and the English and Welsh (27.1 per cent). Thus, the development of an Irish-like school system in Ontario made demographic sense. Moreover, in townships such as Leeds and Lansdowne, which Akenson studied in detail, the local school system "caused the Irish migrants less cultural harm than any other social group in the society and, further, was so arranged that it was easier for the Irish migrants to deal with than for any other group."[34] The books were familiar, the educational structure was understood, and the teachers themselves were often of Irish origin. Not surprisingly, therefore, Ryerson's schools met substantial support in many Ontario communities.

If Ryerson encouraged and received support for the development of an Irish-like school system in Ontario, his use of "British" must be taken as meaning "from the British Isles" and not as implicitly attacking the Irish. His promotion of structures and content from the Irish school system must be considered consistent with his desire "to render this country British in domestic feeling."

The Goal of Voluntary Assimilation. How can we reconcile this goal of cultural standardization with Ryerson's policy of language toleration? Why permit francophone teachers and textbooks if a uniform system based on "British" cultural transfer was under construction? One answer was offered in the 1880s by George W. Ross, who became minister of education in 1883. He explained that Ryerson had anticipated that francophones in Ontario "surrounded as they would be by an overwhelming English majority, would become Anglicised by English teachers and English institutions, and that in this way a social revolution would take place, without any irritation or agitation whatsoever." While admitting that some communities would seek francophone teachers, Ryerson had nonetheless had the "courage to trust to the natural effect of the Anglo-Saxon institutions which surrounded the French." He had been confident that the desire for non-English-language instruction was ephemeral and that francophones, faced with the tradition and character of "British" culture, would soon voluntarily surrender their own distinctiveness and accept instruction in the dominant school mode. In other words, according to Ross, Ryerson believed that time and flexibility were required to allow francophones to integrate themselves into the British context and that coercive measures could wreck irreparably the natural process of "social revolution."[35]

Ross's use of "English" and "Anglo-Saxon" here appears to relate to the sense of "British Isles" we have deduced for Ryerson's own statements. (Otherwise, the rationale offered by Ross would be complete nonsense; Ontario's francophones could have been considered "surrounded" only if the Irish were included as the dominant part of the "English majority.") What Ross meant by "Anglicised" and "social revolution" is more problematic. Nineteenth-century educators in Ontario did not define a concept of assimilation, nor did they indicate the mechanisms through which such a process could occur. Their statements do not suggest that they shared the modern sense of sociocultural fusion involving behaviour such as intermarriage.[36] Rather, they seem to have intended by "assimilated" the usual nineteenth-century meaning of "resembling" or "acting like." If we assume Ross intended this sense, he was claiming that Ryerson anticipated and hoped that, at least from an educational perspective, the perceived difference between anglophones and francophones would naturally over time disappear – specifically, that the desire for French-language schooling would diminish with each passing year. In other words, Ross argued that Ryerson's tolerant language policy was based on a concept of what we would call voluntary assimilation.

Admittedly, George Ross's statement from the 1880s is not the best source for understanding Ryerson's rationale for his policies, since by this time Ross himself was deeply involved in the question of minority-language education. His pronouncements were obviously designed to serve his own ends. Moreover, there is only fragmentary evidence that Ryerson did indeed believe that common schooling could improve French Canadians in the direction of the British standard. One example is his reaction to news of educational progress in Lower Canada. In 1854, Ryerson received a report from which he concluded that "education in that part of the Province [of Canada] is in steady progress" and thus predicted that "the 'habitans' [sic] as a class are likely to come up to their due place in the national attainments."[37] The following year he remarked on the "greater mental culture and wealth" of English-Canadian Protestants compared to French-Canadian Catholics.[38]

Such fragmentary sources can only be considered suggestive but, along with the claims of George Ross, they encourage further probing into the possibility that the policy of toleration was consistent with the goal of a uniform "British ... Domestic feeling."

THE VIEWS OF LOCAL OFFICIALS

The focus of research attention inexorably closes in on the local level. What did local school officials report from areas of francophone settlement? What attitudes and perceptions lay behind the inquiries sent to Toronto?

During the Ryersonian period, the local school superintendents of Prescott County were anglophone, despite heavy francophone settlement in the area. This fact is germane to the history of French-language schooling and will be dealt with at length in later chapters. Suffice it to say at this point that the anglophone community, the largest group of whom were of Irish origin, had grasped the administrative structure of education in Prescott County. It is also significant that the local reports never distinguished among various anglophone groups, despite the reality of Irish, Scottish, and English settlement. In contrast, the reports frequently remarked on the francophone presence. This pattern does not necessarily mean that differences among the anglophone groups were not noticed, but it does suggest that such differences paled in comparison to the perceptions of francophone distinctiveness.

The Prescott County evidence demonstrates a clear connection in the minds of middle-management school officials between tolerance of language diversity and anticipation of voluntary assimilation. Immigration from Quebec was consistently reported to be having an adverse effect on educational development in Prescott County. In the 1850s, the local superintendents were optimistic that this effect was temporary and that francophone settlers would soon contribute positively to the fledgling common school system. The reports of later decades turned pessimistic, however, and their conclusions no longer implied a concept of voluntary assimilation. This development related directly to the new language policies of the post-Ryersonian period.

Midcentury Reports and Expectations

The local superintendents of the mid-nineteenth century recognized that rural communities, such as those in Prescott County, could not be expected to progress educationally as quickly as urban centres, but they also perceived that the general quality of school development was particularly poor in the eastern corner of the province. In 1848, the school superintendent for the Ottawa district lamented, "The state of education is very low, especially in the new settlements."[39] The 1850 annual report documented the status of Prescott County schools in comparison to those in the rest of Ontario. By listing schools as first, second, or third class, the superintendent showed that the quality of schools in certain townships was consistently inferior, thereby contributing to the county's overall unfavourable status. Fewer than 40 per cent of its schools were categorized as first or second class, while the provincial average was more than 60 per cent. No school in Alfred or Caledonia Township had achieved the higher standard.[40] (See Table 1.)

In 1851, John Pattee reported from Alfred Township, the "condition of the schools in this locality exhibits no material improvement."[41] Reports such as these continued in later decades. In the

TABLE 1
Perceived Quality of Schools, 1850 and 1873

| | 1850 | | | | | |
| | 1st Class | | 2nd Class | | 3rd Class ("Inferior") | |
	N	%	N	%	N	%
Alfred Township	0	0.0	0	0.0	3	100.0
Caledonia Township	0	0.0	0	0.0	4	100.0
Prescott County	5	17.8	6	21.4	17	60.7
Ontario	397	16.5	1063	44.4	933	38.9

| | 1873 | | | | | |
| | Good | | Medium | | Inferior | |
	N	%	N	%	N	%
Township of East Hawkesbury	4	16.7	5	20.8	15	62.5
Township of West Hawkesbury	3	27.2	3	27.2	5	45.4
Longueuil Township	2	22.2	3	33.3	4	44.4
Caledonia Township	1	12.5	2	25.0	5	62.5
Alfred Township	0	0.0	3	33.3	6	66.7
Hawkesbury Village	1	33.3	1	33.3	1	33.3
Total	11	17.2%	17	26.6%	36	56.2%

Source: Upper Canada Annual Report for 1850, 98–119, and Thomas Steele, Prescott County, Annual Report for 1873, Appendix 17. (See note 39 concerning bibliographical information on the annual reports of the school superintendents.)

1872 report, Thomas Steele portrayed Prescott County schools as still "generally backward." Steele ranked the schools in the following year to emphasize their poor condition; in his view, more than half of them were of inferior quality, and only 17 per cent ranked as good.[42] (See Table 1.)

In the eyes of school superintendents, the general poor quality of schooling in eastern Ontario was a result of heavy francophone immigration from Quebec. In his 1851 report, Pattee analysed the condition of the Prescott County schools in terms of the "general apathy" of French-Canadian parents toward formal education. He depicted his educational role as best fulfilled by continuing the attempt "to inspire the parents and guardians of children with a conviction of the utility of education."[43]

Local superintendents believed that the new French-Canadian settlers were emerging from an environment in which educational achievement had very little priority, and that they were more reluctant to support the new Ontario school system than were other residents of the eastern counties. In anglophone areas, educational officials reported that enthusiasm for schooling was growing at mid-century. For example, in Caledonia Township, where residents were still predominantly anglophone in the 1850s, the local superintendent observed that "the schools in operation here made good progress" and were expected to improve their "inferior" ranking. The Caledonians were said to be "in favour of the full system of education as one well-calculated to benefit the rural sections and the poorer classes."[44]

Over time, the local school promoters expected the good example of anglophone communities, such as Caledonia, to transform the educational lethargy of francophone regions. Initially, these Pygmalian expectations appeared justified. In 1858, Humphrey Hughes contentedly reported, the number of schools in Alfred Township was "fast increasing," an improvement "which considering the difficulties new settlers must contend with, could hardly have been expected." Hughes identified these new settlers as French Canadians who had, he felt, "heretofore been very careless about the education of their children" but who, in the Ontario environment, were "becoming quite anxious on the subject." The French Canadians were said to be becoming "more acquainted with the school system and [to] like it better."[45]

Other areas returned similarly optimistic reports. The Ottawa District superintendent observed that in 1848, despite the reality of poor schooling, "a feeling is evidently springing up on the part of parents and guardians, and the community generally, that the education of the rising generation is indispensable." In 1851, the residents of predominantly francophone East Hawkesbury were considered to be "becoming more alive to their interest and duty" of high-quality schooling. The French Canadians of neighbouring Clarence Township in 1858 were said to be "becoming sensible of the value of education and seeking the means of sending their children to school."[46]

Growing Disillusionment

Significantly, however, local superintendents did not maintain the perception that francophones were learning to contribute enthusiastically to the school system of eastern Ontario. In his 1861 report, the Alfred Township inspector felt forced to apologize that his schools were not "making the proficiency" he had earlier reported. The main obstacle, he explained, was French-Canadian settlers, the majority in the area, who were not allowing their children "to be benefited by the schools."[47]

Similar reports grew more numerous in the 1870s. The Prescott County inspector did not feel the need to explain the failure of one of his schools to open in 1871; he simply noted that it was in a predominantly French-Canadian township.[48] Even when local officials admitted that francophone areas were not solely responsible for the statistical evidence which clearly indicated that schooling in eastern Ontario had not kept pace with the improvement noted in other regions, they still saw differences between francophone and anglophone behaviour. The Prescott County official blamed a "partial failure in the crops, high wages of labourers, and the low prices of farm and dairy produce" for poor schooling in his area; although these economic difficulties affected all Prescott residents, he said, predominantly French-Canadian areas made the least effort to maintain the schools.[49]

The distinction which inspectors perceived between anglophone and francophone educational behaviour also took on new dimensions in the 1870s. Most significant in this respect was the 1873 Prescott County inspection, which discovered five "inferior" schools in Caledonia Township, where the reports of the 1850s had told of growing enthusiasm for education.[50] In the intervening years, the Caledonia population had changed from predominantly anglophone to predominantly francophone. The evidence from this Township appeared to suggest to officials that an unanticipated transition was in progress! The settlers from Quebec, rather than being transformed by the British character of Ontario, were transforming the character of Ontario, maintaining and extending their traditional educational lethargy. If this pattern continued, educators feared that eastern Ontario would become a cultural extension of Quebec.

PROVINCIAL POLICY AFTER 1876

The growing anxiety of local school officials was not immediately reflected in educational policy in Ontario. Egerton Ryerson's theoretical accommodation of francophones within the common school system was not altered during the uneventful tenure of Adam Crooks as minister of education, from 1876 to 1883. Soon after, however, both Government and Opposition leaders came to view language toleration as the primary reason for the persistent francophone stability in Ontario. Editorials in Toronto newspapers began arguing that the breakdown of French as the dominant language in communities such as those in Prescott County was a necessary and sufficient condition for the total disintegration of the alien culture. In 1886, for example, the *Mail* described language as the "lynchpin" of French-Canadian culture, holding together a "fabric of delusion, superstition, and know-nothingnism." French-language schooling was said to be the "thin edge of the wedge" which, if not rejected, would permit further establishment of "the peculiar institutions of Lower Canada." The ameliorative effect of English-language instruction on francophone children was said to be evident at the other end of the province, in the County of Essex, where English was taught in all schools of French-Canadian communities. As a result, the *Mail* found "reason to believe that in point of intelligence the children there [Essex] will compare favourably with the French children in Prescott and Russell," some of whom attended unilingual francophone schools.[51] Conservative politicians, sitting in opposition, similarly urged an end to French-language schooling in Ontario.[52]

The Liberal government, under Oliver Mowat, was sensitive to attacks on the tolerant language policy; since the early 1870s, its own school officials had emphasized the perceived negative implications of francophone settlement in Ontario. In fact, the Liberal minister of education, George Ross, initiated action on the issue even before provincial concern was widespread. On taking office in 1883, Ross immediately inquired into the number of French-language schools in operation in eastern Ontario and found that there were now twenty-seven exclusively francophone schools located in Prescott and Russell counties. He responded in 1885 – before the start of heavy political pressure – by introducing new regulations to require daily use of two hours of English in the lower grades and four hours in the upper grades of all Ontario public schools. Ross must have recognized, however, that this regulation could not be strictly enforced; no plan of implementation was specified, nor were many French-speaking teachers bilingual.[53]

The 1885 regulations also required, equally in vain, that "every candidate for a teacher's certificate shall be required to pass such examinations in English grammar and in translation as may be prescribed by the Board of Examiners."[54] In 1886, the Prescott and

Russell school inspector blithely admitted to a *Mail* reporter that candidates for teaching certificates were still being examined only in French. The following year, a letter from Prescott County to the *Mail* editor complained that French-speaking candidates continued to enjoy "a special examination, and are not compelled to pass the English examination at all."[55] Ross did make a half-hearted attempt to ensure that unilingual francophone candidates were rejected, but he obviously recognized that strict enforcement would close many French-language schools for lack of teachers and would thereby worsen, rather than improve, schooling in French-Canadian areas.

THE EVOLUTION OF THE NEW POLICY

Although the 1885 regulations were ineffective, their intent amounted to significant revision of Ontario's language policy. The regulations made clear that special efforts to accommodate francophones within the common school system would no longer be made. It was now intended that they be forced to begin conforming to the general public school experience.

Understanding that this fundamental change of policy did not simply result from political pressure is important to understanding the evolution of official attitudes. By the mid-1880s, the Government, by itself, had come to believe that francophones in communities such as those in Prescott County required a stimulus to start down the path of voluntary assimilation. A key concern was immigration from Quebec. Informed by both government publications and newspaper reports, educators believed that counties such as Prescott were receiving large-scale francophone immigration. In 1881, the *Illustrated Atlas of the Dominion of Canada* estimated that francophone immigration to Prescott and Russell counties "at the present time ... is probably more active than at any other period." The *Atlas* writers predicted that "ere another decade goes by, the 'balance of power' will in all probability have passed from the grasp of the Anglo-Saxon to the French element."[56]

Whether the perception of a dramatic, late nineteenth century increase in francophone immigration to Ontario was accurate is a question we will examine in a later chapter. What is important here is that it was believed by both Government and Opposition representatives. However, the two political sides recommended very different responses. The *Mail*, a Conservative paper, claimed that heavy Quebec immigration seriously increased the need for an English-only policy. The apparent ease with which francophones were "invading" Ontario gave urgency to the *Mail*'s desire for their assimilation. The belief that francophone immigrants were uprooting established anglophone settlers piqued the editors considerably. They maintained that the francophone takeover of anglophone communities should not be facilitated by the establishment of French-language schools.[57]

In contrast, Ross used the supposed newness of francophone settlement to explain the continuance (in fact, significant expansion) of French-language schooling in eastern Ontario. Ross believed that the immigrants' recent experience in Quebec prevented them from immediately recognizing the value of assimilation and so they required special measures to speed up their recognition of the superiority of English-language schooling. As a result, Ross modified Ryerson's total confidence in British influence and accepted the need for forced introduction of some English-language instruction. At the same time, however, Ross considered the francophone settlers to be deserving of the same patience and tolerance which Ryerson had exhibited in the mid-nineteenth century. In refusing the English-only alternative for Ontario schools, Ross argued that although the settlers of Prescott and Russell counties did not yet evidence assimilation to anglophone institutions, the stimulus of some familiarity with English would lead them to replicate the pattern of Kent and Essex counties, where language controversy was perceived to be subsiding rapidly.

Initially, Ross hoped that the stimulus would be provided by bilingual teachers, who could introduce English-language instruction in keeping with the 1885 regulations. However, the first attempt to supply properly trained, bilingual teachers was a dismal failure. In the summer of 1886, Ross authorized the opening of a model school specifically designed to render French-speaking candidates bilingual. This authorization was given with the seemingly minimal condition that a bilingual principal with a second-class normal school certificate be secured. Six months later, however, the inspector for Prescott and Russell counties had to admit that the plan had been abandoned when "no suitable and properly qualified principal could be found."[58]

The failure to establish a francophone model school left Ross puzzled, and he began a search for a more successful strategy. After learning that the Fredericton Normal School offered a course designed for teachers of French-language schools, he wrote, in early 1888, to New Brunswick's superintendent for education, inquiring about the extent to which French and English were used as languages-of-instruction and about the course of studies which prepared teachers to give this instruction.[59] The Ministry of Education also corresponded frequently with the inspector and the assistant inspector for Prescott and Russell counties to ascertain their opinions on how English could best be introduced to the schools of their region. Discouragingly, their responses showed no imagination and were little more than regurgitations of the common theme extolling British heritage.[60] In 1887, Ross organized a meeting of inspectors responsible for French-language schools so they could collectively study the problems of introducing English instruction. This meeting also failed to identify new methods of ensuring that francophone children would learn English.[61] Ross was left with no strategy for implementing the 1885 regulations.

PROVINCEWIDE DEBATE

In the fall of 1887, Ross described himself as "very anxious" about the questions he anticipated would be asked in the legislature concerning the progress he had promised for the schools of eastern Ontario.[62] Ross's anxiety proved justified; pointed questions were asked about the number of French-language schools, improvement in English-language instruction, and the pattern of school attendance in francophone communities. In response, Ross protested that he had not been given due credit for "having been the first to make regulations for the study of English in all the schools of the Province." Moreover, Ross reiterated that integration of francophones into the mainstream common school experience had to be done "gradually" in an atmosphere of "sympathy," rather than coercively in a climate of hostility. By showing moderation, Ross promised, "five years would not elapse before every French scholar is able to read our textbooks."[63]

During March and April of 1889, the question of French-language schools dominated debate in the provincial legislature, and it then became a central campaign issue for the election of 1890. The Government leaders protested the Conservatives' vituperative stereotype of francophones in Ontario, but the Liberals did not suggest that the French-Canadian culture was worth preserving except as a supplement to the British-based standard. Premier Mowat claimed to be just as "anxious" as the Opposition "to see their French fellow-subjects speak the English language," but admitted "difficulty" in establishing "how to bring about that result." Mowat rejected the Conservative suggestion of outright coercion for fear of alienating and antagonizing the francophones who would then, he said, learn "not more English ... but less." He dismissed as "absurd" the allegation that the government did not "desire the French population to learn English." While admitting that the government had not yet achieved an effective plan of action for the 1885 regulations, Mowat assured the legislature that he recognized the "necessity for doing something" to introduce English "as speedily as possible." Nonetheless, he warned that English-language instruction "could never be accomplished by exhibiting a spirit of hostility to the French population."[64]

Similarly, Ross emphasized that the attempt to introduce some English-language instruction to all Ontario schools represented modification, rather than desertion, of the goal of voluntary assimilation. Ross continued the traditional argument that "liberality" of educational policy would best produce a homogeneous society.[65]

In defending his refusal to legislate an immediate end to French-language instruction, Ross reiterated Egerton Ryerson's rationale for the early accommodation of both Germans and French Canadians within the common school system. Ross explained that educational assimilation had already been completed within the German communities but was still in progress in certain francophone regions. By maintaining the analogy of French Canadians to Germans, Ross attempted to prevent the conceptual isolation of French Canadians as a unique cultural group needing special, far-reaching educational measures. Knowing that requests for German-language instruction had indeed subsided dramatically after the 1860s, he implied that francophones in eastern Ontario would similarly come to welcome English-language instruction. Thus Ross made frequent reference to the German example. "Is it not natural, is it not human, is it not reasonable," he asked, "that they should be allowed one generation at least in which to make the transition from the forms and habits of the Germany of Frederick the Great to those of the Dominion of her Gracious Majesty?"[66]

In addition, Ross's speeches drew on the experience of other countries. If the Americans, he asked, had

shown a want of faith in their own institutions, a want of confidence in the assimilation power of the dominant race, namely the Anglo-Saxon, would they have maintained so successfully their national dignity and influence? ... From every quarter of the globe, they have invited immigration, trusting in the assimilating power of their own institutions to make out of these immigrants, American citizens.[67]

As representatives of "the dominant race in this province," Ontario's educational leaders could likewise "better assimilate the people and the languages of other nationalities by generosity than by coercion."[68]

Since the Mowat government differed with the Opposition over strategy rather than ultimate goals, Ross was genuinely sensitive to criticism of the language policy. He recognized that his policy had to be substantiated by evidence from eastern Ontario indicating that francophones were increasingly learning English. Frequently, though, the minister could not obtain accurate information about the condition of French-language schools. Several times, the *Mail* succeeded in demonstrating that he had given incorrect reports to the legislature. In early 1889, Ross wrote to both the inspector and the assistant inspector of Prescott and Russell counties for current information concerning "the extent to which English is taught in the schools of Eastern Ontario." After being assured that English was always taught "more or less," Ross told the legislature that at least some English was taught in all Ontario schools.[69] Two days later, the *Mail* gleefully quoted the *Prescott and Russell Advocate*'s embarrassing correction that in "a considerable number of Public Schools, no attempt or pretense whatever is made of teaching anything but the French language."[70]

The Commission of 1889

Ross's inability to define the precise dimensions of French-language education made convincing the Conservative demand for formal investigation of the actual condition of French-language schools, especially those within the public system. On 13 May 1889, Ross appointed a three-man commission to study the public schools and to ascertain "with certainty whether and how far the said regulations [of 1885] are complied with in the counties of Prescott, Russell, Essex, Kent and Simcoe, or what step should be taken for ... more complete enforcement."[71]

The commission presented its report on 22 August 1889. Although evidence had been gathered for all the designated counties, the real focus of the commissioners' attention was Prescott County and neighbouring Russell County, where the francophone presence was considered to be most disturbing. The report reiterated the traditional argument that francophones would in time integrate themselves into the dominant British-based society in Ontario. Although the commissioners had discovered continued use of only French-language textbooks in some schools, they explained that this practice did not reflect "a desire on the part of the French to exclude the English language from the schools." Rather, francophones were said to have "expressed themselves not only as willing but as desirous that their children should learn the English language." The commissioners agreed that the desire for English instruction was most evident in the counties of Essex and Kent, where in a number of schools "English has been well taught for many years, so that they are practically English schools." This evidence supported the commissioners' claim that to raise schools in French-Canadian communities "to a higher standard, and to secure a satisfactory teaching of the English language in them, *time must be allowed and patience must be exercised*."[72]

The commissioners admitted, however, that the francophones in the eastern counties did need special attention. They soothed concern about an "invasion" from Quebec, noting that immigration "has, of late, been very much reduced," but they could report no progress in the effort to transform French-language schools into English-language ones. In fact, they had discovered that some formerly English-language schools were now employing francophone teachers and that a great many French-language schools had been established in the 1880s. The commission concluded that this expansion of French-language schooling was related to a dearth of properly trained English-speaking teachers within the francophone schools. Not only were most of the francophone teachers unilingual, but of the sixty-nine who had been inspected, only three had received a high school education and only two had attended a normal or model school.[73]

The commissioners reasoned that this debilitating situation could be rectified in two complementary ways: by establishing a model school specifically designed to train francophone teachers in the English language; and by convening "special institutes" or workshops for the dissemination of current pedagogical techniques of English-language instruction. The commissioners claimed that implementing these recommendations would resolve the language issue and ensure that the public schools fulfilled their responsibility to prepare all children of Ontario "to credibly occupy the positions in life that they may be called to fill."[74]

The Education Department's response to the 1889 report was swift and positive. First, on 17 October 1889, "all text-books in the French language" were removed from the list of authorized books, leaving only English-language texts plus a group of bilingual readers.[75] Second, a group of normal school teachers lectured on teaching methods at a four-day gathering that included sixty-nine teachers from all parts of Prescott and Russell counties.[76] Third and most important, a French-language model school was opened in Prescott County; a properly certified, bilingual principal was hired and classes began during January 1890.[77]

These measures plus the Liberals' convincing 1890 electoral victory sapped the Conservatives' energy for attacking the Ministry of Education's language policy. Although the cry for English-only in

Ontario schools had not been fully answered, Ross had temporarily stolen the thunder of Conservative forces.

The Commission of 1893

By 1893, Ross was able to introduce evidence that his confidence in a "liberal" language policy was being vindicated. The same individuals who had served on the 1889 commission reconvened to "consider and report what progress, if any, has been made in the study of English." The 1893 commission claimed that concentration on the need for properly trained teachers was paying off handsomely. Describing the benefits derived from the Prescott County teacher-training centre, the report explained that although enrolment at the centre had slowly decreased since the inaugural year, the cause was only "increased severity" in the entrance examination. The report suggested "a decided advance upon the state of things," since the quality of teaching had risen dramatically in the French-language schools of the eastern counties and a full 98 per cent of francophone children were receiving some English-language instruction, compared to only 77 per cent in 1889. The commissioners admitted that a significant number of French-language public schools had joined the separate system since the previous investigation, but overall the findings were said to indicate that "the marked improvement of the past few years will be not only maintained but increased" and that more improvement could be expected since the "whole benefit" of the new model school had not yet been "reaped."[78]

The 1893 report gave temporary credence to Ross's belief that the assimilation of francophones was inevitable, a process primarily regulated by length of settlement. Although his 1887 promise that "five years would not elapse before every French scholar is able to read our textbooks" had not been fulfilled, the 1893 commission's perception of "marked improvement" in the eastern counties seemed to justify the minister's "confidence in the assimilating power of the dominant race." Moreover, the report supported his conviction that chronology of settlement explained why the desire for French-language schools appeared to be subsiding rapidly in Essex and Kent counties but only slowly in Prescott and Russell. The commissioner's claim that the special language measures were now overcoming the impact of heavy 1880s' immigration convinced Ross that he had finally discovered an answer to the nerve-racking language question. The 1893 report further relaxed the interest of politicians and journalists, and by 1896 Ross smugly assumed that the French-language problem in Ontario was solved. In that year, his final one as minister of education, he published a volume describing the historical background and present status of the Ontario school system.[79] Although he had identified the French-language problem as "that most disturbing of all questions" in 1889,[80] Ross devoted only two pages of his book to the issue.

Resurgence of the Language Question

Within a few years, however, observers recognized that Ross had not solved the language question. They reported that the francophone presence in eastern Ontario was continuing to increase, rather than decrease, and that, Ryerson and Ross to the contrary, the "natural effect of the Anglo-Saxon institutions" could not be discerned.[81] In the early twentieth century, the Liberal party, now in Opposition, strove to inflame the unhealed sore of the Ministry of Education. While A.G. MacKay, the Liberal leader from Grey North, took up the old cry for a single language policy,[82] the Opposition Toronto *Daily Star* sent reporters to examine conditions in the francophone schools of Prescott and Russell counties. Their investigation showed that French was still used exclusively in some schools and that the general quality of these schools remained very low.[83] The language question had returned with a vengeance.

Overview

The writings of educational leaders and their local representatives in Prescott County reveal a great deal about minority-language education in Ontario. This evidence suggests that language diversity was not considered important during the early decades of public school construction. Ryerson did not pay much attention to the complicated questions raised by the reality of francophone settlers in a predominantly anglophone society, and his policy of language toleration was never the focus of debate at the provincial level. George Ross's claim is that Ryerson believed in voluntary assimilation, and that concept is consistent with Ryerson's general perspective on the importance and power of British tradition as well as with the attitudes of local school superintendents in Prescott County. Moreover, a variety of sources suggest a logical continuity between the tolerant policy of the Ryersonian period and the later movement toward intolerance and coercion. Despite changing historical contexts, school officials throughout the second half of the nineteenth century saw language diversity as ephemeral, a necessary but temporary phenomenon to be tolerated on the way to the goal of uniform, unilingual schooling.

The writings of school officials also indicate that they saw the population of Prescott County as divided into only two groups: francophones with roots in Quebec and anglophones with roots in the British Isles. Differences between anglophone groups did not compare with this basic division. The perception of two cultural groups provides the appropriate historical framework for exploring the history of French-language schooling in nineteenth-century Prescott County. The following chapters suggest that this complex history extends far beyond and often contradicts official rhetoric and policy. Beyond contemporary perceptions and behind the pronouncements of education officials lived the boys and girls, men and women whose lives gave meaning to the questions of schooling. As will be suggested, anglophone policymakers at best dimly understood these lives and at worst misperceived or ignored them. Nonetheless, they were the crucial underpinnings of the cultural conflict about minority-language education in late-nineteenth-century Ontario.

CHAPTER TWO

"Invaders" and "Fugitives," or Families in Motion?

The position of minority-language education is always debated most vehemently when population patterns are changing. Shifting levels of majority and minority status have a dramatic impact on the ways in which policymakers, journalists, and the public at large define the educational implications of diversity. Historians have long recognized this relationship, and, in the case of Ontario, many studies point out that during the period of intense controversy in the 1880s, the proportion of francophones was rapidly increasing, especially in the eastern corner of the province, and that the contemporary perception of massive francophone immigration was central to the concern of anglophone spokesmen about French-language schooling.[1]

Numerous articles in the Toronto *Mail*, for example, added graphic details to the general, nonpartisan image of a late-century invasion from Quebec. The editors described a three-step process of immigration involving long processions of "pilgrims." The first to arrive were "mostly young men" who "all had wives" in Quebec awaiting the fortune of their husbands. If successfully settled, the male migrants were said then to send for their "kindred across the river."[2]

The *Mail* suggested that the arrival of young newlyweds from Quebec was strengthening the French-Canadian presence in the eastern counties and even making uncertain the eventual boundaries of Quebec migration to Ontario. The editors feared that young French Canadians, without the burden of responsibility for children, might live only temporarily in the eastern counties and then move to the heartland of Ontario. The vision of dislocated young men and women gave a vagabond character to the Quebec exodus and further emphasized the unsettling impact which these new immigrants were said to be exerting on Ontario society. Moreover, the *Mail* pointed out, the youth of the French-Canadian "invaders" meant that the "kindred across the river" who might follow included parents, siblings, and other relatives. In this view, each immigrant couple would be trailed by two distinct families, adding to the tide. Thus this third step in the French-Canadian migration was perceived to have an endless quality that engendered anglophone retreat. The editors warned, "No force now revealed to human sight is likely to impede the steady and even rapid westward march of the French Canadian."[3]

Such reports grossly overestimated and sensationalized the possibilities of francophone settlement in Ontario. Migration from Quebec to Ontario simply contributed to the establishment of a bilingual belt, and although the number of francophones in Ontario did increase from 102,743 in 1881 to 158,671 in 1901, no great westward march ever materialized.[4] Nonetheless, the perception of an invasion and the contemporary descriptions of how this invasion was occurring provide the basic point of departure for analysing the social history of the language question in Prescott County.

SOURCES OF DEMOGRAPHIC EVIDENCE

The identification of critical watersheds of population change is an important first step in this analysis. Was there a late-nineteenth-century francophone invasion? Did anglophones flee in the face of a "westward march"? Did immigration from Quebec have a vagabond character? Did chain migration of extended families produce an almost endless francophone "pilgrimage"? These questions lead beyond aggregate trends to the level of individuals and families.

A valuable source for considering such questions is the census enumerations of the nineteenth century.[5] They reveal demographic patterns from 1851, when individual-level information was first collected on the ages, genders, birthplaces, and (from 1871) ethnic origins of the population. Because the available manuscript enumerations list the members of each residence as distinct entries, analysis at the individual, family, and household levels is possible. The following discussion pursues this information for the 1851–81 period in two townships of Prescott County. Alfred Township was a region in which francophones predominated within a few years of first settlement. In contrast, neighbouring Caledonia Township attracted a substantial anglophone population which remained quite constant for most of the nineteenth century, despite steady francophone immigration. Taken together, these townships offer a comparative view of settlement patterns in Prescott County. Their manuscript census enumerations allow a systematic examination of

TABLE 2
Population Growth in Prescott County, 1824–1901

	Population	*Increase from Previous Enumeration*
1824	2,377	–
1831	3,603	1,226
1841	6,093	2,490
1851	10,487	4,606
1861	15,499	5,012
1871	17,647	2,148
1881	22,857	5,210
1891	24,173	1,316
1901	27,035	2,862

Source: Census of Canada, 1851–1901; pre–1851 from 1871 report.

both the French-Canadian and the British-Isles-origin population. In this way, the specific timing and character of immigration, the levels of cultural concentration, and the nature of persistence and transiency in certain communities can be defined. This Prescott County evidence can be used to test the perception of two distinct demographic patterns composed of "invaders" and "fugitives."[6]

THE OVERALL PATTERN OF
SETTLEMENT

Early settlement of the lower Ottawa Valley clearly lagged well behind that of both the St Lawrence Valley and south-central Upper Canada. By the 1840s, however, population growth was underway, and Prescott County attracted steady immigration. Between 1841 and 1861, the number of residents increased two and a half times, from 6,093 to 15,499. Another large increase followed in the 1870s, and then, surprisingly, the rate of growth slowed considerably. During the time of the reported invasion from Quebec, Prescott County's growth was even less than in the 1820s, when settlement was only scattered. Between 1881 and 1901, the population increased by only about 8.5 per cent, from 22,857 to 27,035. (See Table 2.)

The overall pattern of population growth was, in other words, one of late settlement followed by rapid increase during the 1840s, 1850s, and 1870s, and then only small advances during the remainder of the century. What was the cultural component of this pattern?

TABLE 3
Cultural Composition of Prescott County Population, 1871–1901

	Total Population	French-Canadian Population		British-Isles-Origin Population	
		N	%	N	%
1871	17,647	9,623	54.5	8,024	45.5
1881	22,857	14,601	63.9	8,256	36.1
1891	24,173	16,250	67.2	7,923	32.8
1901	27,035	19,190	71.0	7,845	29.0

Source: Census of Canada, 1871–1901.

The evidence does reveal two quite distinct trends, but not those perceived in Toronto. These trends can be discerned by using the census data to form two categories: the British-Isles-origin population and the French-Canadian population. The first trend involved anglophone immigration before the 1850s and relatively little of it thereafter. The second trend was almost the exact opposite; relatively little francophone settlement before the 1840s and heavy settlement thereafter, especially during the 1850s and 1870s. The result was that the 1870s were a critical watershed for the linguistic composition of the eastern corner of Ontario. From that time, francophones increasingly dominated Prescott County, and by 1901, they were 70.9 per cent of the population. (See Table 3.)

This transformation makes understandable the late-nineteenth-century perception of a francophone invasion. Indeed, the number of francophones was increasing and their relative importance was growing. However, the engine of this growth was not a surge of immigration from Quebec. In fact, the largest increase in the French-Canadian population had occurred in the 1870s. Moreover, the aggregate data do not support the contemporary perception of anglophone flight. The British-Isles-origin population stayed quite constant, with only small decreases after 1881. The relative numerical importance of francophones in Prescott County increased by only 7.1 per cent in the last two decades of the century.

EARLY ANGLOPHONE SETTLEMENT

During the years of predominantly anglophone settlement in Prescott County, the most important group was the Irish, followed by the Scottish and, to a lesser extent, the English and the Americans.

Local histories provide examples such as David Holmes and Thomas Pattee, who took up land just after 1800 near the trail which was later named Alfred Road. James Proudfoot arrived in Caledonia Township from Scotland in 1831. Humphrey Hughes and his wife came to Alfred Township from Ireland in 1823 and settled on the south side of Lake George. These pioneers were followed in 1830 by Thomas and John Brady, Irish immigrants who established the community of Bradyville with several other frontier families.[7]

Other early settlers in townships such as Alfred and Caledonia came from the northern United States or were descendants of United Empire Loyalists. John Cashion was the son of a New England colonist who had settled in Ontario during the late eighteenth century. Cashion came to Alfred in 1823, and he married and established his own household there in 1837. The Americans who immigrated to Prescott County during the 1820s and 1830s included Charles Gates, who came with his father to Caledonia from Massachusetts.

Other settlers in Prescott County were members of families that had earlier pioneered in Quebec or in more southern parts of Upper Canada. Duncan McLeod, who had been born and raised in Glengarry County, settled in the southwestern corner of Caledonia Township. Another McLeod family immigrated through Glengarry to Caledonia in 1844, and Thomas Lytle permanently settled with his family in Alfred Township in 1831 after arriving in Cornwall from Ireland.

By 1851, the various routes of migration to Prescott County had produced a British-Isles-origin population of about seven thousand residents. Most were native to British North America but a sizeable number had been born in the British Isles (especially Ireland) and the United States (see Table 4).

The Importance of Family

These examples suggest that the family unit was a basic element in the process of British-Isles-origin immigration. Local histories often mention young couples and families with several children as the characteristic immigrants to Prescott County, and their arrival appears to have accounted for much of the population growth during the early nineteenth century.

The importance of the family in immigration seems to have extended beyond the mobility of conjugal units. The actual dynamics of settlement are very difficult to measure precisely, but the evidence clearly suggests that kinship attachments often attracted and certainly facilitated immigration to specific areas. Such attachments were

TABLE 4
Birthplaces of British-Isles-Origin Residents,
Prescott County, 1851

	Number	Percentage
Province of Canada	4745[a]	67.3
Atlantic Canada	14	0.1
Ireland	1264	17.9
Scotland	647	9.1
England/Wales	198	2.8
United States	152	2.1
Other	29	0.4
Total	7049	99.7[b]

[a] Based on a recorded French-Canadian population of 3438.
[b] Does not add to 100 because of rounding.

Source: *Census of Canada*, 1851.

particularly important in the early decades of settlement, when younger brothers and sisters were often drawn by the encouragement of previously settled siblings. The chain migration of three brothers and their families, for example, resulted in the community known as Smith Settlement, which straddles the border between North and South Plantagenet Townships. Similar kinship settlement was reflected in the names given other local areas: for example, James Settlement, Holmes Settlement, Allen Settlement, and, as previously mentioned, Bradyville.

British-Isles-origin immigration became less pronounced as the years went on, but it was important in establishing the anglophone presence during the first half of the nineteenth century.[8]

The anglophones settled in all townships of Prescott County, but they engendered an ethnic residential pattern in the early decades of the nineteenth century by concentrating in its central and northeastern parts.[9] During the 1830s the most densely settled township was Longueuil, which began as a seigneury first granted in 1674 to François Provost, a military man and later governor of Trois-Rivières. Through a series of inheritances, the land passed into the hands of Paul-Joseph Le Moyne, chevalier de Longueuil, and then to his son, who was in possession at the time the area became part of Upper Canada. Some settlement by French Canadians occurred during the eighteenth century, but the greatest development took place after the seigneury was sold in 1796 to an American immigrant, Nathaniel Hazard Treadwell. He and his son acquired township status for the area and were able to attract other American settlers. As a result, Longueuil included a relatively important anglophone community throughout the rest of the century. Together with later immigrants from the British Isles, these settlers encouraged development of Longueuil and established the village of L'Orignal as an important nexus of the area.

Ethnic Patterns

Other areas of concentration in the early settlement of Prescott County were the townships of Hawkesbury East and Hawkesbury West. Their anglophone populations closely reflected the overall county proportions of Irish-, Scottish-, and English-origin settlement. This area of the county became the most well-developed during the nineteenth century, and from the early years of settlement it attracted immigrants from the British Isles and the United States. The Hamilton family, who were from Ireland, purchased the Hawkesbury Mills in 1807, beginning many decades of social and economic leadership in the entire Ottawa Valley. The power of this family had no equal in Prescott County, but, at the local level, other families were able to build upon success during the period of early settlement. Four Higginson brothers and their families, for example, were attracted to Prescott County by the Hawkesbury Mills in 1817; they played important roles during the region's formative period with frequent involvement in religious, educational, and political activities.[10]

Scottish immigration was particularly important in Caledonia Township. Its southern part largely settled by Highlanders, some of whom had previously resided in Glengarry County. As a result, Caledonia included a plethora of McLeods, McCuaigs, Morrisons, and Macdonalds throughout the century.[11]

Although early development was focused on the central and northeastern regions of Prescott County, the western townships also included anglophone communities by the mid-nineteenth century. Irish settlement became substantial there. In one case, these immigrants arrived not simply as families but as part of a group migration. John J. Bigsby describes a group of 200 Irish immigrants, consisting of the "very aged, those in middle life, and the babe at the breast," who were seen camping for the night near Point Fortune "in a wood, under a few loose boards and bushes, pushed carelessly together." These immigrants, who had walked much of the way from Montreal, took up land which became known as the Irish Settlement in the

TABLE 5
British-Isles-Origin Settlement, Prescott County, 1871

Township / Village	Origin		
	Irish	Scottish	English
Alfred	305	28	18
Caledonia	268	494	73
East Hawkesbury	901	815	216
West Hawkesbury	598	602	218
Hawkesbury Village	464	169	167
Longueuil	240	132	225
North Plantagenet	891	154	56
South Plantagenet	388	152	283
Total	4055	2546	1256

Source: *Census of Canada*, 1871.

townships of North and South Plantagenet.[12] South Plantagenet also included a relatively substantial English-born population. None of the western townships received sizeable Scottish immigration, although all three British-Isles groups had some representation in each subdivision of the county. (See Table 5.)

Denominational Patterns

British-Isles-origin settlement brought a wide variety of religious denominations to Prescott County. The largest group among the anglophones was the Presbyterians, followed in order by the Catholics, the Anglicans, and the Methodists. The Baptists also maintained a small but steady adherence in the county. The Congregationalists were somewhat important early in the century, at the time of American immigration, but thereafter steadily lost ground. In 1851, almost one-third of the anglophone population was Presbyterian and a slightly smaller percentage was Catholic. Together with the Anglicans, these denominations included more than four-fifths of the British-Isles-origin community in Prescott County. (See Table 6.)

The individual-level data of the manuscript census returns show that religious denominations were generally associated with specific anglophone groups, although the pattern was complex. For example, examination of the 1881 data reveals thirteen distinct combinations

TABLE 6
Religious Affiliation of British-Isles-Origin
Residents, Prescott County, 1851

| | Adherents | |
Denomination	N	%
Presbyterian	2304	32.7
Catholic	1898[a]	28.2
Church of England	1356	19.2
Church of Scotland	264	3.7
Methodist	736	10.4
Baptist	203	2.9
Congregationalist	175	2.5
Other	113	0.3
Total	7049	99.9%[b]

[a] Based on a total Catholic population of 5336 and a recorded
French-Canadian population of 3438.
[b] Does not add to 100 because of rounding.

Source: Census of Canada, 1851.

of origin and religion among the anglophones of Alfred and Caledonia townships (see Table 7). The Irish settlers included many adherents to Roman Catholicism and to the Church of England. More
than three-quarters of the Scottish population were Presbyterians.
The less numerous English residents were divided more evenly among
the Church of England (a bare majority), Methodism, Presbyteri-
anism, and Roman Catholicism. The result was that among Alfred
and Caledonia anglophones, three groups were particularly important: Scottish Presbyterians, Irish Catholics, and Irish Anglicans. By
1881, each of these groups was well established, and with their counterparts in other townships, they formed the backbone of the anglophone community of Prescott County.

EARLY FRANCOPHONE SETTLEMENT

From the mid-nineteenth century, the arrival of francophones from
Quebec radically changed the cultural complexion of all the Prescott
County townships. Substantial immigration from nearby areas across
the Ottawa River began in the late 1830s and 1840s, and within a
few decades French Canadians had reduced British-Isles-origin res-

TABLE 7
Ethnic and Religious Identity of British-Isles-
Origin Residents, Alfred and Caledonia
Townships, 1881

	N	%
Irish		
Roman Catholic	298	50.1
Church of England	214	36.0
Methodist	41	6.9
Presbyterian	36	6.1
Baptist	6	0.1
Total	595	99.2%[a]
Scottish		
Presbyterian	378	77.5
Roman Catholic	62	12.7
Church of England	40	8.2
Methodist	8	1.6
Total	488	100.0%
English		
Church of England	66	50.0
Methodist	35	26.5
Presbyterian	16	12.1
Roman Catholic	15	11.4
Total	132	100.0%

[a] Does not add to 100 because of rounding.

Source: Manuscript census, 1881.

idents to minority status throughout most of the county. By 1871, the francophones were more than half the total population (see Table 3) and a considerably larger percentage in certain townships. Like the anglophone settlers, the francophone immigrants clustered in particular areas, engendering distinct language-based residential patterns. The sharpest contrast developed in the adjoining townships of Alfred and Caledonia. By 1871, francophones were more than three-quarters of the residents in Alfred, but only one-third in Ca-

TABLE 8
French-Canadian Settlement in Prescott County,
1871

Township / Village	Total Population	French Canadians	
		N	%
Alfred[a]	1,697	1,349	79.5
Caledonia[a]	1,262	438	34.7
Hawkesbury East	4,611	2,601	56.4
Hawkesbury West	1,977	545	27.6
Hawkesbury Village	1,671	844	50.5
Longueuil	1,835	1,223	66.6
Plantagenet North	3,000	1,892	63.1
Plantagenet South	1,575	734	46.7
Total	17,628	9,626	54.6

[a] Figures from manuscript schedules.

Source: *Census of Canada*, 1871.

ledonia. Similar, if less startling, variations occurred in some other townships. Strong francophone majorities were established in Longueuil and Plantagenet North, while much less French-Canadian settlement took place in Hawkesbury West. The remaining areas of Prescott County approximated its overall proportions of francophones and anglophones. (See Table 8.)

Family Migration

The pattern of the francophones' settlement in Prescott County resulted at least in part from the process of their migration, which, like that of the anglophones, was based on the arrival of families.[13] This pattern can be examined systematically, beginning with the manuscript census of 1851. It suggests the importance of family migration by indicating the presence of Quebec-born children. Families that list both Quebec- and Ontario-born children can be assumed to have migrated during the period between the birth of the youngest Quebec-born child and the oldest Ontario-born child.

The enumerations also provide a minimum estimate of the immigrants who arrived with children. The birthplace data suggest that, for example, Aimable Druer emigrated with his wife and at

TABLE 9

Estimated Family Migrations from Quebec to Alfred Township, 1851–71

	French-Canadian Population of Township	Number of Families	Certain Family Migrations		
			N	%	Average Number of Children
1851	295	42	16	38.1	3.2
1861	997	108	61	56.5	5.7
1871	1349	194	88	45.4	3.9

Source: Manuscript census, 1851–71

least two children in the early 1840s. Similarly, the Laviolette family arrived from Lower Canada with no less than five offspring. By identifying such families, it is possible to count the number of French Canadians who appear to have migrated as family units. For this purpose, I have defined "certain family migrations" as francophone families that included at least one Quebec-born child. Table 9 shows these certain family migrations as a proportion of all French-Canadian families for Alfred Township – more than half in 1861 and almost that many in 1851 and 1871.

The number of children which families brought with them from Quebec to Alfred Township varied considerably during the 1851–71 period. At midcentury, half the family immigrants included just one or two children and only 12.5 per cent included more than five. In contrast, the 1861 evidence shows that almost half (47.5 per cent) of the Alfred families left Quebec with at least six children. By 1871, the structure of family migration had returned to the midcentury pattern. (See Table 10.)

The variations in the sizes of families which left Quebec during the 1851–71 period are also evident in the changing average number of children in families at the time of immigration. This average is produced by dividing the number of Quebec-born children by the number of immigrant families. The 1851 census data for Alfred Township suggest that a mean 3.2 children arrived with their parents, while in 1861 a dramatically increased average of 5.7 children came in each family unit; this figure is then reduced to 3.9 in the 1871 data. These findings suggest that especially during the 1850s Alfred Township attracted not only small families but also sizeable ones that must have been established in Quebec for at least a decade.[14]

TABLE 10
Number of Children in Each Certain Family
Migration, Alfred Township, 1851–71

Children	Families		
	1851	1861	1871
1	3	14	23
2	5	3	18
3	2	10	15
4	0	12	5
5	4	3	11
6	1	12	9
7	1	4	3
8	0	6	3
9	0	3	0
10	0	4	0
11	0	0	1
Total	16	61	88

Source: Manuscript census, 1851–71.

The moves I have called certain family migrations represent a minimum estimate of this form of settlement. I cannot go further because of imprecise data on the arrival of other families headed by Quebec-born parents. Theoretically, three possibilities exist for such French-Canadian families: (1) they may all have immigrated with children who left home (or died) before the next census; (2) they may have all been newlyweds who came to eastern Ontario without children; or (3) they may all have resulted from marriages formed in Ontario by individual Quebec immigrants or the grownup children of earlier family-group arrivals. Undoubtedly, French-Canadian families with only Ontario-born children were a combination of these possible patterns; some had been family migrations, some had come as young couples, and some resulted from marriages formed in Ontario.

Similar estimates of the importance of family settlement are not possible for the anglophone population since by 1851 the birthplaces of their children were usually Upper Canada. Nonetheless, it is clear that, however migrants of different cultural groups arrived in Alfred

Township, they characteristically resided as members of assembled families during the mid-nineteenth century.

Relatives, Boarders, and Co-Resident Families

In the 1851–71 period, the number of households which included relatives and boarders – that is, people outside the conjugal family – was not substantial, although an upward trend is evident for both francophones and anglophones.[15] This trend was related to the growing establishment of the township and to the subsequent immigration of kin. In Alfred Township, the proportion of French-Canadian households with relatives rose slightly from 9.5 per cent in 1851 to 12.8 per cent in 1871. English-Canadian households with relatives increased from 5.0 per cent to 14.5 per cent during the same period.

Some households in Alfred Township also included unrelated individuals, although this phenomenon was not important after 1851 and was almost entirely limited to the French-Canadian male population, for whom boarding was a feature of the migratory process. At midcentury, young men from Quebec often initially arrived alone and rented lodgings while they prepared to establish their own families. Thus, in 1851, 22.1 per cent of Alfred Township's male residents were French-Canadian boarders, and, of this group, 38.4 per cent were married. Although the boarding of individuals was very rare after 1851, at the time of the next enumeration, a significant proportion of households were serving as temporary residences for immigrating families. In Alfred Township, the percentage of households with more than one conjugal family unit in 1851 was 9.5 per cent for French Canadians and 7.5 per cent for their counterparts of British-Isles origin. As a result of the heavy immigration of the 1850s, the proportion for francophone households increased to 16.5 per cent in 1861, before declining to 3.4 per cent in 1871. It was 15.0 per cent in 1861 for anglophone residences, which by 1871 included no multiple-family households.[16]

Persistence of Settlement

During the second half of the nineteenth century, when francophone immigration and settlement became significant in Prescott County, the extent of anglophone immigration was very limited. However, the established anglophone population exhibited astonishing rates of persistence after 1851. The number of British-Isles-origin residents who stayed in the same Prescott County township for many years compares favourably not only to the data for other rural communities at the time but also to that of the Prescott County francophone community.[17]

Persistence can be examined by linking the records of each of the manuscript census enumerations from 1851 to 1881. Unfortunately, the complete pattern during these decades cannot be demonstrated since the tracing of females from one enumeration to the next is often thwarted by name changes in marriage. In addition, the linkage of francophone names rendered by anglophone enumerators can only be carried out confidently for 1861 and 1871, years for which record-linkage is facilitated by additional information on residential location provided in the agricultural schedules.[18] The following analysis considers the French-Canadian pattern for these enumerations as well as more complete linkage of British-Isles-origin residents for the censuses of 1851 through 1881. (The data are not adjusted for estimates of mortality, so the findings slightly overemphasize emigration, which, as will be shown, was relatively low.)

The example of Alfred Township suggests the complexity of population movement and stability in Prescott County. Between 1851 and 1881, the anglophone settlers of this township exhibited remarkable rates of persistence. Of the 276 such individuals living there in 1851, 64 per cent were enumerated in 1861, 33 per cent again in 1871, and 20 per cent yet again in 1881. The demographic context of this persistence was the family unit. Of the thirty-nine households represented in 1851, thirty were maintained by the same head in 1861 and nineteen continued to 1871. This stability was further enhanced by many instances in which an inheriting son took over from his father and through his own marriage and children renewed the family's attachment to the township.

General persistence was less common among francophone settlers in Alfred Township than among their British-Isles-origin counterparts, but the maintenance of established households was similarly significant. Of 1,041 French Canadians enumerated in 1861, 30 per cent continued to reside in the township in 1871. This surprisingly low proportion is partially explained by the high rate of emigration for families and individuals who had been boarding in 1861. Seventy-seven per cent of French Canadians who were not members of families with their own households in 1861 were no longer present by 1871. In contrast, more than half (52 per cent) of the households established in 1861 were still represented one decade later. This evidence suggests that, despite ongoing emigration, French-Canadian communities were being established by a sizeable proportion of stable households.

It should be noted however, that the attraction which Alfred Township held for immigrants was sometimes short-lived. While some new settlers became part of the stable core of persisters, others remained present for only one enumeration. This pattern can be shown systematically in the case of anglophone settlers. Of the ninety-one immigrants to Alfred in 1861, 64 per cent were not there ten years later. Of those who came to Alfred during the 1861–71 period, 40 per cent were no longer resident by 1881. Some may have died, and it is certainly possible that others were more or less transients, people for whom migration was an ongoing feature of life and who may have come to Alfred planning to stay only a few years or even weeks. It is also likely, however, that Alfred Township did not always live up to the newcomers' expectations. A portion of those who had come to settle apparently reconsidered and moved on.

FAMILY STRUCTURE

The census data indicate that individual decisions to stay or to leave were made within the context of family and household. By examining together the manuscript census data for Alfred and Caledonia townships, we can look at specific age cohorts of anglophones and francophones for both marital status and family size.

Of course, this examination is only possible if families were specifically either anglophone or francophone; if intermarriage were occurring, a culturally dichotomous comparison would not be appropriate. In fact, almost all marriages were endogamous with respect to ethnic origin and especially to religion. The 1851, 1861, and 1871 enumerations reflect virtually no marriages involving spouses of different origin and religion. By 1881, some exogenous marriage was occurring but on a very limited basis: in Alfred Township, almost all marriages involved spouses of similar identities; the pattern was similar in Caledonia Township although the proportion was slightly smaller. (See Table 11.)

Within the limited number of ethnically-mixed marriages, exogeny among the various anglophone groups was more frequent than between anglophones and francophones. Of the sixty-four ethnically mixed marriages in Alfred and Caledonia townships in 1881, only 31.2 per cent involved francophones. Given the numerical predominance of francophones in these townships by this time (75 per cent), this evidence reveals the extent to which the population was composed of two demographic solitudes. Families were, indeed, either francophone or anglophone. This reality makes possible a compar-

TABLE 11
Marriage Patterns, Alfred and Caledonia Townships, 1881

	Married Couples			
	Alfred Township		Caledonia Township	
	N	%	N	%
Spouses with same religion and ethnic origin	486	93.8	248	87.6
Spouses with same religion but different ethnic origin	28	5.4	26	9.2
Spouses with different religions and ethnic origins	3	0.6	7	2.5
Spouses with different religions but same ethnic origin	1	0.2	2	0.7
Total	518	100.0%	283	100.0%

Source: Manuscript census, 1881.

ative examination of family structure as a background to further analysis of the patterns of persistence and migration during the 1851–81 period. These patterns must be understood in terms of both individuals and families.

Family Formation and Size

The manuscript enumerations provide evidence on the timing of family formation by way of individual data on age and marital status. The following discussion presents collective evidence from the 1851 through 1871 enumerations since the patterns of these years are quite consistent. (As will be shown, the 1881 enumeration includes some noteworthy distinctions related to the changed demographic context of the day.) For Alfred and Caledonia townships, the 1851–71 data reveal a systematic difference in marriage patterns between anglophones and francophones. Among both males and females, francophones married on average at a younger age than anglophones. Most male francophones married by their late twenties, but their anglophone counterparts did not reach the same proportion

FIGURE 3

Age by Marital Status, Alfred and Caledonia Townships, 1851–71
(percentage married, three-year moving average)

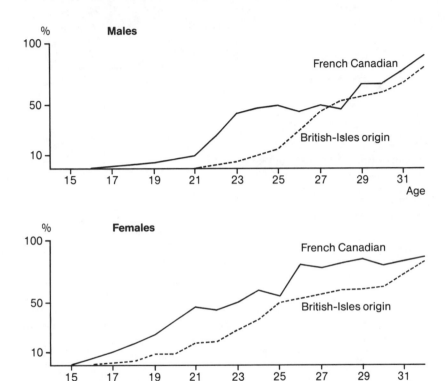

until their early thirties. The pattern is similar for females, although the average age for brides was two to three years less than for grooms. (See Figure 3.)

The difference in the timing of anglophones' and francophones' family formation is reflected directly in the average family sizes of various age cohorts. Since French Canadian women in Alfred and Caledonia began childbearing at an earlier age than women of British-Isles origin, their families consistently included a greater average number of children throughout the life course. The demographic pattern can be shown by dividing the number of unmarried, resident children by the number of families represented in each age cohort of married women. This division produces the average number of children for familes at different stages in the life course of mothers.

FIGURE 4

Average Family Size by Age of Mother, Alfred and Caledonia Townships, 1851–71

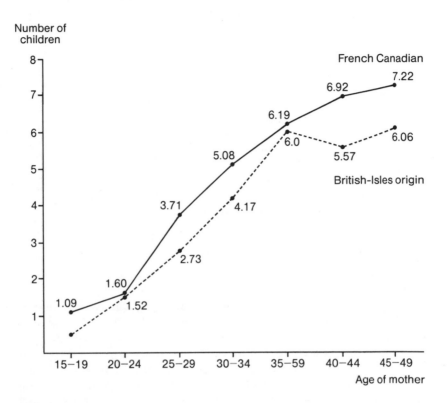

The resultant curves are similar for the two populations, but the difference in the timing of family formation meant that francophone women characteristically had families that were one child larger than those of anglophone women of the same age. (See Figure 4.)

Out-Migrants and Persisters

Differences in age-at-marriage and the consequent size of families are noteworthy since an important balance to the persistence of settlers in Alfred Township was the out-migration of large numbers of sons and daughters, who left their parents' household as they reached young adulthood. It appears that mature children most often left as newlyweds or with young families of their own, rather

TABLE 12

Children Who Left Their Parents' Households between 1861 and 1871, Alfred Township

	Age in 1861				
	10–14	15–19	20–24	≥ 25	Total
British-Isles origin					
Sons	0	6	10	4	20
Daughters	4	8	5	1	18
Average age: sons = 21.35; daughters = 17.50					
French Canadian					
Sons	9	12	12	7	40
Daughters	12	16	5	1	34
Average age: sons = 19.37; daughters = 16.20					

Note: These young people either established their own households in Alfred Township or emigrated while their parents and siblings persisted in the township.

Source: Manuscript Census, 1861 and 1871.

than as individuals. In the 1860s, for example, the average age of sons who moved out of the parental household in Alfred Township was twenty-one for anglophones and nineteen for francophones; for daughters, it was seventeen-and-a-half for anglophones and sixteen-and-a-half for francophones. (See Table 12.) Not surprisingly, these differences are consistent with the general differences in the timing of marriage. Interestingly, most of these young adults left not only their parents' households but also the township. Among British-Isles-origin sons, only one-quarter established new households in Alfred; the French-Canadian proportion was a similar 23 per cent.

The suggestion that out-migration included young couples and families, rather than simply individuals, is supported by evidence on the frequency of emigration by established family units. Although the census data reveal that many households were maintained from one decade to the next, there was also a constant flow out of Alfred Township, and emigrants usually left with other family members. Between 1861 and 1871, 53 per cent of anglophone emigrants left with either parents or children, and most others seem to have been accompanied by siblings or spouses. The likelihood of family migration was even greater for francophones. Of those who emigrated during the decade, 72 per cent appear to have departed as part of a family unit or at least with close relatives.[19]

FIGURE 5

Persistence and Transience of Individuals, British-Isles-Origin Population of
Alfred Township, 1851–81

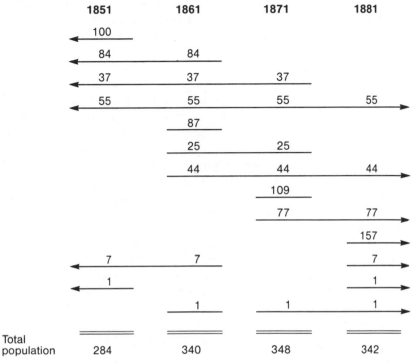

Source: Manuscript census, 1851–81.

Clearly then, families were on the move in Prescott County. Since census enumerations underestimate population turnover and represent minimum measures of family migration, we can safely conclude that geographic mobility was often negotiated with immediate relatives. Moreover, the replacement of older families by younger ones was an ongoing feature of family migration and thus a central component of the constant population turnover.

In sum, these data suggest that the Prescott County population at any one point in time included both transients and persisters and must be analysed in terms of several demographic groups. The Alfred Township enumerations suggest the relative importance of these various groups for anglophone residents during the 1851–81 period. Figure 5 reflects the enumerations for which each individual resident was present. For example, the top bar shows that of the 284 anglophones enumerated in Alfred in 1851, one hundred were present for that census but not the next; the second bar shows that eighty-four persisted at least through 1861 but not until 1871, and so on. (The backward pointing arrows indicate lack of data about these individuals' presence or absence in previous years.) At the bottom are bars for individuals whose presence for the census was intermittant.

This analysis permits clear identification of the components of the Alfred anglophone community at the start of each decade. Particular clarity is available for 1861 and 1871 because the enumerations from a decade earlier and a decade later are also available.

In 1861, for example, the Alfred population can be divided into two general groups: (1) persisters from 1851; and (2) people who appear in the census for the first time, including the young children of persisters and of immigrants to the township. Each of these groups can be further analysed according to their subsequent length of residence. Persisters from 1851 can be separated into (1) those who do not reappear in the 1871 enumeration; (2) those who lived in Alfred for at least another decade but were not present in 1881; and (3) those who remained in the county throughout the 1851–81 period and perhaps longer. Similarly, individuals who appear on the 1861 enumeration for the first time include three possibilities: (1) those who do not reappear in the 1871 census; (2) those still present in 1871 but not in 1881; and (3) those who remained through at least to 1881.

The Overall Population Patterns

When Alfred Township's specific demographic pattern of settlement and migration is viewed in this way, its impact becomes readily apparent. The most significant overall result was the maintenance of an approximately constant anglophone population size in the second half of the nineteenth century. The fall-off in new settlers meant that the group did not grow from immigration; the out-migration of a large proportion of mature children ensured that the persistent population did not increase naturally. Thus, after the early decades of settlement, the anglophone population of Alfred Township reached a numerical level which did not increase or decrease significantly for the rest of the century. The British-Isles-origin population of Alfred Township was 284 in 1851 and 270 in 1901. The same phenomenon was apparent at the county level, where the population consistently included seven to eight thousand British-Isles-origin residents. This relatively constant size was not, however, the result of internal de-

TABLE 13

Quebec-Born Residents of Prescott County, 1871–1901

| | | Quebec-Born Residents | | |
	Total Population	French-Canadian Residents	N	% of French-Canadian Residents
1871	17,647	9,623	4,991	51.9
1881	22,857	14,601	6,771	46.4
1891	24,173	16,250	5,935	36.5
1901	27,035	19,190	5,415	28.2

Source: Census of Canada, 1871–1901.

mographic homeostasis but rather the complex product of persistence and transience.[20]

Geographic mobility also affected the francophone population of Prescott County, but in a pattern quite distinct from that of the anglophones. For the French Canadians, emigration was more than balanced by heavy immigration from Quebec during the mid-nineteenth century, and thus the group increased dramatically. By 1871, there were 9,623 French Canadians in Prescott County; by 1881, this number had grown to 14,601.

THE LATER PART OF THE CENTURY

The demographic regime of rapid growth in the francophone population ended abruptly in the early 1880s. The major change was a marked decline in French-Canadian immigration; only a relatively small number of new arrivals balanced the impact of emigration and mortality after this time. Just as 1851 had been the peak year for the number of British-Isles-born residents in Prescott County, 1881 was the high point for Quebec-born newcomers. Their number declined from 6,771 to 5,935 between 1881 and 1891 and then fell to 5,415 by 1901. The result was that the francophone population of Prescott County was predominantly Ontario-born by 1881, and this trend increased year by year. At the start of the new century, almost three-quarters of those in Prescott County who listed their origin as French Canadian had been born in Ontario. (See Table 13.)

At the same time, substantial out-migration from Prescott County continued during the late nineteenth century. The importance of

FIGURE 6

Population Growth, Prescott County, 1881–1901

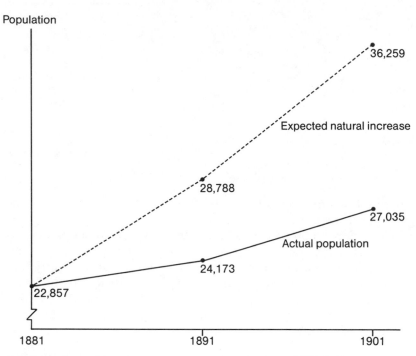

Note: Expected natural increase curve assumes zero net migration and 1901 fertility rate (40.13/1000) and mortality rate (16.79/1000).

Source: Actual population from Census of Canada 1881–1901.

the exodus between 1881 and 1901 can be estimated with a projection of population figures that assumes no immigration or emigration occurred and that is controlled for natural increase. Using the 1901 vital rates for the previous two decades, I produced such a minimum estimate. It shows that Prescott County's population of 22,857 in 1881 should have grown to 28,788 in 1891 and 36,259 in 1901. In fact, it was 24,173 in 1891 and rose to only 27,035 by 1901. Figure 6 graphs these data; the gap between the two lines represents estimated out-migration. (Since some immigration obviously did occur during the period, this is a very conservative indication of the actual out-migration of the 1880s and 1890s.) Clearly, after decades of heavy and rapid population growth, Prescott County quickly became an undesirable region, and its residents were encouraged to seek survival and security in other areas.

The kind of detailed analysis offered for the decades of substantial population increase in Prescott County is not possible for the late nineteenth century since the manuscript census schedules are not available for examination. The 1881 enumeration, however, shows that demographic change was already under way, and the details of this evidence are consistent with the aggregate trends apparent in 1891 and 1901 censuses. Taken together, these sources suggest that a changed demographic regime characterized the late nineteenth century in Prescott County. Strong elements of continuity, however, are evident for family and household structure.

Family and Household Structure

The failure of Prescott County to attract continued immigration after the 1870s combined with changes in the timing of family formation and thus with average family size. These changes affected anglophones and francophones in the same way; as a result, the differences exhibited by the two groups endured from previous decades while the overall pattern shifted. Young people of both cultural groups were delaying marriage. In 1881, the proportion of males and females who were married increased slowly for individuals in their twenties, and many were still not married in their early thirties. Francophones continued to marry earlier than their anglophone counterparts, but neither group were forming families in 1881 with the frequency of earlier years. (See Figure 7.)

As one would expect from the evidence of delayed marriage, families in the area were smaller in 1881 than in earlier decades. The average number of children in both French-Canadian and British-Isles-origin families decreased for each age cohort of mothers between fifteen and forty-nine years old. The 1881 data also indicate that parents were attempting to avoid pregnancies in the later years of the childbearing period. Unlike the period of rapid settlement, when childbearing continued among women older than thirty-nine, maximum family size was now, on average, reached by mothers in the cohort of thirty-five- to thirty-nine-year-olds. It then declined because the home-leaving of older children was not compensated by additional births. This pattern, which was similar for francophones and anglophones, means that average size for families with mothers in their forties was approximately one child less than it had been during the 1851–71 period. (See Figure 8.)

Although the timing and size of families was changing by 1881,

FIGURE 7
Age by Marital Status, Alfred and Caledonia Townships, 1881
(percentage married, three-year moving average)

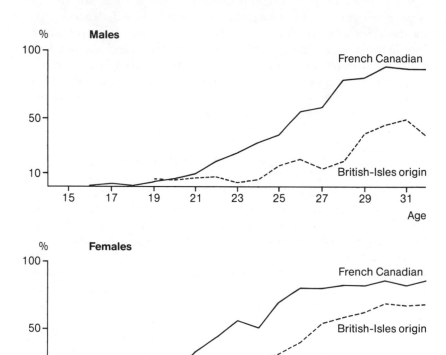

the structure of households continued the pattern of earlier decades. The characteristic household in Alfred and Caledonia townships still included only a single, conjugal-family unit. Multiple-family households were rare; only twenty of the 518 households in Alfred Township and fifteen of the 283 in Caledonia Township included more than one conjugal family unit. Similarly, the most common household members beyond parents and children continued to be relatives, rather than unrelated boarders. This pattern was somewhat less pronounced in Alfred Township, where continued immigration from Quebec was reflected in the presence of boarders who were young francophone males. However, these and other boarders still

FIGURE 8

Average Family Size by Age of Mother, Alfred and Caledonia Townships, 1881

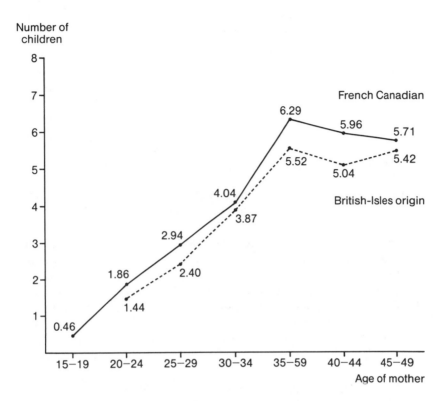

made up only 3 per cent of the population. The importance of relatives was somewhat greater, with 4.4 per cent of the total population consisting of relatives beyond the family of the head of the household. In Caledonia Township, household structure was even more dominated by single, conjugal-family units; only 1 per cent of the population were residing as unrelated boarders while 6.4 per cent were relatives beyond the head of household's family.

The patterns of household structure in 1881 suggest that both change and continuity characterized the demographic context of Prescott County in the later nineteenth century. Emigration became far more important than immigration. Family formation and family size were undergoing significant alteration, but households contin-

TABLE 14

Family / Housing Ratio and the Sex Ratio, Prescott County, 1851–1901

	Families	Houses	Family / Housing Ratio	Males	Females	Male / Female Ratio
1851	1,567	1,461	107	5,408	5,079	106
1861	2,316	2,274	102	7,963	7,536	106
1871	2,874	2,777	103	9,013	8,634	104
1881	3,814	3,747	102	11,688	11,169	105
1891	4,138	4,005	103	12,402	11,771	105
1901	4,861	4,700	103	13,827	13,208	105

Source: Census of Canada, 1851–1901.

ued the established pattern of single families. Only a small proportion of residents lived outside the nuclear family, as relatives or boarders.

The general predominance of single-family households was still evident at the end of the century; in fact, the aggregate evidence for Prescott County suggests remarkable continuity throughout the second half of the nineteenth century. During the 1851–1901 period, the number of families in Prescott County always approximated the number of inhabited houses. At the outset, only 106 families did not have their own dwellings, and this number increased only to 161 in 1901, despite the overall tripling of families in the county. (See Table 14.)

The constant integrity and importance of the family as a demographic unit is also suggested by the low and unchanging sex ratio of the 1851–1901 period in Prescott County. The proportion of males was always slightly greater than of females, and no change over time is apparent. (See Table 14.) This evidence supports the conclusion that families provided the predominant context of individual existence throughout the century.

At the same time, however, the families who stayed in Prescott County had fewer children as the century closed. The number of children less than five years old per 1000 women between ages fifteen and forty-nine declined from 731 in 1881 to 674 in 1891 and 648 in 1901. This trend combined with out-migration to decrease slightly the average size of Prescott County households. In 1881, each dwelling averaged 6.10 residents; this figure declined to 6.04 in 1891 and 5.75 in 1901. It should be noted, however, that the natural growth of Prescott County was still very high, with vital rates similar to those in present-day developing countries. The 1901 fertility rate was 40.13 births per 1,000 population while mortality was 16.79 deaths per 1,000, resulting in a natural annual growth of 2.3 per cent. This situation was quite similar to that in much of Quebec but very unusual for Ontario, where the overall fertility for the same year averaged 23.91 births per 1,000 population. In comparison to data from elsewhere in the lower Ottawa Valley, the Prescott County data are very unlike those from the Ontario county of Glengarry (28.46 births per 1,000 population) but quite similar to those from Quebec's Soulanges (39.89 births per 1,000 population).[21] Undoubtedly, this pattern fuelled Ontarians' perception of a francophone invasion in the late nineteenth century. However, it was natural increase, rather than immigration from Quebec, that was now the engine of population growth in Prescott County. The real invasion had occurred before the early 1880s.

CONCLUSIONS

The character of settlement in Prescott County has several important implications for the cultural and social relations that will be detailed in the following chapters. The most important conclusion is that the country's demography can be explained by a single interpretive framework based on considerations of family and kinship. One can best understand Prescott County as composed of persistent households and families in motion rather than two distinct demographic configurations of French-Canadian and British-Isles-origin residents. From the time of each group's initial settlement, similar family strategies were in place. In this sense, the Prescott County data also do not support an image of individual pioneers blazing trails and building shanties single-handed. Indeed, migration and settlement were much more than the experience of intrepid adult males. The process involved substantial interdependence among all family members, including women and children. Certainly, the relocation of a family took more organization and planning than would have been required for an individual, but the Prescott County evidence suggests that the settlers found the additional effort was more than balanced by the advantage of mutual aid and support. The value of family relationships is especially accentuated by the data suggesting that even those mature children who left the county usually married before emigrating.

In brief, geographic mobility was rarely a solitary affair for the residents of nineteenth-century Prescott County. Rather than independently striking out to seek opportunity, both anglophones and francophones sought whatever security and sense of place they could garner from collection pursuit. Similarly, migrants relied on family and less immediate kinship attachments to ease their initial reception in the county. For example, siblings were important connections for those who wished to settle in various townships. Specific locales thus became identified with certain family names, especially for early anglophone arrivals.

The importance of family migration is particularly noteworthy for the francophones, whom contemporary observers tended to consider as vagabonds. The arrival of French Canadians in Prescott County was part of a massive diaspora in which almost a million French Canadians left Quebec to settle in other parts of Canada and the United States.[22] This movement concerned leaders not only in Ontario but also in Quebec, where, at least initially, major political figures scorned the emigrants as the riff-raff of French-Canadian society.[23] The francophones who immigrated to Prescott County, however, came not as vagabonds but as family units. The county attracted newlyweds, young couples with just a few children, and also sizeable families that had been established in Quebec for at least a decade. Thus, the settlement of townships such as Alfred can be said to have involved, in many cases, conscious decision and firm commitment to a new setting.

The Prescott County experience further reveals that early Irish, Scottish, American, and English immigration engendered settlement that remained important throughout the century. The anglophone presence was especially meaningful in the later part of the century, when this group had been pushed into minority status by francophone immigration. Of course, it would be wrong to claim that no British-Isles-origin residents actually left Prescott County as a result of heavy immigration from Quebec. Certain individuals probably found the reality (or anticipation) of minority status impossible to accept and, as a result, moved from the County. Perhaps some members of this group encouraged the perception of widespread cultural alienation (maybe a few such families spent time in Toronto). Nonetheless, the image of an exodus inspired by Quebec immigration simply does not apply. Indeed, observers should not even have held ideologically based emigration responsible for the small net losses that the British-Isles-origin population experienced for the first time in the late nineteenth century. Cultural considerations may have been weighed carefully during these decades, but, as will be demonstrated in later chapters, this phenomenon can be fully explained by the general social evolution of Prescott County.

The demography of Prescott County also puts in question the

usual view of nineteenth-century eastern Ontario as simply a battle-
ground of Irish Catholics and French Canadians. The anglophone
population certainly included Irish-origin Catholics, but Irish-origin
Protestants were also quite evident, especially in such important communities as the Village of Hawkesbury. Moreover, Scottish-origin
and English-origin residents, some of whom were Catholic, were
present in Prescott County. The result was an ethnic mix not unlike
that found within anglophone populations in other rural Ontario
communities. For this reason, questions of schooling must be examined with respect to a British-Isles-origin population and not simply Irish Catholics.

Moreover, the early numerical majority of French Canadians in
Prescott County suggests that the language-of-instruction controversy was not a straightforward problem in minority education. Francophones dominated most townships by the 1870s and were a majority
at the county level. On the other hand, they remained a decided
minority provincewide. Thus, the francophone situation was de-
mographically complex with distinct majority *and* minority positions
at different administrative levels.

What were the educational implications of this complexity? How
did these various demographic positions affect the impact of local
and provincial authorities? Such questions further suggest the possibility that the French-Canadian settlers may have differed with each
other on school questions. Since francophones were soon numerically dominant within Prescott County, an interpretive framework
focusing only on anglophone-francophone conflict may be incom-
plete. Clearly, French Canadians were a small minority in Ontario,
and thus they had to face the control of an anglophone majority.
Nonetheless, the demographic evidence of Prescott County emphasizes the extent to which francophones dominated many school sections by the 1880s. What were the results of such numerical
domination? Was a consensus on local goals achieved? The importance of the latter question is suggested by the complexity of French-
Canadian settlement, persistence, and out-migration. The francophone population of Prescott County in the late nineteenth century
included a wide range of residents, from new arrivals to "indigenous"
members of long-established families. Such diversity suggests that a
variety of attitudes and behaviour may have characterized francophone educational activity. An analysis that examines only anglophone-francophone relations does not make demographic sense in
Prescott County.

CHAPTER THREE

Farms, Forests, and Family Economies

A crucial result of the population patterns we saw in the last chapter was that firm demographic foundations supported both the minority anglophones and the majority francophones of Prescott County in their pursuit of social, economic, and political ambitions in the later part of the century. The question of identity and thus schooling emerged at the core of these local ambitions. To understand the context of this process, we must next examine the changing economy of Prescott County.

The engine of the Ottawa Valley economy in the nineteenth century was the forest industry. In the first years of the century, the British demand for square timber and the availability of pine trees made the Ottawa River the axis of a new economic zone connected to the vital centres of Montreal and Quebec City. This zone was based on two forms of land exploitation: the use and sale of timber and lumber, and the establishment of agriculture. By the 1840s, the Prescott County economy operated as a système agro-forestier, as in certain areas of Quebec and New Brunswick.[1] Not surprisingly, therefore, the eventual retreat of the forest frontier transformed the region's economy. The period of transition was the 1870s, when the participation in the lumber industry became much less feasible. Few alternatives were available, and Prescott County's système agro-forestier produced frequent hardship and only limited opportunity throughout the end of the nineteenth century.[2]

Thus, two periods characterize Prescott County's economic evolution during the nineteenth century: the years from the 1840s to the early 1870s, when the lumber industry and land availability offered a measure of economic opportunity to settling families, and the years thereafter, when the northwestward retreat of the forest frontier produced an economic crisis. This general economic change can be demonstrated by aggregate data from sources such as the census and from documentary evidence, including local newspapers. However, a more detailed analysis is required to appreciate the evolving material environment's implications for schooling. Was the impact of general economic changes the same on francophones and anglophones? What were the connections among the demographic differences, the distinct patterns of settlement, and the economic experiences of the two groups? Most important, to what extent can a single explanation account for differences in the economic status of Prescott County residents? Or, to tackle the same point somewhat differently, do comparisons of data for French-Canadian and British-Isles-origin residents support the view that Quebec immigration had brought a "foreign" element to Ontario society?[3]

Such questions probe to the level of individuals and households and to topics such as the role of children and the process of family formation. A variety of sources indicate that the farming and forestry economy of nineteenth-century Prescott County must be analysed in terms of the family as an economic unit. Families were characteristically formed on the basis of agricultural ambition, while the forest industry offered seasonal employment for certain family members, a market for agricultural produce, and some compensation for the onerous task of land clearing. All able family members were expected to participate in some form of agriculture or lumbering and, by pooling the contribution of each member, a family sought survival and security. This phenomenon can first be explored by examining the evidence on occupation provided by the manuscript censuses. As will be discussed, the evidence must be used with care, but the provision of occupational data for individuals, as well as information on age, gender, and origin, makes the census a valuable source for understanding the changing economy of Prescott County.[4]

BOOM: THE 1840S TO
THE EARLY 1870S

The Occupational Structure for Men

For the period from the mid-nineteenth century to the early 1870s, the example of Alfred Township indicates the importance of farming and the forest industry to family economies in the lower Ottawa Valley. In each year of census enumeration between 1851 and 1871, farmers and labourers predominate among those residents listed with occupations. These titles were closely associated with age for both anglophone and francophone males. In 1851 and 1861, many

TABLE 15
Age of Farmers and Labourers, Alfred
Township, 1851–71

	Age	Francophones		Anglophones	
		Labourer	Farmer	Labourer	Farmer
1851	10–24	34	0	27	0
	≥ 25	29	31	7	32
1861	10–24	27	6	22	0
	≥ 25	58	102	15	43
1871	10–24	20	81[a]	0	25[a]
	≥ 25	38	174	2	65

[a] Some of these individuals were farmers' sons working on family land; they would have been listed as labourers in the earlier censuses. See the text for a discussion of this distinction.

Source: Manuscript census schedules, 1851, 1861, 1871.

labourers were younger than age twenty-five, and most farmers were older. (See Table 15.) This pattern was very strong among the residents of British-Isles origin. It also existed among French Canadians, although this group did have a significant number of labourers age twenty-five and older, particularly in 1861.

The apparently weaker movement of francophones away from "labouring" after early adulthood is also evident in the 1871 census (see Table 15). It should be noted, however, that enumerators for this census were instructed to consider all males who worked on family farms to be "farmers," whereas in 1851 and 1861, the son of a farmer was defined as a labourer if he worked "for the benefit of his parent."[5] Consequently, farmers predominate among working males in the 1871 census, even among the teenage population. Since the enumerator did not use "labourer" to describe domestic contribution, the two anglophone and fifty-eight francophone males so listed must have been employed outside their own households or engaged to farm land belonging to others. This evidence, like that of the 1851 and 1861 enumerations, suggests that more francophone than anglophone settlers continued as wage-earners as they grew older. Anglophone youths who did not acquire land in early adulthood tended to leave their families in Alfred Township and seek their fortune elsewhere.

The number of males in the township who were neither labourers nor farmers was never significant during the 1851–71 period and, in fact, diminished after midcentury. In 1851, most nonagricultural occupations listed by the enumerator involved woodworking; there were a carpenter, a shingle-maker, a sawyer, a wood dealer, and seven lumberers. In addition, there were three weavers, one shoemaker, one thresher, and one innkeeper, all of whom were anglophone, plus one francophone and one anglophone blacksmith. By 1861, artisans and lumberers had all but disappeared from Alfred Township; in that enumeration, only one francophone teacher and one francophone blacksmith joined the plethora of men who were labourers and farmers. Despite tremendous growth in population, the absence of significant nonagricultural titles continued in 1871. Some woodworking industry returned, as reflected in the presence of five francophone carpenters and one anglophone lumber dealer, but they were joined by only a teacher, a blacksmith, and a storekeeper among francophones and a merchant and a clerk among anglophones.

The predominance of labourers and farmers in Alfred Township was partly related to the sparsely settled character of the area at the time of intensive Quebec immigration. Perspective on the issue comes from contrasting the experience of neighbouring Caledonia Township, where considerable British-Isles-origin settlement in the early nineteenth century had led to a well-established community by 1851. In the enumeration for that year, the occupational structure included eighteen different designations for anglophone males, including carpenters, tavern keepers, teachers, and blacksmiths. Among francophones, only one male servant and one shoemaker were listed. By 1861, however, the variety of occupational titles for anglophone residents in Caledonia had decreased by half, but there were now two francophone shoemakers, a blacksmith, a carpenter, a cooper, and an innkeeper. Nonetheless, the overall occupational structure of Caledonia had simplified considerably, with only ten distinct occupational titles being listed. This variety remained unaltered in 1871, leaving labourers and farmers to dominate the township's occupational structure as they already did in Alfred.

The decrease in artisan activity in Alfred and Caledonia townships resulted from the growth elsewhere of specific centres of economic activity. The development of service centres, such as Hawkesbury, incorporated as a village in 1867 and having a population of 1,671 by 1871, and of the smaller communities of L'Orignal and Vankleek Hill, centralized the residences of blacksmiths, carpenters, coopers, and weavers and caused a simplification of the occupational structure of neighbouring farming-lumbering areas. Certain townships of Prescott County became increasingly rural and tied to land exploitation.

Farming – A Family Endeavour

The relationship of agriculture and the forest industry meant that land availability was a critical factor in determining the extent of economic opportunity in Prescott County. Land was required as a basis for the family economies, which could then participate seasonally in the forest industry. Although land ownership clearly did not exempt anyone from constant material uncertainty, it was perceived as the best hedge against the economic insecurities of the time since farming offered the possibility of collective family endeavour. Productive opportunities for women and children outside the rural family economies were limited. At each census year, only a small number of women were considered by themselves and the enumerator to have occupations. These females were usually servants, teachers, seamstresses, or farmers, and their positions were closely associated with age and marital status. A woman with an occupation was either saving for marriage or supporting a family after her husband had died. In Alfred Township, for example, two francophone female adolescents were servants in 1851, and seven young women and one widow were servants in 1861. By 1871, "working" francophone women in the township included one young servant, four single-parent or widowed farmers, two young weavers, and two dressmakers.

The more established character of the anglophone community in Caledonia was reflected in a greater number of females with occupations, but the variety of their titles only slightly exceeded the francophone example. In 1851, seven young anglophone females were employed as servants, and four older single-parent women were listed as farmers. In 1861, there were five young servants, one older farmer, a widowed weaver, and three young teachers.

This small number of women considered to have occupations was representative of the general pattern in Prescott County during the mid-nineteenth century. The 1861 census listed only fifty-three seamstresses, 187 female servants, and twenty-two female teachers.[6]

Similarly, it was the farm that best allowed children to contribute to the family economy.[7] Local sawmills offered some opportunity for boys, but there were few income-producing possibilities for young girls. Yet, the nimble fingers and simple skills of children could be well utilized in a domestic agricultural setting. The writings of settlers, travellers, and other observers emphasize that full family participation was characteristic of all phases of settlement.

Each family member had specific tasks throughout each process. Land clearing first involved the cutting of underbrush and small trees, a job accomplished by the adolescents of settling families. Younger children, supervised by mothers, then piled the small trees, underbrush, and branches into heaps, where they remained until decay facilitated burning off. As this work progressed, the father and older sons began chopping the large trees, which were afterwards stripped of their branches and cut into logs.

Once a piece of land had been cleared, planting was begun immediately, with each member of a family contributing to the agricultural process. The female head of household organized the planting of vegetables, such as turnips, potatoes, and peas, which would supply a newly settled famly with its initial food requirements, while the men of the family concentrated on hay and oats, the products most easily grown during the first years of settlement. This work was paralleled by the labour of younger children, who worked together in the fields in a division of labour appropriate to their size and strength. "We raised potatoes all day. Jane and Esther helped us to pick them up."[8] Children also helped cultivate fruits and vegetables such as "bleuets, fraises, framboises, et groseilles sauvages." The produce of the children's gardens was then made into "des plats exquis, des confitures et des liqueurs" by the female household head.[9]

During the winter months, the land was further cleared and threshing and milling were accomplished, usually by the male household head and one or two of the family's male adolescents. During this time, women and children continued the domestic economic activity, often including the production of textiles for family use. As soon as possible after settlement, women began weaving blankets, rugs, and fabrics for clothing in response to the needs of their families. They organized this domestic industry on the basis of full participation by their sons and daughters; young children frequently contributed by spinning. The majority of families produced their own fabric for clothing, generally about twenty-five yards per year of "home-made cloth and flannel."[10]

The character of the family economy in Prescott County suggests why the first and most immediate attachment of producers was to the family unit, even though participation in the système agro-forestier connected individuals to an international economic structure. Moreover, the attachment of family members to a collective household economy helps explain why land hunger was a common characteristic in Prescott County as elsewhere in North America in the nineteenth century.[11] Families were seen as crucial to the survival and security of individuals, and land was considered to offer the best opportunity for the family economy.

Settlement Patterns

The availability of certain soil types affected the settlement patterns of anglophone and francophone immigrants in different ways. The observations of contemporary writers and the actual location of individual residences show that anglophone and francophone families differed in their opinion of what constituted favourable or even arable land.

Prescott County has two distinct kinds of arable soil. Glaciers covered all the eastern counties long after the land of central and western Ontario had surfaced; as a result, soil development in the eastern region is several thousand years behind that of the rest of the province; more than half of Prescott County is covered with sand and gravelly soils. Most of this less-fertile land is in the higher plains of the county. In lower regions, the land is largely clay loam, a soil type with great productive potential. These loams are water-laid, however, and must be drained artificially before they produce well. Therefore, most Prescott County soil requires preparation before cultivation can begin: the moist, clay land must be drained, and the drier, sandy land must be improved by fertilization.[12]

The pattern of anglophone and francophone settlement in Prescott was closely related to this topography. Anglophone settlers consistently displayed a preference for the dry, sandy plains. In 1881, the *Dominion Atlas* observed that "vast tracts of low lying land" had been "shunned by settlers of the Anglo-Saxon race," who had, it reported, chosen the land of regions that reached an "altitude of some dignity."[13] This preference had been true from the earliest days of anglophone immigration. For example, Simeon Vankleek, a United Empire Loyalist from New York, was travelling in "the Laurentian hills north of the Ottawa when he noticed high land on the south side of the river." He crossed the Ottawa and became an early settler in Prescott's township of West Hawkesbury.[14]

Vankleek's decision to settle on "high land" may have been influenced by the many English-language settlers' guides that warned pioneers to avoid swampy land. These guides emphasized the importance of limiting the initial time and effort needed for cultivation and consequently discouraged settlers from acquiring land which needed drainage. Anglophone advisers felt that the required fertilizing of sandy soil, though not desirable, was far less time-consuming and laborious than the digging of trenches in marshy fields.[15]

In contrast, francophone leaders urged habitants to take up tracts of wet land. In encouraging settlement in the Ottawa Valley, francophone writers described the land being ignored by the anglophone settlers.as a "magnifique région." While the *Dominion Atlas* reported that "very extensive areas in Prescott and Russell approach so nearly the definition of the term 'swampy' as to render them almost unfit for cultivation," francophones were praising the "grande fertilité" of the same counties.[16] Even later in the nineteenth century, one Quebec leader reported that "la région des belles terres est très considérable" in the Ottawa Valley.[17]

The perceptions of francophone leaders concerning desirable land were shared by Quebec immigrants who settled in the Ottawa Valley in the nineteenth century. Donald Cartwright has systematically examined Prescott and Russell counties and concludes that the characteristic French-Canadian colonist exhibited a "preference ... to settle on the wetter clay soils." Cartwright also finds that settlers of British origin showed a "preference for the higher and drier lands associated with the sand and till plains."[18]

Part of this distinction appears to have resulted from culturally based perceptions and part from necessity. As we have seen, the heavy Quebec immigration followed earlier anglophone settlement. By the time many francophones arrived in Prescott County, low-lying land was all tht remained available. (This fact was also important to Irish immigrants of the 1840s, who sometimes had to accept wet soil.)

Land selection in the earlier nineteenth century was also influenced by the county's roads, whose placement made elevated land the most accessible. Much of the county was densely wooded, and travel was exceedingly difficult and often dangerous for many months of the year. (The Ottawa River was a vital communications artery, but it could not be relied upon for safe travel year round.) Prescott County's principal road paralleled the river.[19] Like most early roads in Prescott County, it began as an Indian trail that was blazed during the fur-trade period. Many of these trails were located on high-lying plains, especially the east-west ridge spanning the land that became Prescott County. Consequently, this area attracted early residents; in the 1820s about 90 per cent of the settled lots of the townships of East and West Hawkesbury were located on sand and till plains.[20] Low-lying areas, such as Alfred Township, which includes large stretches of swamps and marsh, remained very sparsely settled. These areas became the focus of francophone settlement.

Land potential was not the only ecological factor that influenced settlement patterns. For some, the Ottawa Valley's severe climate was a further consideration. One immigration agent admitted that anglophone immigrants characteristically regarded the cold weather with "so great a horror." In contrast, francophone leaders viewed the Ottawa Valley's climate as quite familiar, and comparison to conditions in northern Quebec made Prescott County appear desirable; one report stressed that "le climat dans la vallée de l'Ottawa est des plus favorables à l'agriculture parce qu'il est aussi doux que dans le district de Montréal."[21]

The chronology of immigration, the accessibility of land, and the climatic conditions made the different perceptions of soil particularly important in determining the cultural pattern of settlement in Prescott County. Even in the early nineteenth century, when all types of land were still available, observers noticed a cultural distinction in settlers' locations. In 1827, the deputy surveyor of the Canada Company reported that land in the Township of West Hawkesbury, which was "generally swampy," was being rejected by Scottish settlers; "such lands, however, the [French] Canadians are fond of clearing, and make certain kinds of swamps the best for tillage." Similarly, the deputy surveyor noted that the "swamps in Caledonia are generally such lands as Canadians are partial to, and good for cultivation, when cleared in their way of clearing and completely drained." The land in Alfred Township, he emphasized, was "generally swampy but good lands for Canadians or such as they make good by their mode of clearing."[22] Some early anglophone settlers did attempt to take up low-lying land but failed to bring the soil into cultivation and consequently migrated elsewhere.[23]

The 1851 census enumerators reported that the anglophone-francophone pattern was continuing into the mid-nineteenth century. Albert H. James, the Alfred Township enumerator, noted:

part of the township bordering on Longueuil is of a clay soil and the west part of the township is for the most part sandy and the southern part of the township across which runs Horse Creek which empties itself into the South Petite Nation River is low and swampy, a portion of that section from the Part of the Great Tamrock Marsh which pervades this township ... Alfred is generally considered to be a township of the most inferior in regard to the quality of soil but parts [sic] of it is good land and produces pretty good crops.

The enumerator suggested that the "good land," defined as the sandy areas, had already been fully taken up by anglophone settlers and that no more anglophone arrivals should be expected. He predicted that whenever the township became "settled to any further extent or importance, it will be settled by the French-Canadians of Lower Canada mainly – or rather it is most like such to be the case."[24]

Philip Downing, the 1851 enumerator for Caledonia Township,

also recognized the relationship of soil type to patterns of settlement. He estimated most of the Caledonia land to be of very inferior quality: "generally swampy and cold soil – it embraces on the North for several concessions, the great Caledonia marsh which pervades 3 or 4 townships and is of no value." However, he noted, a "tract in this township called the Caledonia Flats through which runs Caledonia Creek is well settled and the soil is of superior quality." It was here that anglophone immigrants had established significant settlements. They were attracted to the "soil of this lay of land which is a sandy loam." That this kind of land was now fully settled meant to the enumerator that the future of Caledonia township was not promising. After describing the unsettled land as "of little value," Downing concluded that "it appears useless to make any further remarks in regard to this township."[25]

As we have seen, the 1851 enumerators' predictions that further anglophone settlement would not occur in Alfred and Caledonia townships were fulfilled during the later decades of the nineteenth century, when the number of anglophone residents remained almost constant, despite the rapid growth of francophone settlement. In 1881, the *Dominion Atlas* explained that the "peculiarities of soil and surface" characteristic of Alfred township had "militated against the rapid development" of this township by anglophones and for the heavy immigration of francophones. The *Atlas* writers analysed this phenomenon in terms of cultural tradition, explaining that francophones had been "long accustomed to life on the flat lands of the Lower Province" and were thereby prepared for the "cultivation of the semi-swamps" which the early British settlers had ignored. Francophone heritage also was said to have provided immigrant habitants with appropriate techniques of land clearing. The *Atlas* writers admitted that French Canadians had "proven their efficiency" in the "preliminary clearing" of the difficult low-lying land. This efficiency resulted, they said, from French Canadians' specific agricultural tradition, which had evolved in the fertile but very moist St Lawrence Valley. In other words, the *Atlas* compilers explained the willingness of Quebec immigrants to settle in Alfred Township on the basis of the appropriateness of their agricultural tradition to the available land in the township.[26]

This explanation of settlement patterns in Alfred Township is supported by evidence concerning the Quebec backgrounds of the francophone immigrants. Parish records from St-Victor-D'Alfred show that the eighty-six families the Church considered "des pionniers" of the parish mostly came from neighbouring counties in Quebec, especially Soulanges, Vaudreuil, and Deux Montagnes (see

Figure 9). Emigrants from such counties met very familiar agricultural conditions in Prescott County, which, in the extent of its low-lying land, maintained continuity with the St. Lawrence lowlands. Moreover, almost all these settlers brought farming backgrounds to Alfred Township. (Significantly, Montreal, despite its close proximity, was the place of origin for only one of the francophone pioneer families.)

Thus, the decisive factors in the settlement patterns of Prescott County seem to rise well above the level of physical determinism. Each family's decision involved a judgment of advantage, involving familiarity with specific agricultural skills, which made settlement in Prescott County attractive to some and unattractive to others. Such an analysis suggests why the number of anglophone families remained relatively constant in Prescott County after the 1840s. An inheriting offspring took over each farm; siblings, faced with the prospect of being able to obtain only low-lying land, decided to seek their fortune elsewehere. Land that seemed desirable to francophones, however, was available for several more decades.

Family Formation and Family Size

The pattern of settlement relates directly to the variation in age-at-marriage and, therefore, family size between anglophone and francophone settlers in Prescott County. Marriage depended on the ability of aspiring couples to form separate households and consequently on their ability to acquire land. For a few young adults, this need was easily satisfied by a timely inheritance, but for most young men and women, especially anglophones, land acquisition was uncertain by the mid-nineteenth century. By this time, the less expensive acreage was predominantly in low-lying areas, so settling on elevated soil required substantial capital. The abundant low-lying land now also had to be purchased and, for most couples, represented an important investment.[27] Thus, age-at-marriage tended to be delayed for both anglophone and francophone couples despite the apparent availability of land during the midcentury. Before establishing a household, aspiring anglophone couples who chose not to emigrate had to wait for an inheritance or a vacancy in some other established household, and their francophone counterparts had to accumulate savings. During the 1851–71 period, these factors delayed family formation for both groups, especially the anglophones.

The process of family formation is central to the social history of Prescott County since the nonmechanized nature of production in the système agro-forestier meant that family size had a significant

FIGURE 9
Origins of the Pioneering French-Canadian Families in the Parish of St-Victor-d'Alfred

PLACE	NUMBER
Soulanges	18
Vaudreuil	17
Deux-Montagnes	16
Laval	9
Terrebonne	6
Montcalm	6
Laprairie	4
Jacques-Cartier	3
Beauharnois	3
Kamouraska	2
Montreal	1
Lac St-Jean	1
TOTAL	86

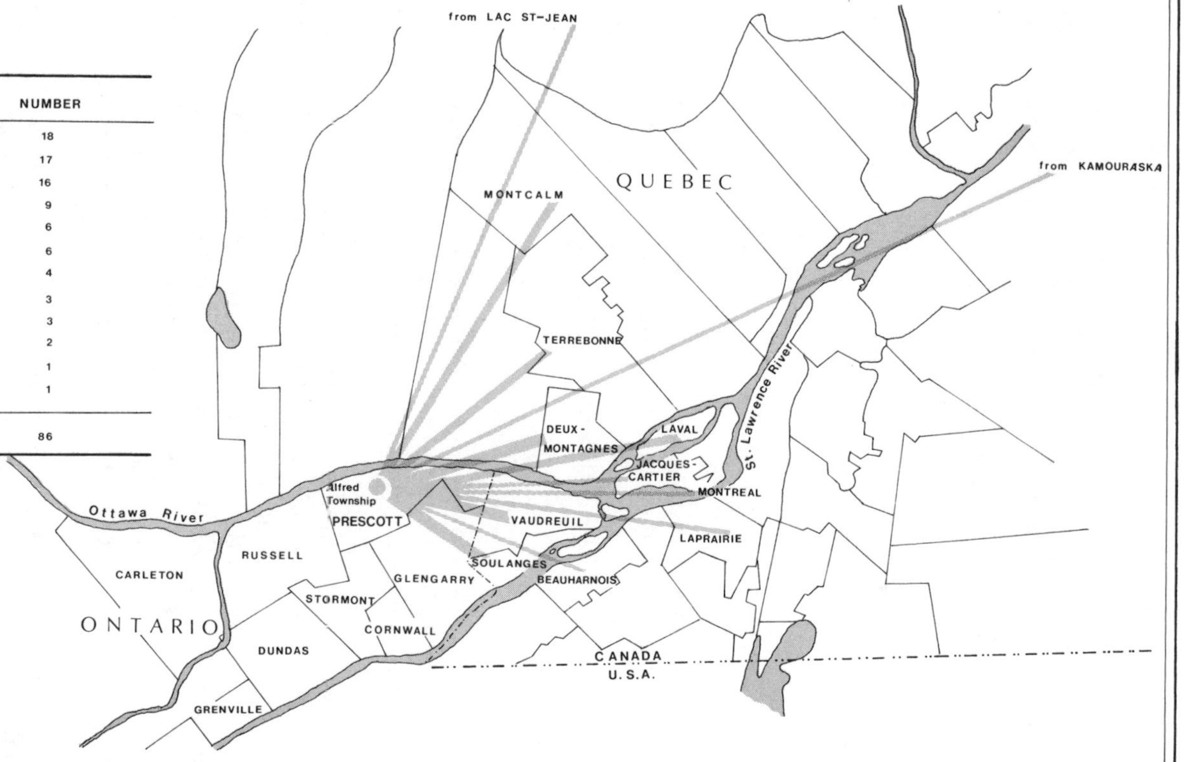

impact on family destiny. The number of able-bodied members that a family could draw on determined the scope of its economic activities and the extent to which it could take advantage of material possibilities in the county. It is not surprising, therefore, that married women, both anglophone and francophone, gave birth at regular intervals throughout their childbearing years and that the average established family within either group could draw upon the labour of several young teenagers. (Francophone families averaged a one-child advantage over anglophone families, but, as has been discussed, this difference, especially for families with mothers younger than age forty, was simply the result of francophones' earlier family formation.)

Participation in the Forest Industry

The establishment of farms was a point of entry to the forest industry. During the mid-nineteenth century its activities were combined with those of agriculture in three major ways: (1) marketing of the products of land clearing; (2) farmers' or their sons' taking seasonal employment in sawmills and shanties; and (3) the sale of agricultural produce to sustain the shanties during winter.

Land Clearing. Research suggests that most early settlers in Ontario were hostile to the dense forest which covered most of the province; trees were considered obstacles to agriculture, and landclearing was looked on as an onerous task.[28] In the Ottawa Valley, however, the forest was an important natural resource available to settling families and aided more than hindered the establishment of viable domestic economies. This phenomenon was particularly important in Prescott County because of the changing nature of the Ottawa Valley forest industry during midcentury. At the outset of the 1800s, it had primarily produced square timber, the product desired in Britain, where the export market was almost totally focused. Several decades later, however, the forest cover of the northeastern United States was rapidly declining, and the Americans were looking for new areas of lumber supply. They turned to the Ottawa Valley as the most likely source of additional wood. Available Canadian supply and heavy American demand inspired the 1854 Reciprocity Treaty, by which Canadian lumber products gained free access to market in the United States. Canadian lumber export now increased to satisfy both the traditional British demand and the new American market.[29]

The growth of an American market for Canadian export had significant implications for the forest industry in the Ottawa Valley.

Rather than square timber, the United States wanted sawn lumber. Thus, the 1840s witnessed a rapid growth in the manufacture of, for example, deals, pieces of lumber sawn to about three inches thick, ten inches wide, and ten to twenty-four feet long. Deals were exported to both the United States and Britain and were also sold to Canadian sawmills, which recut them for the housing market. Hamilton Brothers of Hawkesbury was a major supplier of deals and during the mid-nineteenth century held a major place not only in the Prescott County economy but also among all the lumber companies of the Ottawa Valley.

To some extent, the growth of the sawmill industry gave new value to wooded areas which had already been exploited. These areas, which included much of the lower Ottawa Valley as early as the 1830s and 1840s, had been stripped of the enormous, quality trees needed for preparation of square timber, but many retained lesser trees from which sawmills could produce deals, planks, and boards. Consequently, the rapid rise of the demand for sawn lumber prolonged the forestry potential of the lower Ottawa Valley after it was no longer considered part of the forest frontier.[30]

The disregard of all but the best trees by the square timber industry left some townships in Prescott County still wood-covered at midcentury. In 1847, a surveyor, sent to establish a route for road builders to follow through the county, reported that his efforts were impeded by "a dense forest, mostly of pine, with a thick growth of underwood."[31] Although this forest was reduced in the following years, a 1873 description estimated that "il y a encore environ 250,000 arpents de terre couverte de bois d'une excellente qualité" in the counties of Prescott, Russell, and Vaudreuil.[32]

Thus, the lumber industry of the Ottawa Valley enabled families that arrived in Prescott County at midcentury to reap some initial profit from land clearing, which was still underway in 1871. The enumerator of the agricultural census for Caledonia Township noted for certain households "land cleared last summer – too late for crop" or "land cleared but was not cropped last summer." Then, apparently tiring of including these notations, the enumerator simply wrote, "Such circumstances will occur on many of the sheets [of the manuscript census]."[33]

In response to the availability of adequate trees and the demand for sawn wood, sawmills were established at crossroads throughout Prescott County during the 1840s and 1850s, ready to purchase whatever supply could be generated by local families. In 1851 in Longueuil Township, a small sawmill "using five hands part of the time" processed "about 2,000 logs yearly, mostly manufactured boards." Similarly, Caledonia Township had a small sawmill by 1851, while Alfred Township acquired its own mill, valued at $800, by 1861. The impact of the sawn lumber trade was even more significant in later years, and the number of sawmills in Prescott County reached sixteen in 1871.[34]

An additional way in which Prescott County families could attempt to benefit from land clearing, especially before the mid-nineteenth century, was by burning trees and selling the ashes for their potash. For this process, logs which had been chopped and stripped were piled strategically for easy combustion. After burning logs, family members carefully gathered the resultant ashes in a kettle. By pouring water into the kettle, settlers could obtain lye, which they could use for making their own soap. As late as the mid-nineteenth century, they could also sell the lye for soap production in a small local market or sell barrels of soap to a small cloth factory.[35] More important, they could boil down the lye and then cool it in an iron pot, producing the solid potash sought by Canadian and New England markets. If a settling family did not have a potash kettle and coolers, the ashes could be sold to a more fortunate neighbour. However, since the manufacture of potash required little skill or capital investment and dramatically increased the reward of land clearing, new families often strove to obtain the necessary appliances on credit, using ashes or expected farm produce as collateral.[36]

The cash return from either selling ashes or producing potash was considered by some a worthwhile reward for land clearing, initially providing "la principale ressource" of settling families in the Ottawa Valley.[37] One English-language source estimated that clearing two-and-a-half acres would produce one barrel of potash, which, after expenses, would return $30. A French-language source indicated more conservatively that each barrel brought about $20.[38] The number of acres of land that could be cleared each year depended both on the land itself and on the amount of labour each family could provide. During the winter months, two men reportedly could clear "quinze arpents de terre neuve" (about twelve and a half acres), but in the spring they could chop two acres of average land in the course of a week.[39] No extant records document the size of the reward for individual settling families, but in 1861, it is clear that potash production was still possible for small, local firms in eastern Ontario. In Prescott County, six "factories" produced 220 barrels of potash, valued at $7,000. By 1871, potash production in the eastern counties appears to have been centralized partially in Glengarry County, which had had only two asheries in 1861 but now had ten, producing potash valued at $14,220. In contrast, the number of

TABLE 16

Size of Lots Held by Farmer-Owners, Alfred and Caledonia Townships, 1861–71

	Caledonia Township		Alfred Township	
	1861	*1871*	*1861*	*1871*
Francophones holding				
0–19 acres	1	0	1	0
20–49 acres	0	3	15	20
≥ 50 acres	10	41	75	132
Total francophones	11	44	91	152
Anglophones holding				
0–19 acres	0	0	0	2
20–49 acres	3	10	1	3
≥ 50 acres	103	109	39	58
Total anglophones	106	119	40	63
Total farmer-owners	117	163	131	215

Source: Manuscript census, 1861–71.

potash factories in Prescott County was reduced to three in 1871; nevertheless, they managed $7,030 in production value.[40]

Each family's income from marketing logs or potash was related to the size of its property, but settlers characteristically acquired lots sufficiently large to ensure a return for at least several years. This was true for early-century anglophone settlers and for midcentury francophone arrivals. Among farmers in both Alfred and Caledonia townships during the 1850s and 1860s, most anglophone and francophone settlers owned land of more than fifty acres. No more than 10 per cent of the Caledonia farmers held lots of fewer than fifty acres. In Alfred, a slightly larger proportion of francophones owned twenty to forty-nine acres, but a substantial majority held larger parcels, and by 1871 more than 87 per cent of the francophone farmers had acquired at least fifty acres of land. (See Table 16.)

Seasonal Employment. The marketing of wood products garnered from land clearing was the first way in which families in Prescott County could profit from the lumber industry at midcentury. The second way was by having the male head of household or, more usually, older sons seek employment on a seasonal basis. The major employer with headquarters in Prescott County was Hamilton Brothers of Hawkesbury. Local historians have preserved some of the company's business records, and they include details on its labour force.[41] One set of extant records includes employment summaries for all the company's workers during 1856 and 1857, permitting calculations of length of employment and wages for workers in the company's shanties in the regions of the Gatineau and Rouge rivers and in the sawmills at Hawkesbury. The documents are fragmentary and they only offer names as personal identification, but considered together with census evidence on the ages and marital status of lumber-industry workers from Prescott County, they help to specify the role of seasonal labour within family economies.

Participation in the Ottawa Valley lumber industry involved employment in shanties during winter and in sawmills from spring to fall. Shantymen generally received wages for three or four months before work was completed in early April. At this time, some shantymen returned to prepare for opening the sawmills, and some stayed for the log drive. Those workers who stayed usually received pay increases, an indication of both the competition of other employment opportunities as winter ended and the added skill and courage required to transport the timber down the Ottawa River and its tributaries. Sawmills, such as the one at Hawkesbury, were in full operation from spring to fall, and many employees were paid for as much as five months. In addition, sawmills hired agricultural workers who were available for short periods during less active phases of the farm cycle. These workers might be at the sawmills for only a few weeks, usually those before the harvest was ready.

The Hamilton Brothers' records show that the company employed about 450 workers in each of 1856 and 1857. At any one time during the year, however, the actual number of workers was smaller since employment patterns were dictated by the rhythm of the lumber industry. Of the 200-odd men hired for the shanties, about two-thirds also worked in the sawmills at Hawkesbury; additional workers brought the total of sawmill employees to an average of 360 in these years. (See Table 17.)

The usual wage in the shanties was $10 to $13 per month, plus room and board. Most sawmill workers received a higher wage of $12 to $15 per month but had to provide for their own food and lodging. Some sawmill employees, however, received as little as $4 to $5 per month, reflecting child labour at the mill. Boys of twelve or fourteen acted as messengers, carried pails of drinking water,

TABLE 17
Hamilton Brothers' Labour Force, 1856–7

	Number of Workers		
	Total	Employed in shanties	Employed in sawmills
1856	415	194	333
1857	483	221	387

Note: Shanty workers and sawmill workers do not add to the total because many individuals were employed successively in both capacities (see text).

Source: Hamilton Brothers of Hawkesbury employee records, 1856 and 1857, now held by Hawkesbury [Ont.] Public Library.

swept offices, and acted as assistants to the older labourers. The Hamilton Brothers' records do not specify the ages of their employees, but the 1871 census indicates that approximately 15 per cent of the recorded 388 sawmill workers in Prescott County were less than sixteen years of age. These figures include the Hamilton Brothers' operation as well as local sawmills that relied even more heavily on young workers. In 1871, for example, Alfred Township boasted a sawmill employing twenty adults and ten youngsters under age sixteen.

In contrast, shanty work required physical strength beyond the capability of children. The census did not officially seek information on shantymen in Prescott County, but fortuitously, their demographic profile is suggested by the 1851 manuscript census for Caledonia Township. For normally resident individuals who were absent at the time of the census, the enumerator not only completed the required column but also noted "in shanty" as appropriate. These extra notations indicate clearly that the shantymen from rural areas were characteristically young adults. The twenty-nine shantymen from Caledonia were predominantly unmarried sons of independent farmers or agricultural labourers. Most were in their late teens or early twenties; only two were under the age of sixteen. Clearly, shanty work was for those in their physical prime. (See Table 18.)

Food Supply for the Shanties. Another way in which Prescott County families could participate in the lumber industry was by responding to its demand for food supplies, particularly during the winter months. At this time, the lumber shanties were in full operation, and the

TABLE 18
Shantymen, Caledonia Township, 1851

Household Status	N	Average Age
Head	5	40.0
Son	24	21.7
Total	29	24.8

Source: Manuscript census, 1851.

tremendous need for meat, grain, and vegetables drove the price of agricultural produce to high levels. Some supplies were imported from the United States and from other regions of Canada; for example, pork was usually brought in from Cincinnati while flour came from western areas of Ontario. Certain desired products, however, were too cumbersome to be transported long distances, and consequently the lumber industry was forced to rely on local markets. Hay, oats, and potatoes were the most important of these products, and throughout midcentury farmers of the lower Ottawa Valley enjoyed ready markets for any surplus they could generate.[42] In 1867, the shanties of Hamilton Brothers consumed 2,000 tons of agricultural produce, including 750 tons of hay, 25,000 bushels of oats, 5,000 bushels of turnips, 6,000 bushels of potatoes, 1,000 barrels of pork, 9,000 barrels of flour, and 2,000 bushels of oatmeal.[43] Some of these supplies were produced by Hamilton Brothers' own farms, which it operated on the north side of the Ottawa River. However, only major companies had their own farms, and the extent of the lumber industry's needs engendered a substantial reliance on small-scale production.

Contemporary writers recognized that this kind of demand promised a substantial reward to enterprising settlers. An English-language immigration agency, established in Ottawa in 1857, distributed pamphlets which stressed the huge market created by the lumber industry, predicting, "The vast amount of lumbering ... will require more than the Settlement can yield for years."[44] Similarly, a Carleton County resident reported in 1876, "The farmer here has a home market where he can dispose of his coarse grain to a better advantage than to use it for fattening cattle, on account of the large lumbering interest carried on here."[45] Difficulties in transportation because of poor roads ensured that local farmers could receive top prices for the bulk produce which they supplied to the shanties. In 1847, the commissioner of public works remarked that in the Ottawa Valley

TABLE 19
Agricultural Produce, Alfred and Caledonia Townships, 1851–71

	Hay (tons)	Oats (bu.)	Potatoes (bu.)	Wheat (bu.)	Peas (bu.)	Barley (bu.)
Alfred Township						
1851[a]	–	–	–	–	–	–
1861	446.0	18,660	13,900	4,890	3,950	642
1871	919.0	21,802	17,021	5,025	5,134	[b]
Caledonia Township						
1851	813.0	9,464	10,924	3,777	757	122
1861	1,148.0	29,359	22,571	5,746	2,936	820
1871	1,502.5	35,626	44,697	6,972	3,646	[b]

[a] These figures are not available because they were aggregated with the totals of Longueuil Township for the purposes of the printed census volumes. The manuscript census of the agricultural schedules for all of Prescott County in 1851 are missing.
[b] Not given in the census schedule.

Source: Census of Canada, 1851–71.

"the highest prices are paid ... for every description of agricultural produce." He claimed to "have seen £10 per ton paid for hay; 6s. per bushel for oats and the same for potatoes."[46] Farmers and their sons could bring supplies to the shanties and, if they wished, then hire out themselves and their sleighs. In this way, families could doubly profit during the winter months.

Because the Prescott County families participated in supplying agricultural produce to the lumber industry, their crops were precisely those most heavily in demand in the shanties. Throughout the mid-nineteenth century, hay, oats, and potatoes were the staples of their cultivation. By 1871, hay farming occupied twice as much land as any other crop in both Alfred and Caledonia townships. In that year, Caledonia yielded 1502.5 tons of hay, while Alfred, more recently settled, produced 919 tons. The cultivation of oats and potatoes was also extremely important in these townships. Other significant crops were wheat, peas, and barley, but their production never rivalled the importance of hay, oats, or potatoes. (See Table 19.)

Because of the availability of the forestry market, Prescott County farmers aimed to achieve surplus production. A prerequisite was a significant amount of cleared land, and many farmers, anglophone and francophone, had it, particularly by 1871. The earlier settlement

TABLE 20
Improved Land on the Lots of Farmer-Owners, Alfred and Caledonia
Townships, 1861–71

	Caledonia Township		Alfred Township	
	1861	1871	1861	1871
Francophones				
Number	11	44	91	152
Acres improved				
0–19	90.9%	56.8%	52.7%	34.9%
20–49	9.1%	34.1%	45.1%	52.0%
≥ 50	0.0%	9.1%	2.2%	13.1%
Anglophone				
Number	106	119	40	63
Acres improved				
0–19	19.8%	16.0%	10.0%	25.4%
20–49	49.1%	41.2%	65.0%	60.3%
≥ 50	31.1%	42.8%	25.0%	14.3%

Source: Manuscript census, 1861–71.

of anglophone immigrants was clearly reflected by the number of
farms which included more than twenty acres of cleared land in
1861 and 1871. Throughout this period, the vast majority of anglophone farmers held land which was used for commercial purposes.
The pattern was slightly different for many francophones, who in
1861 had not yet had sufficient time to establish commercial farms.
Only one French Canadian in Caledonia Township held a sizeable
portion of improved land in that year, while in Alfred Township
fewer than half the habitant farmers cultivated twenty or more acres.
By 1871, however, many more francophone farmers in these townships had that amount of improved land and were capable of producing surplus crops. (See Table 20.)

BUST: THE LATE 1870S ONWARDS

The relationship of farming and lumbering in the mid-nineteenth
century led contemporary observers to agree that the lower Ottawa
Valley offered economic opportunity to family units. In 1854, a
government official in the Ottawa Valley remarked, "The population
are more able, and do consume more and live better than any other
country population that I am acquainted with ... I never saw elsewhere money more plenty, and the means of comfort more univer-

sally diffused." John MacTaggart considered French Canadians along the Ottawa River to be "by far the most respectable people in the country ... and to live in comparative happiness." Similarly, Joseph Guigues, the bishop of Ottawa, remarked during a tour of Prescott County in 1860 that "les terres sont excellentes" and that as a result "les Canadiens affluent."[48]

Over time, however, the true nature of a système agro-forestier became evident in the Ottawa Valley. Dependency on the lumber industry ensured an inherent structural weakness in family economies.[49] Contemporary observers did not recognize this weakness and it was not a serious problem in the mid-nineteenth century, but it should be appreciated as background to the later history of Prescott County. Family economies depended on the lumber industry since, by itself, agricultural opportunity in the area was quite limited. Not only was shanty and sawmill labour often necessary to achieve farm establishment, but the county's land and location worked against full reliance on independent farming. The more elevated land required the removal of stones and rocks, a strenuous job necessitating enormous collective effort. On 26 September 1846, eighteen-year-old Thomas Tweed Higginson "took the oxen and steers and worked all day raising and drawing stones" with a brother and two relatives. The job was not easily achieved and had to be faced with grim determination. After decades of attempting to overcome this obstacle, Higginson expressed both frustration and resignation. In 1878, he was

preparing ground for corn; the everlasting boulders in the way. Nothing but perseverance will ever remove them from their beds. It was an unlucky freight those icebergs carried here in the olden time when the world was young. Well, here they are and must remain until some agency stronger than wishing sets about their removal.[50]

The richer, low-lying land, on the other hand, often suffered from flooding, especially during the crucial spring season. Farms in swampy areas could be ruined after a severe winter, leaving families to depend on friends and relatives for survival.

In addition, the lack of good roads and general transportation facilities meant that Prescott County farmers could not market surplus produce except in the lumbering regions to the north. Without this market, farming in Prescott County would not have surpassed the subsistence level at any time in the nineteenth century. For these reasons, participation in the système agro-forestier may have appeared to be a rational economic strategy from the perspective of most mid-nineteenth-century families, but over time it placed these families in a very dependent position. This dependency was especially precarious since work in the lumber industry was inherently temporary, and job security extended only from day to day. Employers such as Hamilton Brothers hired labourers for the precise amount of time they were needed; the needs of the lumber companies, more than the needs of family economies, determined the pattern of employment.[51]

Moreover, although Hamilton Brothers offered a variety of employment opportunities, it also dominated the village marketplace in Hawkesbury and through the company store recovered a substantial amount of its employees' wages. The store reportedly overpriced its products and stocked luxury goods, which were offered on credit to Hamilton Brothers' workers; by payday at the end of each month, earnings could have been expended. Furthermore, seasonal labour exacted a heavy physical toll. The lumber industry was only for the strong and healthy, but even for the physically able, seasonal labour presented constant risks. Frostbite, machine-related accidents at the mill, and the well-known dangers of the log drive were only some of the dangers of lumber-industry participation. For some young men, brief acquaintance with these working conditions was sufficient to inspire pursuit of economic opportunity elsewhere, despite the promise of relatively good wages. For example, Michel Dupuis worked three days in 1856 and then "ran away."[52]

Thus, the importance of seasonal labour to family economies could be insidious in several ways. Shanty and sawmill work might support preparation for household formation and, thereafter, the first years of childbearing, but the work was inherently insecure and represented a tenuous economic niche. Within its context, the establishment of family economies did not always move forward smoothly but often lurched sideways and sometimes backwards, bounced by the vicissitudes of economic instability. This phenomenon helps explain the relatively late age-at-marriage in Prescott County in the mid-nineteenth century, when couples continued to approximate the traditional European pattern of delaying marriage until their midtwenties. This pattern has been explained for Europe in terms of the limited opportunities offered by a relatively closed economy.[53] Although this explanation cannot be applied directly to Prescott County, the widespread dependency on seasonal labour made the establishment of a separate household a considerable achievement and thereby engendered significant apprehension about family formation. These obstacles to viable household establishment, even during relatively good economic times, further explain the ongoing pattern of emigration during the mid-nineteenth century. The economy was in a period of general growth, but, as discussed earlier, many young adults chose to settle their families elsewhere.[54] This decision reflected the negative aspects of the système agro-forestier, which became increasingly important in the 1870s.

The Retreat of the Forest Frontier

The actual economic crisis began with the retreat of the forest frontier northwest, away from Prescott County.[55] It steadily became much more difficult for the county's families to piece together a viable existence from their collective labour, and by the 1880s local reports described an "almost universal cry of hard times."[56] Farmers found it less profitable to supply the shanties as it became cheaper for the timber companies to procure food from more western areas, which profited from successful completion of the long-delayed roads to the lumbering areas and a network of railways connecting southern Ontario with northern regions. The local suppliers of Prescott County lost their previously sheltered position and were now forced to compete with producers from all Ontario and the northern United States.[57]

For lack of other opportunities, some Prescott County farmers continued to travel to the forest frontier during the winter months, but the proportions who went became smaller over time. One way to measure this travel during the 1870s is offered by the census of 1871 and 1881. Each of these enumerations included questions which established the month of birth of all children born during the year. If we assume a normal gestation period, these data can be associated with the months of conception, thereby suggesting the married males' patterns of residence in and absence from the county. Obviously, this analysis can be considered no more than suggestive since the population of Prescott County males involved in the lumber industry and the population of males responsible for Prescott County births in 1871 and 1881 overlap only partially. Moreover, a variety of factors influence the time of year in which children are born, especially first children whose arrival may be linked to a seasonal pattern of marriage. (In the case of Prescott County, however, this factor is not too worrisome since the overall fertility levels were quite high.)

Table 21 shows the data from 1871 and 1881. (The published volumes for 1871 aggregate the data into two-month periods, but the general pattern is still clear.) In both years of enumeration, the estimated proportion of conceptions was lowest during February and March, the months when absence in the forest would be most likely for Prescott County men. The following two months, when men were returning, exhibit a quick increase. Moreover, although the

TABLE 21
Seasonal Pattern of Conceptions and Births, Prescott Country, 1871–81

| | 1871 Births | | 1881 Births | | | | |
| | 2-Month Total[a] | | 2-Month Total | | 1-Month Total | | Conception |
Birth	N	%	N	%	N	%	(est.)
Jan.					84	9.2	April
	121	20.8	172	18.9			
Feb.					88	9.6	May
Mar.					86	9.4	June
	100	17.2	183	20.0			
April					97	10.6	July
May					57	6.8	Aug.
	96	16.5	135	14.8			
June					78	8.6	Sept.
July					72	7.9	Oct.
	102	17.5	161	17.7			
Aug.					89	9.8	Nov.
Sept.					72	7.9	Dec.
	93	16.0	140	15.4			
Oct.					68	7.4	Jan.
Nov.					52	5.7	Feb.
	69	11.9	121	13.3			
Dec.					69	7.6	Mar.
Total	581	100.0%	912	100.1%[b]	912	100.0%	

[a] Data for 1871 are available only in two-month aggregates.

[b] Does not add to 100 because of rounding.

Source: Census of Canada, 1871–81.

pattern is similar for the two years, the extent of the variation is somewhat less for the later enumeration, which was taken when the forest frontier was becoming more out-of-reach for Prescott County men. In 1871, 11.9 per cent of the year's conceptions occurred during February and March, and in 1881, 13.3 per cent. The proportions of conceptions during April and May jumped almost nine percentage points in 1871 but only about five and a half points in 1881. Since the data implicitly include all Prescott County married men, rather than just those involved in travelling to the forest, these changes are indeed meaningful.

Some support for the hypothesis comes from a fact that might have been expected to confuse the issue. Historians have found that a variety of religious practices affect the monthly pattern of child-bearing in many societies. Of relevance here is the contemporary Catholic Church's requirement of abstinence from sexual intercourse during Lent, the forty days (excluding Sundays) preceding Easter. If the adherents in the county actually followed this dictum, a trough should have appeared in the number of births nine months later, given the large number of Catholics in the Prescott County population. Unfortunately for our analysis, the season of Lent and the usual months of absence in the forest overlapped significantly, making it difficult to separate economic and religious factors in the change in the estimated incidence of conception. However, the monthly data for 1881 are revealing. Easter is a moveable feast that occurs sometime in the four weeks following 21 March. In 1881, it fell quite late – on 17 April – and thus more than half of April occurred during Lent. If religious factors were substantially responsible for the patterns of conceptions, the April data should reflect a significantly lower proportion of conceptions than the May data. In fact, however, the proportions for April and May are very similar and among the highest for any months of the year. Thus, the data appear to emphasize the importance of economic, rather than religious, factors in determining the seasonal pattern of conceptions and births. The inference about declining absence in the forest during the 1870s is also reasonable. Fewer farmers were travelling to the shanties during the winter to sell their produce. The forest frontier was truly retreating from Prescott County.

Exacerbating Problems

A prime characteristic of a système agro-forestier is the lack of agricultural integration into commercial markets other than the immediate lumber industry. In Prescott County, the withdrawal of shanty markets was certainly not compensated by the availability of other commercial outlets. An obvious market for farm produce was across the southern border, especially in New York State, but Prescott

County farmers faced an export tax, which hindered their competitiveness. A local newspaper suggested that the Reciprocity Treaty of 1854 should be revived, calculating that, as a result, each farmer would save $150 per year "sur les produits de son exploitation." Although this strategy was promoted as "le seul moyen que nous ayons d'améliorer notre position, le seul moyen de nous enrichir," reciprocity with the United States was not revived, and Prescott County farmers were left without effective market alternatives.[58]

Lumbering opportunities within Prescott County also declined after the mid-nineteenth century. By the end of the 1870s, the lower Ottawa Valley had been thoroughly exploited. As a result, families who were contemplating settlement could no longer plan on immediate financial benefits from land clearing. Only a few logs were left for market at local sawmills or for production of potash.[59]

Moreover, by the later nineteenth century, the arable land in the townships of Prescott County had been cleared; the land that was not under cultivation was truly useless swamp. Although francophones had shown that many acres of low-lying land could be agriculturally productive, certain regions could not be reclaimed. Prescott County could not even profit from the legislation of 1869 which provided funds for the drainage of swamp and marsh land. The Ontario Drainage Act authorized $200,000 for this purpose, but none of it was spent in Prescott County because the wet lands not yet developed were considered beyond reclamation. Studies by the Public Works Department concluded that these lands could not be drained by gravitation and that underdraining would be hindered by rock a few feet below the surface.[60]

Thus, in the changed economic world of late-nineteenth-century Prescott County, the problems of land shortage began to affect francophones much as they had anglophones during the midcentury. Young francophones could no longer plan to take up lots in regions neighbouring the households of their parents as they had in earlier years when low-lying land was still available in townships such as Alfred and Caledonia. After the 1870s, the shortage of even this land left little opportunity for the achievement of independent farming.

Land shortage thus exacerbated the economic problems begun by the retreat of the forest frontier. The attraction of the système agro-forestier during the mid-nineteenth century had rapidly fulfilled local agricultural potential, leaving only the poorest soil still available for settlement in later years. The amount of occupied land in Prescott County doubled between 1851 and 1881, but it increased by only

TABLE 22

Land Use, Prescott County, 1851–1901

| | Acres | | | |
	Held	Under Cultivation	Under Crops	Under Pasture
1851	113,035	32,920	21,415	11,319
1861	145,223	53,934	34,474	19,237
1871	179,287	78,272	53,649	23,955
1881	220,692	122,168	76,487	44,764
1891	251,330	188,089	127,097	59,761
1901	264,781	183,797	128,557	73,683

Note: For 1851–91, the amount of land listed as "under cultivation" is slightly larger than the total of the land listed as "under crops" and as "under pasture." This is exactly what one would expect since land "under cultivation" includes lands used for buildings, barnyards, and so on as well as for crops and pasture. The data for 1901, however, pose a problem in that the amount "under culture" is smaller than the sum of land "under crops" and land "under pasture." Yet none of the three figures given has an obvious error. I am unable to explain this anomaly.

Source: Census of Canada, 1851–1901.

another 20 per cent during the remaining two decades of the century. The amount of land under cultivation continued to increase substantially during the 1870s and 1880s as settlement spread and families devoted more energy to farming, but by the 1890s, the economic crisis was apparent; between 1891 and 1901, the acreage under cultivation actually decreased slightly. (See Table 22.)

This fall was in part the legacy of the shanty market, which had encouraged the immediate and constant cultivation of hay and oats, a type of farming that fast depletes the richness of the soil. It necessitated "clearing off the farm ... everything most likely to maintain its productivity," thereby engendering a "gradual drain upon and reduction of the quality of land." For this reason, farming for shanty supply was "temporarily profitable" but its impact on the soil was "exhausting."[61] As a result, the land of Prescott County became increasingly poor for agricultural production. By the end of the century, it was beginning to resemble the Quebec soil of the 1830s and suffered similar insect attacks. The "potato bug" hit the Prescott County crop in the 1870s, and later in the century farmers found "un nouveau fleau" in the form of "un petit ver dans la racine du grain."[62]

TABLE 23

Cheese and Butter Production, Prescott County, 1881–1901

	Home Production		Cheese Factories	
	Butter (lb.)	Cheese (lb.)	N	Hands Employed
1881	685,226	39,194	6	16
1891	502,336	11,102	29	40
1901	456,820	*a*	72[b]	115

[a] Data not requested by the 1901 census.

[b] Eight of these factories also produced butter; the 64 factories producing only cheese employed 100 hands.

Source: Census of Canada, 1881–1901.

Strategies for Remedies

In response to the agricultural difficulties of the late nineteenth century, Prescott County farmers began forming societies to discuss possible remedies for their situation. One agricultural society grew from eighty-two members in 1883 to 236 members in 1894.[63] The Alfred Township society included sixty-three paid members at this date, but its meetings attracted much larger audiences, indicating that interest and support exceeded the ability to contribute financially to the organization.[64] For the most part, such agricultural societies focused on the possibilities of using land for pasture and producing cheese and butter. During the 1870s, these possibilities were pursued in earnest. The acreage under pasture in Prescott County almost doubled between 1871 and 1881 and increased by another 65 per cent over the next two decades (see Table 22), and cheese factories were established throughout the townships, with six in operation by 1881 and seventy-two by 1901 (see Table 23).[65]

The transition for dairy farming provided some financial relief in Prescott County, but even this development had a negative impact on the collective potential of the family economy. The establishment of local cheese and butter factories meant that this activity was removed from domestic control. The impact of these factories was immediately felt with family economies. In 1871, the settlers of Prescott County had produced 49,005 pounds of homemade cheese; by 1891, the amount had dropped to 11,102 pounds, and the next census did not even request this information.[66] The new factories did create some employment opportunities, but the number of jobs

TABLE 24
Sawmills, Prescott County, 1871–1901

	Establishments	Hands Employed
1871	16	388
1881	12	544
1891	17	537
1901	10	530

Source: Census of Canada, 1871–1901.

was limited. In 1901, only 100 workers were employed in the cheese factories of Prescott County. (See Table 23.)

In the late nineteenth century, the lumber industry continued to be the major employer in Prescott County since major companies of the lower Ottawa Valley still found it profitable to drive timber down the Ottawa River.[67] However, the number of employment opportunities remained constant after the 1870s (see Table 24) and, because of population growth, represented a relative decline.[68]

Moreover, the character of lumber industry employment altered with the diminishing possibility of independent farming in Prescott County. Before the 1870s, many young men could expect to work in local sawmills for a short period in the course of each year, thereby supplementing the collective economies of their families and preparing themselves financially for marriage and formation of a separate household. These ambitions continued in the later nineteenth century, but the chances of them being fulfilled in Prescott County were less and less favourable over time. In the changed economic environment, young adults could no longer anticipate independent farming supplemented by lumber-industry participation.

The Changing Occupational Structure. Land shortage and the retreat of the forest frontier thus created a social layer of labourers for whom there was little prospect of improvement. At midcentury, the vast majority of young men had been able to make the transition from labourer to farmer by their mid-twenties; now the achievement of independent farming became less likely. This development was similar to the earlier impact on anglophone society of the shortage of well-elevated land, which had by the 1840s already necessitated substantial adjustment in the form of out-migration or delayed age-at-marriage for those who stayed. Among francophones, however, the only precedent was what had happened in Quebec decades earlier.[69]

TABLE 25
Age of Farmers and Labourers, Alfred Township, 1881

Age	Francophones		Anglophones	
	Labourers	Farmers	Labourers	Farmers
10–24	87	27	6	6
≥ 25	105	285	8	63
Total	192	312	14	69

Note: For comparative data from earlier census years, see Table 15.

Source: Manuscript census, 1881.

The combination of diminished economic opportunity and rapid population growth quickly engendered francophone labouring families that had no hope of independent farming in Prescott County. For Alfred Township, this process of proletarianization was reflected in the 1881 census. Unlike earlier enumerations, it identified a substantial group of older francophones who had not acquired their own land. The occupational structure of the township was still dominated by farmers, but now there were also 105 francophone labourers over the age of twenty-four. The appearance of this group was not paralleled among anglophones, who continued to leave the county rather than remain as labourers after early adulthood. (See Table 25; for data from previous decades, see Table 15.)

This development meant that, as a group, anglophones maintained their general economic advantage over francophone settlers, who now included both secure and insecure families. By the 1880s, some francophones had well-established farms, and others had acquired positions as local merchants and tradesmen as new service centres developed, such as Lefaivre and the actual community of Alfred. There had also arisen, however, a sizeable group of francophone proletarians for whom uncertain tenant farming and wage labouring was all that could be achieved in Prescott County. It was this group of families that became the object of derision and scorn among Toronto newspaper editors by the mid-1880s and, as will be discussed in later chapters, inadvertently encouraged new educational policies for all Ontario.

Demographic Adjustment and Stability. As would be expected, economic difficulties in Prescott County were exacerbated by the fact that the flow of immigration did not immediately adjust to the new conditions in the area. The 1881 census showed that heavy immigration from Quebec had continued during the 1870s. However, some demographic adjustments were becoming quite apparent. As discussed in the previous chapter, family size was declining from the pattern of the 1850s and 1860s. Francophone families continued to be larger than their anglophone counterparts, but both groups were limiting their completed family size.

By 1881, the smaller size of families offered some demographic relief for Prescott County residents as they struggled to adjust to their changed material environment. However, the most serious problems were faced by those who were attempting to form their own families. The census evidence suggests that age-at-marriage was relatively late for men and women and that marriage had become especially difficult for anglophones. The process of family formation was not facilitated by any weakening of the established equation of a separate household for each family. The norm in Alfred and Caledonia townships continued to be a household that included only a single conjugal family unit. Multiple-family households were rare.

By 1881, the new conditions were also affecting the experience of childhood, especially the role of children within the family economy. As Prescott County lost its frontier character, the local economy offered less and less productive opportunity for children. Families still depended on collective contributions, particularly from older sons and daughters, but the extent of activities possible for children decreased as Prescott County became an "old" agricultural area.[70]

The economic crisis of Prescott County is only suggested in the patterns of the 1881 census, but evidence of material hardship is starkly apparent in later decades. One clear indication is the sudden decline of immigration from Quebec. After coming in large numbers for several decades, francophone migrants began bypassing the lower Ottawa Valley to seek opportunity elsewhere.[71] Moreover, substantial out-migration from Prescott County began in the 1880s. After years of heavy and rapid population growth, the region had quickly become an undesirable one that encouraged pursuit of survival and security elsewhere.

Of course, many anglophones and francophones did stay in Prescott County throughout the late nineteenth century, undoubtedly with very complex motivations. They continued to use demographic adjustments. The decline of immigration and the extent of emigration relieved some of the demographic pressure, and parents continued to have fewer children. At the same time, the family unit remained the basis of social organization, and certain important features of the mid-nineteenth century remained unchanged. Families continued to avoid co-residence as a strategy for offsetting the economic hard times. The continued attachment to the custom of a separate household for each family emphasizes the ongoing stability of the family, even in the face of severe economic pressure. Similarly, the economic crisis, with its sudden decrease in immigration and increase in emigration, did not affect the established sex ratio. Throughout the 1851–1901 period, the number of males in Prescott County was always slightly greater than of females, and no relationship to economic conditions is apparent. The pursuit of survival and security involved couples and family units, rather than individuals, throughout the century.[72]

Attempts at Economic Solutions. The stability of the family as a social unit provided a foundation upon which residents could seek some sense of security in late-nineteenth-century Prescott County. With the maturing of local communities, networks of family and kin became extensive for both anglophones and francophones, and even though emigration was a constant factor, these networks continued to offer at least the hope that collective effort could compensate individual difficulty. By the 1880s, this hope was nourished by local leaders, who began promoting a sense of place among Prescott County residents. Anglophone and francophone community leaders began claiming that the lower Ottawa Valley had special needs and interests which demanded specific articulation and action. The initial editorial of the *Eastern Ontario Review*, published in Vankleek Hill, promised in 1893 that the "local interests of these Eastern Counties will ever be our first solicitude, and in whatsoever we can do to promote the welfare of its people, that shall engage our most earnest labors."[73] Similarly, the region's first French-language newspaper, *La Nation*, appeared in 1885 as the "organe des intérêts canadiens dans la partie Orientale de la province d'Ontario."[74]

In articulating an attachment and belief in the region, local leaders engaged in two somewhat contradictory activities: uncritical boosterism, and the devising of solutions to the readily apparent material problems. The agricultural difficulties encouraged a belief that the development of towns held the solution to the area's economic problems. In Prescott County, Vankleek Hill, L'Orignal, and Hawkesbury all aspired to leadership. Since the sawmill industry ensured that Hawkesbury was less affected than the others by the changes in the système agro-forestier, promotional spirit was most apparent in Vankleek Hill and L'Orignal. The leaders of each community admitted that it had not yet achieved much stature, but they all foresaw bright futures. Optimism was high despite the reality of grim times.

The enthusiasm in Vankleek Hill was based on geographic location and institutional strength. Since the Hill was located right between Montreal and Ottawa, it was described as the "natural centre of the trade and business of eastern Ontario." Moreover, it was "in the foremost rank as an educational centre" with not only common schools but also a model school to train teachers and a high school to train county leaders. Churches and societies such as the Freemasons were also fully represented, "while the women are busy in their own good way, having organizations of their own, for various purposes." These features combined to support a heady assessment of the town's future:

As yet, "the Hill" is a comparatively small community, but if progress made in the past be an earnest indication of the future, the day is not far distant when it will claim a first place in the list of go-ahead (what shall we say?) — cities.[75]

At the same time, leaders in L'Orignal were convinced that it was their village that would rescue the county and, indeed, the lower Ottawa Valley from economic disaster. In the later 1870s, this conviction was based on anticipated railway construction which would link L'Orignal with the world beyond and produce a rippling burst of economic development:

Our farmers will find provided convenient, cheap and speedy means of conveyance for their produce to places where it will find a ready market. Our merchants will have increased facilities for bringing in their goods; supply will create demand. Ready access to L'Orignal will bring in additional customers. Additional customers will afford a stimulus to increased exertions to supply their various needs. The necessity for additional house accommodation will encourage capitalists to invest in buildings. Building sites will be in demand, new streets will be opened, and the sites already in the market will be rapidly taken up and utilized. With the natural advantages of L'Orignal coupled with the increased facilities of communication with our great centres, L'Orignal will become a summer resort. Trade that has been languishing will revive and the county town of the united counties of Prescott and Russell will become one of the most thriving spots in the Ottawa Valley. The high tide is beginning to set in, and taken at the flood, will lead on to fortune. L'Orignal will take the place which a county town should hold — the thriving centre of a busy, important, and flourishing community.[76]

The boosterism and community spirit of Prescott County newspapers was intended to encourage families to stay, rather than to leave the "state of utter paralysation [sic]," as it was called.[77] The local French-language press deplored "le triste sort, la funeste manie d'un nombre encore trop grand de familles canadiennes qui chaque mois prennent la route des Etats-Unis, le chemin de l'exil."[78]

Of course, those who stayed could not simply feed on optimism, and there were constant attempts to devise strategies for survival and security. In addition to railway promotion, major farmers and town leaders pursued an array of avenues toward possible material improvement. Some ideas were not too helpful. One suggested "remedy for hard times" was thrift; "stop spending so much on fine clothes, rich food and style. Buy good, healthy food, cheaper and better clothing; get more real and substantial things of life every way."[79] Other ideas were more to the point. The transition to dairy farming, especially cheese manufacturing, was promoted by leading farmers, who held meetings throughout the 1870s to share information about this new activity and to listen to guest speakers, such as an "experienced Dairyman from Vermont" who promised in 1876 that dairy farming would lead to replenishing of exhausted soil.[80]

A second survival strategy involved a common refuge of unproductive places: tourism. In addition to L'Orignal's potential as a summer resort, Prescott County's claim centred on the mineral springs in Caledonia Township, which earlier in the century had attracted vacationers and health seekers from faraway regions. At one time, Caledonia Springs boasted a Grand Hotel as well as several smaller hotels and boarding houses, but a series of fires and other misfortunes ruined the resort by the early 1870s. The Grand Hotel was reopened under new ownership in 1876, and through advertising was even able to achieve an export to Europe of one hundred barrels per week of mineral water. This activity confirmed local belief in these years that Prescott County did indeed possess tourist possibilities which could be exploited to energize the stagnant economy.[81]

The transition to dairy farming and tourism promotion held some hope for Prescott County residents, but the most astute diagnosis of economic weakness focused on the lack of diversification. Some community leaders were convinced that the establishment of factories was needed to balance the production of staples. They were not fussy about the type of factory desired:

Our situation upon the Ottawa River with the Railway on the North Shore, makes it a most desirable position for a manufactory of any kind. We hope to see the attention of our village Councillors turned to this project at an early day.[82]

La Nation also foresaw a bright future for Prescott County and neighbouring Russell County as a result of the anticipated economic diversification. The editors predicted that with "la multiplicité de leurs manufactures, les deux comtés de Prescott et Russell deviendront dans un avenir rapproché un pays florissant et prospère."[83]

The desire for factories was, however, widely shared in late-nineteenth-century Canada, and Prescott County residents soon learned that they would have to offer inducements if they wanted even to enter the competition for industry. The prospect of special concessions, usually in the form of low-cost or free land with reduced taxes, tested the level of desperation among the county's established economic leaders, who would have to continue without similar concessions. Their concern delayed action for a while, but as conditions worsened, the prospect of inducements had to be faced.

Would it not be well to ascertain the feeling of the electors of the County town towards offering inducements to any company desirous of erecting a factory at L'Orignal, that would employ from one to two hundred hands? A slight consideration of the kind might be productive of much good in directing the attention of persons having capital to invest."[84]

By 1880, village leaders in L'Orignal were ready to take the initiative.

With the object of inducing the erection of manufactories or workshops within the village limits the Reeve urged upon the Council the passage of a measure relieving any capitalists who may erect workshops within the village limits, from taxation for twenty years. The subject met with the unanimous approval of the Council and a resolution authorizing the introduction and passage of a By-Law for the purpose was carried with the condition however that such a factory should not employ less than twenty laborers on an average each year.[85]

The economic strategies employed in Prescott County were not, however, equal to the task of material regeneration. The lack of markets prevented dairy farming from compensating for the changed système agro-forestier, and although cheese and butter production increased substantially, the rural townships of Prescott County continued to struggle. Tourist ambitions for Caledonia Springs were never fulfilled. Just as new ownership re-established the resort in the late 1870s, a mysterious illness struck the area; news of it spread quickly, and the resort closed as new visitors failed to arrive.[86] Although there was a report on new mineral springs at Caledonia in 1883, Prescott County's potential as a major tourist centre was no longer even discussed.

Efforts to diversify economically were no more successful than the other survival strategies of Prescott County residents. Beyond the establishment of cheese and butter factories, there was little economic development in the late nineteenth century. The lumber industry continued to be the only significant employer in the county. In addition to the sawmills at Hawkesbury, a number of firms made wooden boxes, wood pulp, and other lumber products; they were small, however, and in 1901 there were only fourteen such establishments. Other manufacturing activity was restricted to a few flour and grist mills, several carriage and wagon factories, and four brick, tile, and pottery producers. The employment opportunities offered by all industries combined amounted to only 1,277 jobs.[87] Given the failure of economic diversification, towns such as Vankleek Hill and l'Orignal did not grow into cities. There was little urbanization despite the rural economic crisis. The county was left without a meaningful place in the economic world of central Canada.

CHAPTER FOUR

Language and the Social Structure of Schooling

Demographic and economic change in Prescott County during the second half of the nineteenth century formed the context of controversy about minority-language education. In the period from the 1840s to the early 1870s, the anglophone population generally formed more mature communities than did the francophone, as a result of the former's earlier settlement and, in some cases, more advantaged backgrounds. Meanwhile, heavy immigration from Quebec led to French Canadians' assuming a numerically dominant position in areas such as in Alfred Township, but in other areas, such as Caledonia Township, the anglophone population remained better established. This complexity raises questions about the character of schooling in various communities of Prescott County. Did the establishment of French-language schools immediately follow the spread of settlement? Did francophone children have educational opportunities in all townships? Did francophone and anglophone children attend the same schools?

The changing structure of the Prescott County economy also had educational implications. The système agro-forestier functioned in part as a collection of family economies that sought full participation from every family member. Therefore, the experience of childhood and youth involved integration into productive activity. In the period from the 1840s to the early 1870s, the family economy determined the nature of growing-up, from participating in land clearing, spinning, and gardening for boys and girls to employment in sawmills and shanties for young men. The economic restructuring which began in the 1870s affected family economies and thus the social organization of Prescott County. This development suggests that we must analyse the history of schooling from a perspective which considers the status of the pupils and their families. Who went to school?

At what ages? In what social and economic circumstances? These questions should be posed for both the middle and later decades of the nineteenth century in order to explore the ways in which the language controversy represented a convergence of larger historical phenomena.

Sources for the history of schooling in Prescott County are quite extensive. The manuscript annual reports of the local superintendent of common schools for 1850 to 1870 provide school-by-school information on a wide variety of topics, including teachers and textbooks. In 1871, a new school act led to the creation of boards of examiners, and thus, for the years from 1871 to 1897, manuscript reports of the board meetings in Prescott County offer an array of information about local schooling. This type of evidence on the structure of education is complemented by data from the manuscript censuses on school participation by specific children. Such evidence indicates the extent to which the history of schooling in Prescott County was related to the history of its families and the changing social structure of the nineteenth century, a relationship not emphasized in the view from Toronto.

FACTORS IN MIDCENTURY FRENCH-LANGUAGE SCHOOLING

The point of departure for investigating the character of schooling in Prescott County is the actual meaning of the official acceptance of language diversity in the public schools. Did the provincial Council of Public Instruction's policy really remove language as a consideration of school establishment at the local level? The evidence from Prescott County clearly suggests it did not. In fact, francophones faced formidable obstacles to the formation of French-language schools. A key obstacle was the membership of local boards of school trustees. Particularly in areas of recent francophone immigration, trustees often did not reflect the changed composition of school districts. Not surprisingly, anglophone trustees continued to provide only English-language schooling.

The importance of trustees is illustrated by the 1871 francophone protest against the hiring of only English-speaking teachers in Prescott County's Township of East Hawkesbury.[1] When asked to intercede on behalf of the francophones, J. George Hodgins, Egerton Ryerson's assistant, explained, "The employment of French teachers in our Public Schools is merely permissive and not obligatory." Hodgins, who was secretary of the Council of Public Instruction at the time, said that the Department of Education could not dictate to trustees on the matter of teacher selection; the solution to this controversy was "to elect such trustees as will carry out the wishes of the ratepayers in this respect."[2] Thus, the significance of the Council's pronouncements on the French-language issue depended largely on the decisions of local school trustees. Consequently, the educational experience of francophones in Prescott County was significantly determined by the membership of those boards.

Even when francophones controlled the school board of a particular community, establishing a French-language school was not easy. At least some residents had to learn the rules and regulations of the provincial school system, and francophone trustees had to file formal reports on English-language forms and generally function under the supervision of unilingual anglophone local superintendents and school inspectors.

The information available about each school in Prescott County emphasizes the importance of the factors undermining francophone educational opportunity in the mid-nineteenth century. Despite the policy of toleration, only two of the thirty-eight schools in the county were instructed in French in the early 1850s. Over time, as francophone settlement spread, this disproportion was only partially corrected. Thirteen of the seventy schools in 1870 were based on French-language instruction, and they were located in those townships where francophones had gained representation among the school trustees. In 1850, Longueuil was the only township with French-language schooling, although francophones had already settled throughout the county. By 1870, French-language schools had been established in three more Townships, but there were still none in Caledonia, West Hawkesbury, and North Plantagenet townships, where anglophone communities were strong. (See Table 26.)

School Enrolment and the Language of Instruction

The paucity of French-language schools in mid-nineteenth century Prescott County might be interpreted as evidence of educational disinterest among francophones rather than of the inevitably intolerant structure of a standardized school system. Perhaps francophones were simply not interested in formal education and thus did not take advantage of the possibilities for establishing schools. This explanation would be entirely consistent with the official school reports, which emphasized the need to transform the educational lethargy of the Quebec immigrants. Of course, the relative absence of French-language schools might also have resulted from the willing-

TABLE 26
Number of Schools, Prescott County,
Mid-Nineteenth Century

Township	All Schools		French-Language Schools	
	1852	1870	1852	1870
Alfred	2	9	0	4
Caledonia	3	8	0	0
Longueuil	5[a]	6	2[a]	2
East Hawkesbury	11	18	0	6
West Hawkesbury	9[b]	9	0	0
North Plantagenet	5[b]	11	0	0
South Plantagenet	3	9	0	1
Total	38[c]	70	2[c]	13

[a] 1854 data.
[b] 1850 data.
[c] Because data for some townships are for years other than 1852, these totals must be regarded as for the early 1850s, not for 1852.

Source: Annual reports of the local superintendents. (For bibliographical information, see Chapter 1, note 39.)

ness of francophone parents to send their children to English-language schools. This possibility would require some explanation of why the school reports focused on francophone disinterest, but it would support the official expectation of voluntary integration into the common school system.

The most direct way to analyse the relative importance of local motives and provincially determined structure is to examine actual school attendance patterns. The evidence provided by the manuscript census shows clearly that the ability of francophone settlers to establish their own French-language schools had a dramatic effect on the educational experience of their children. This impact is starkly apparent in the contrasting experiences of the neighbouring townships of Alfred and Caledonia.

School sections did not completely correspond to cultural neighbourhoods – a fact that caused considerable difficulty – but many schools reflected the language and religion of nearby residents. The strong francophone presence in Alfred meant that by 1870 four of

TABLE 27

Children Ages 5 to 16 Enrolled in School, Alfred and Caledonia Townships, 1851–71

	Alfred Township		Caledonia Township	
	Francophone	Anglophone	Francophone	Anglophone
1851	7%	17%	11%	36%
1861	40	36	9	50
1871	55	46	25	72

Source: Manuscript census schedules, 1851–71.

the township's nine schools were intructed in French. (In addition, School No. 1 and School No. 5 were supported by anglophone Catholics, while School No. 2 was attended by anglophone Protestants.) In Caledonia Township, however, the early British-Isles-origin settlement, especially of Scottish immigrants, had led to continued anglophone control over educational administration. Although the schools in Caledonia reflected certain ethnoreligious differences within the anglophone community, there was no accommodation of francophone residents, who represented one-third of the township's population according to the 1871 census. At this time, the only choice was among nine English-language schools.[3]

For Alfred Township, the census enumerations from 1851 to 1871 suggest that there was little cultural distinction in the enrolment figures.[4] French-speaking and English-speaking children enrolled in a similar pattern, especially by 1871. In 1851, when the township included only two schools, both of which were English-language, neither group enrolled in sizeable proportions, although, as would be expected, anglophone children were more likely pupils. Of children between the ages of five and sixteen, 7 per cent of francophones and 17 per cent of anglophones were listed by the census enumerator as going to school. As additional schools in each language were built during the next two decades, the proportion of children who went to school increased substantially for both groups. By 1871, about one half of all children were enrolled in school. (See Table 27.)

In Caledonia Township, however, schooling had a quite different cultural meaning. The absence of French-language schools throughout the period meant that most francophone children rarely received common schooling, especially before the 1870s. In 1851, when Quebec immigration to Caledonia had just begun, only 11 per cent went to school, and in 1861, the figure was 9 per cent. Quebec immigration to the township was heavy during the 1860s, especially along the border shared with Alfred and Longueuil townships. Some francophone families in Caledonia could take advantage of French-language schools in the neighbouring townships; the children of Alphonse Duhamel, for example, walked two miles from Caledonia Springs to Ritchans in Longueuil because the local teacher was not able to teach them "French or their Catechism."[5] This strategy was not feasible for most French Canadians, however, and, in 1871, only one-quarter of their school-age children were enrolled in school.

The exceedingly low rate of school participation by francophones in Caledonia Township contrasts sharply with the high level of anglophone enrolment. From 1851 to 1871, the proportion of school attenders among five- to sixteen-year-old children jumped from 36 per cent to 72 per cent. These high rates, which exceeded those for anglophones in Alfred Township, do not seem to have been simply the result of heavy Scottish settlement, a phenomenon that usually engendered energetic educational activity. Rather, all anglophone groups exhibited similar school-enrolment patterns; in 1871, the proportion of school-age children registered for class was 69 per cent for those of Scottish origin, 86 per cent for those of English origin, and 78 per cent for those of Irish origin. These high proportions reflected the anglophones' general domination of common schooling in Caledonia; throughout the mid-nineteenth century, they controlled all the school trustee positions and thus could ensure the establishment of English-language schools wherever they were needed.

Significantly, however, Egerton Ryerson's policy of linguistic toleration did not necessarily protect anglophones who found themselves in a minority situation; like the French-Canadians elswhere, they found that their educational experience depended on the decisions of local trustees. On 4 February 1861, James McCaul, local superintendent in neighbouring Russell County, wrote to Ryerson asking if "where the majority of the Inhabitants are French, and all the Trustees and Teacher French, can the English portion of the School Section compel the Trustees to furnish the means of education for their children?" Ryerson responded negatively, confirming the policy of leaving the question of language in the hands of local leaders.[6] As a result, the minority anglophones of Alfred Township had considerably less influence on schooling than their majority counterparts in Caledonia Township.

The contrasting experiences of Alfred and Caledonia vividly illustrate the extent to which the issue of language of instruction played a critical role in determining the extent of formal education in Prescott county during the mid-nineteenth century. The relatively small number of French-language schools was associated with generally low rates of school enrolment among francophones. However, in Alfred Township, where French Canadians formed the majority of the township's population and French-language schools were established, francophone children participated in school in increasing proportions between 1851 and 1871. This pattern was markedly different from that of neighbouring Caledonia Township's francophone children, most of whom never went to school.

As francophone immigration changed the cultural balance of Prescott County, however, anglophones in certain areas faced difficult educational decisions. The policy of language toleration meant that anglophones in minority situations might have to send their children to neighbouring school sections to receive English-language instruction. As a result, the generally high anglophone school enrolment rates varied considerably, from about one-half to three-quarters of school-age children by 1871.

Schoolhouse Location

The cultural dimension of schooling in Prescott County did not end with the language-of-instruction issue. A further factor involved schoolhouse location – specifically, the anglophone preference for elevated land. According to official policy, moist soil was totally inappropriate for the building of schools. Trustees learned that "damp places in the vicinity of stagnant pools or unwholesome marshes ... should be carefully avoided." Instead, schools "should be placed on firm ground, on the southern declivity of a gently sloping hill."[7]

The value of carefully situating rural schools was emphasized throughout the nineteenth century. In 1885, regulations formally reiterated that "every school site should be on a well-travelled road, as far removed as possible from a swamp or marsh, and so elevated as to admit of easy drainage." The next year, J. George Hodgins, who was now the deputy minister of education, stressed the "great importance" exercised in the choice of a situation for the site of a schoolhouse. He quoted the educational motto of the state of Iowa, "A School House on Every Hill-top," in order to emphasize that every school site in Ontario should be "on an elevated piece of ground, a knoll, or a gentle slope."[8]

In Alfred Township, this policy was followed with the result that the schools of this predominantly low-lying region were generally situated, as Figure 10 indicates, on the elevation which divides the Township centrally, on a southern ridge, and on hills near the Ottawa River. These locations corresponded with the areas of high, sandy

FIGURE 10

Schools of Alfred Township in the Late Nineteenth Century

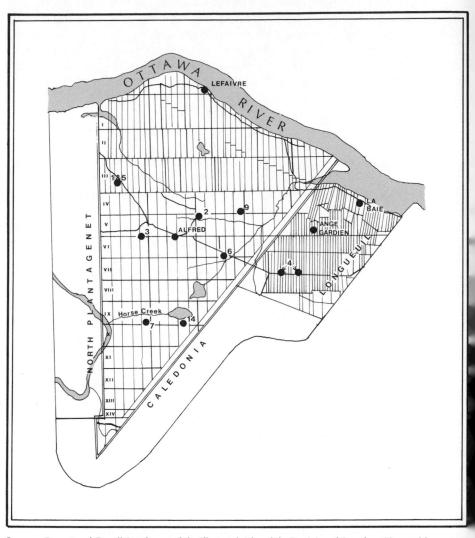

Sources: *Prescott and Russell Supplement of the Illustrated Atlas of the Dominion of Canada, 1881:* parish reports. St-Victor-d'Alfred and St-Jean-Baptiste. L'Original. Archives of the Archdiocese of Ottawa.

soil, where most anglophone immigrants chose to settle. Thus, the formal education policy on school-site location combined with the cultural pattern of settlement so that schoolhouses were centrally

situated in anglophone regions and often on the borders of francophone areas. This phenomenon suggests that the cultural ingre-
dient of the common school system may have helped to undermine
the ambitions of its anglophone architects. Although they believed
that schooling was particularly important for diverse social and cultural groups, they did not recognize the full implications of this
diversity.

Family Economies

The potential for widespread controversy as francophone settlement
changed the cultural geography of Prescott County was not realized
during the 1850s and 1860s. The major reason was that schooling
was simply not a crucial concern in local society at this time. Since
the predominant experience of growing-up involved increasing integration as a productive member of a family economy, learning to
spin, garden, and cook, to plant, chop, and harvest at home was
much more important than having the chance to learn reading,
writing, and discipline at school. This priority is evident in the age
structure of school enrolment. Only a minority of children continued
in school as teenagers. In Alfred Township, the most important
increase in enrolment between 1851 and 1871 was the result of more
active participation of seven- to twelve-year-olds. Both francophone
and anglophone parents sent an increasing number of children in
this age group to school. A much lower proportion of older children
attended. (See Figure 11.)

The age structure of school attendance in Caledonia was similar.
Although most francophones did not register for class, parents who
lived within reasonable distance of French-language schools in other
townships did make an attempt to send seven- to twelve-year-olds.
By 1871, 34 per cent of francophone children in this age group were
enrolled in school, but only 18 per cent of younger children, 15 per
cent of thirteen to sixteen-year-olds, and none over the age of sixteen. Although much larger proportions of anglophone youngsters
were enrolled, a similar age structure obtained. At the time of each
enumeration, seven- to twelve-year-olds exhibited much higher enrolment rates than older children, and, by 1871, almost all the children in this group (87 per cent) were registered at school. A majority
of thirteen- to sixteen-year-olds were also pupils, but only a small
proportion (10 per cent) continued after age sixteen. (See Figure
11.)

The pattern of actual attendance emphasizes that, for most families, even those children who were enrolled in school went to class

FIGURE 11

Age Structure of School Attendance, Alfred and Caledonia Townships, 1851–71

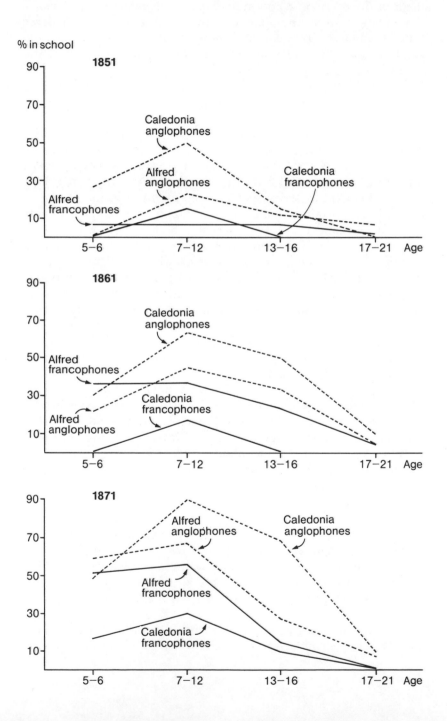

only during certain times of the year. The rhythm of the seasons controlled educational as well as economic life in Prescott County. The nature and pace of daily activity changed with the seasons. Spring, for example, was a hectic time. Streams became rivers, the little villages bustled, families reunited, flowers bloomed. In the countryside, not a moment could be lost as soil was turned, seeds positioned, fences mended. The activity encaptured everyone. Young sons tested the new strength of another year's growth, perhaps by releasing a mud-stuck wagon. Daughters accepted new chores to match their increased maturity. In villages, the din of the sawmill was renewed, and hands rushed to cope with the onslaught of timber from up-river. Wagons and carriages were substituted for sleighs, clothes were washed, mattresses aired. School was forgotten.

Summer, fall, and winter included times of tranquility as well as feverish periods of activity, and it was during the slow periods that classrooms would be filled. From the perspective of children, there were purely social reasons for attending when they could be spared from the family economy. The constant togetherness of family life undoubtedly became oppressive at times, especially during the cold winter months when outside activity had to be curtailed. Both parents and children waited eagerly for the winter to end.[9] Going to school was at least something to do at this time of year, and it offered the potential (if not the reality) of intellectual challenge. Moreover, other opportunities for socializing with peers were not plentiful. Children in agricultural areas only rarely visited villages, such as Hawkesbury; for the most part, their lives were limited to the farm. (Church attendance could be an important exception to this generalization, for it did have a strong social dimension, but children would be more likely to be able to select their own friends while walking to and from school and during recess.) This motivation to attend class was undoubtedly particularly strong in immigrant children, for whom school was a way to meet other youngsters and to escape the work of clearing the land.

Of course, all children in Prescott County were not needed to the same extent as members of family economies, and a small minority were available for the classroom throughout the year. Between 1860 and 1870, 8 to 10 per cent of registered pupils attended school more than 200 days per year. This minority was dominated by the children of the anglophone elite, some of whom would go on to university at McGill or Queen's. For most children, however, formal education was limited to certain months. Although the schools were open almost all year, Prescott County children who were registered were usually in class fewer than half of the schooldays in 1860–70 period.

TABLE 28

Annual Attendance of Enrolled Students, Prescott County, 1860–70

Days in School	1860 (N = 2658)	1865 (N = 1865)	1870 (N = 3620)
< 20	12%	12%	11%
20–49	20	20	22
50–99	23	24	23
100–49	20	20	19
150–99	17	14	15
200–51	8	10	10

Source: Annual Report for the years indicated. (For bibliographical information, see Chapter 1, note 39.)

(See Table 28.) Schooling was not yet a dominant social institution in Prescott County.[10]

The relationship of the rhythms of the Prescott County economy to school participation further suggests why the relative lack of French-language schooling did not lead to cultural confrontation during the mid-nineteenth century. French-Canadian settlement in Prescott County was dominated by family economies participating in the système agro-forestier. In the labour-intensive attempt to achieve survival and security, most francophone children worked at home, in the woods, and perhaps at the mills. School was simply not important. Some highly motivated francophone children even became "educated" in the course of economic activity. A son of Henri Lefaivre, who settled in Alfred Township in 1848, "had only attended school eight months when eight years of age but while lumbering acquired a fair business education in both English and French by studying during the evenings."[11] Such initiative must be considered unusual, but it is clear that in Prescott County during the mid-nineteenth century, most francophone children were primarily producers, rather than pupils. Thus it is understandable that the relative absence of French-language schools did not cause immediate conflict.

MIDCENTURY SCHOOLING: A
GENERAL SURVEY OF CONDITIONS

That schooling was not a high priority among francophones from the 1840s to the early 1870s was not unusual in Prescott County. Anglophone settlers were not educationally enthusiastic either, judging by the quality of their schools. Although the annual school reports remark on anglophones' initiative and energy in comparison with francophones,' the actual data showed that all schooling in Prescott County was quite inferior to the provincial norm.

Schoolhouses and Equipment

The circumstance of this inferiority began with the condition of schoolhouses, which often did not conform to the officially desired model. Thomas Steele, the Prescott County inspector, found "great deficiency" with regard to the level of schoolhouse accommodation in his area. In 1873, he reported "a large number of inferior schoolhouses in this County, many of them being small and uncomfortable."[12] The most characteristic complaint of inspectors concerned the readiness of trustees to approve the building of log schoolhouses, rather than the preferred brick or stone constructions. In 1855, for example, all the schools of both Alfred and Caledonia townships were housed in log cabins. Officials were not optimistic that this pattern could be improved. An 1858 report promised no immediate change since Prescott County residents were "so plentifully supplied with pine logs for building purposes and materials."[13]

The predominance of log school-houses continued in later decades. An 1873 report showed that almost 80 per cent of the county's schools were built of wood. This proportion improved only slightly during the next five years; in 1878, 72 per cent were still of frame or log construction.[14] Education officials continued to report that accommodation was very poor. These wood schoolhouses were often "poorly ventilated, proper outbuildings [were] rarely provided, and but a few of the yards [were] fenced."[15]

Inadequate teaching equipment exacerbated the situation. The Prescott County inspector complained that in 1874 "far too many schools report no maps." By 1878 he could finally report that most of the schools were "tolerably supplied with maps," but the level of expectation for Ontario schools had grown to more sophisticated teaching aids and Prescott County schools remained inferior in this respect: "Other apparatus such as globes, calculators, tablet lessons, and geometrical forms, are confined to a few." In addition, many of the blackboards were of "very inferior quality."[16] The inspector for Caledonia Township emphasized, "Our greatest drawback is the want of libraries."[17]

The trials and tribulations of actually instructing school during the 1850s and 1860s have been graphically recounted by two teachers from Prescott County. J. George Hodgins prompted their reminiscences in 1896, when he was working on a documentary history of the school system, by making a general request that "Old Teachers" write to him about the "early period of their service." Both responses from Prescott County were from anglophones, and they described the difficulty of teaching in an educationally inhospitable environment.

The most detailed response was from Joseph Kyle, who began his Prescott County service during 1854 in a "miserable little log shanty." The shanty was equipped with a stove in the centre so that "in cold weather the backs of the little ones were moderately warm whilst their faces were freezing." The stove was also "set so that one of the pipes passed close under a beam and every cold day when the boys fired up [the stove] they used to set the beam on fire." Kyle was resourceful, however, and he "improvised an extinguisher in the shape of a bundle of rags tied on a broom handle which we dipped in a pail of water and applied to both beam and stove pipe."[18]

Such distractions were compounded by instructional challenges. The books of Kyle's classrooms were "very nearly as varied as the pupils' names" having been "handed down from their ancestors." He constantly pleaded with parents to pay for a "regular series of books," as well as some maps, but "the majority did not see the use of teaching children things that their fathers never had occasion for." Kyle taught in various schools in Prescott County over the years, and some were better than others, but the overall pattern reflected the low quality reported by the local superintendents. Kyle's "last and least" school showed no progress, being only fifteen feet by thirteen feet wide and having the usual heating problems. With as many as thirty children "crowded into this hole in Winter," Kyle had to open both the windows and door "no matter how cold the weather was" in order to relieve the smoke from the centre stove. He admitted he had accepted this situation only because the school was close to his farm, so he could work there "before and after School hours."[19]

Kyle's recollections are quite similar to those of Samuel Derby, the other teacher who wrote to Hodgins in 1896. The letter from Derby, who began teaching in Prescott County in 1847, was quite brief in comparison with Kyle's response, but it remarked on the lack of funds for school support and the small schoolhouses. However, Derby also remembered that the "small children" attended "pretty regularly" and that they "progressed favorably." Also he noted that, over time, "the country began to improve" and that he received "more pay" while the school was supplied with "necessary things."[20]

Teachers

The memories of these teachers emphasize the difficulties of conducting schools in the 1850s and 1860s, but, at the time, local superintendents considered teachers to be part of the problem of, rather than the solution to, educational inferiority in Prescott County. Although superintendents worried about the debilitating effect of log schoolhouses and ill-equipped classrooms, they were most concerned about the negative influence of the teachers they found there, who rarely conformed to the ideal of school officials.

Status and Salaries. Inspectors frequently criticized local residents' reluctance to attribute much status to the position of teachers and considered this failure a major obstacle to improvement. Provincial educators were particularly annoyed at the tendency of trustees to hire female teachers. In 1861, a superintendent in Cumberland Township, on the border of Prescott County, explained that so many teachers were women because "teaching has not yet been regarded as a profession sufficiently respectable to draw young men of talent in to it."[21] This analysis exaggerated the importance of female teachers, but the concern accurately reflected the increased number of females who entered teaching each year in eastern Ontario. In Prescott County, the proportion of female teachers had reached 67 per cent by this date and was more than 90 per cent by 1873; both figures were roughly double the provincial averages. (See Table 29.)

School officials did not suggest that women were inherently inappropriate for school teaching, but they did stress that the availability of young females seriously undermined the status of the occupation. This effect was most apparent in the matter of salaries. Educators suggested that the readiness of young women to accept teaching positions contributed to low salary levels. Throughout the nineteenth century they showed that most Prescott County teachers, male and female, worked for wages that were significantly less than the Ontario average and that were considered extremely low. In the early 1880s, the inspector for Prescott and Russell countries remarked, "Labourers and domestic servants are paid higher wages than many of our teachers."[22]

Most school reports related the inferior salaries of the eastern counties to the predominance of female teachers, who could be hired inexpensively. In Prescott County, as in the rest of Ontario, women instructed for about half to two-thirds of what men received. (See Table 30.)

Educational administrators were very much concerned about fe-

TABLE 29
Gender of Teachers, 1851–73

	Males		Females		Total	
	N	%	N	%	N	%
1851						
Ontario	2551	77.8	726	22.1	3277	99.9[a]
Prescott County	22	52.4	20	47.6	42	100.0
1855						
Ontario	2568	72.0	997	28.0	3565	100.0
Prescott County	23	46.9	26	53.1	49	100.0
1861						
Ontario	3031	69.9	1305	30.1	4336	100.0
Prescott County	19	32.8	39	67.2	58	100.0
1872–3						
Ontario (1872)[b]	2626	48.0	2850	52.0	5476	100.0
Prescott County (1873)[b]	7	9.7	65	90.3	72	100.0

[a] Total is not 100 because of rounding.

[b] The year in parentheses is the one in this time span for which information is available for this jurisdiction.

Source: Annual Report for the years indicated. (For bibliographical information, see Chapter 1, note 39.)

male willingness to work for low pay because they knew that most Prescott County trustees were ready to hire the least demanding applicant for a teaching position. The superintendent from neighbouring Cumberland Township complained that "too often the cheapest man is looked upon as the most desirable," describing this practice as "one of the greatest hindrances to the working of the system" in eastern Ontario, a "pernicious error."[23] Some officials explained the desire to seek the most inexpensive teacher in terms of legitimate financial concern. James Gamble, reporting on the Township of East Hawkesbury in 1851, suggested that the undeveloped nature of the area explained why "the people cannot be prevailed upon to give such salaries as would secure the services of competent and efficient teachers."[24] However, the hiring of low-salaried teachers was reportedly not confined to areas in which budget restraint was a real necessity. The inspector for neighbouring Renfrew County remarked in 1871 that there were "many sections, which are comparatively speaking wealthy, whose trustees go forth, as it were to market, in quest of the cheapest teacher."[25]

TABLE 30
Average Salaries of Teachers, 1847–78

	Males		Females	
	With Board	*Without Board*	*With Board*	*Without Board*
1851				
Alfred Township	£17 10s	–	–	£12 7s
Caledonia Township	–	£32	£11 15s	–
Prescott County	£24 17s	£37 15s	£14 1s	£25 12s
Ontario	£33 7s	£52 4s	£21 9s	£31 1s
1855				
Alfred Township	–	–	£15 18s	–
Caledonia Township	£30 10s	£40	£12 10s	–
Prescott County	£34 12s	£53 19s	£18 9s	£30 14s
1860				
Prescott County	$145	$251	$ 85	$154
Ontario	$188	$457	$124	$242
1872–3				
Ontario (1872)[a]	–	$360	–	$213
Prescott County (1873)[a]	–	$325	–	$150
1877–8				
Ontario (1877)[a]	–	$398	–	$264
Prescott County (1878)[a]	–	$282	–	$160

[a] The year in parentheses is the one in this time span for which information is available for this jurisdiction.

Source: Annual Report for the years indicated. (For bibliographical information, see Chapter 1, note 39.)

In describing the quest of school trustees for the cheapest teacher, educators expressed great disappointment at the way in which considerations of teacher quality were disregarded. In 1861, the Cumberland Township school official, puzzling about what he considered the paradox of teacher selection, was inspired to transcend the characteristic prose of local educators:

Men who would not engage an inefficient ploughman to furrow their fields and commit to them the seed which is to result in a harvest of time, make little inquiry as to the efficiency of the teacher who is to commit to the mellow soil of the heart of the child, seed which is to bear fruit for eternity.[26]

Certification. School officials in eastern Ontario supported their description of a poorly trained teaching force with empirical evidence about certification. Prescott County teachers characteristically had less training than was average for Ontario. In 1851, more than half had third-class certificates, the lowest form of teacher accreditation. In 1860, more than a third still carried only the low-level certificates, while the all-Ontario proportion was less than 20 per cent. By the late 1870s, when emphasis on teacher training increased, Prescott County fell even further behind the provincial pattern. (See Table 31.)

Turnover. From the perspective of local school promoters, the constantly changing membership of the teaching force further worsened the negative effect of poorly trained teachers in the classroom. Prescott County's teachers not only lacked proper credentials; they also tended to give up instructing after a few years. Thus, most of its teachers had neither formal training nor practical experience. In the second half of the nineteenth century, inspectors became increasingly aware that the teachers of eastern Ontario were predominantly young adults who were teaching in anticipation of marriage or better employment. A Russell County inspector best described the life-cycle pattern: "The daughters of respectable farmers teach a few years, and as they gain in experience, generally get married, and just as they become truly efficient, give up the profession." The pattern for males was similar. Instead of treating teaching as a career, "Young men of talent and ambition make teaching a stepping-stone to some other more lucrative profession."[27]

The life-cycle nature of teaching is illustrated by the rapid turnover of teachers in both Alfred and Caledonia townships during the 1856–71 period. In these years, sixty-two individuals taught in Alfred, while the schools grew only from four to nine. The change of teachers was even greater in Caledonia, where sixty-three individuals taught the four to seven schools. Rarely did an individual teach more than two years in either township. (See Table 32.) One exception was Antoine Lemery, who instructed for at least eleven years in Alfred Township. His example does not suggest, however, that teaching by itself was a viable career in Prescott County; in addition to instructing, he operated a forty-acre farm. Similarly, Mary Gauthier had instructed for eighteen years by the late nineteenth century, but these years were not all successive; rather, they included time before marriage and after becoming a widow. During the latter period, she owned a hundred-acre farm. In this sense, teaching was a supple-

TABLE 31
Formal Qualifications of Teachers, 1851–71

	Normal School Training		First-Class Certificate		Second-Class Certificate		Third-Class Certificate		Interim Certificate		Total
	N	%	N	%	N	%	N	%	N	%	
1851											
Ontario	0		378	11.8	1272	39.8	1547	48.4	0	0	3197
Prescott County	0		5	11.9	15	35.7	22	52.4	0	0	42
1855											
Prescott County	0		3	6.4	17	36.2	27	57.4	0	0	47
Alfred Township	0		0		2	50.0	2	50.0	0	0	4
Caledonia Township	0		0		2	50.0	2	50.0	0	0	4
1860											
Ontario	0		962	25.9	2034	54.8	718	19.3	0	0	3714
Prescott County	0		10	18.9	24	45.3	19	35.8	0	0	53
1872–3											
Ontario (1872)[a]	828	13.1	1337	21.2	1477	23.4	2084	33.1	578	9.2	6304
Prescott County (1873)[a]	0		4	6.3	11	17.2	32	50.1	17	26.6	64
1877–8											
Ontario (1877)[a]	1084	14.4	250	3.3	1304	17.3	3926	52.0	988	13.1	7552
Prescott County (1878)[a]	0		8	11.4	4	5.7	35	50.0	23	32.9	70

[a] The year in parentheses is the one in this time span for which information is available for the jurisdiction.

Source: Annual Report for the years indicated. (For bibliographical information, see Chapter 1, note 39.)

TABLE 32
Turnover of Teachers, Alfred and Caledonia Townships, 1856–71

Township	Number of Different Teachers	Years Taught by Each Teacher, 1856–71					
		1	2	3	4	5	> 5
Alfred (4–9 schools)	62	30	22	5	4	0	1
Caledonia (4–7 schools)	63	43	15	3	0	2	0

Source: Manuscript annual reports of the local superintendents for the years indicated. (For bibliographical information, see Chapter 1, note 39.)

mentary or temporary occupation even for those who taught more than a few years.

The Social Context

The evidence from Alfred and Caledonia townships and the general Prescott County data on schoolhouses, instructional equipment, and teachers emphasize that there was no clear divide between the language groups' support for schooling from the 1840s to the early 1870s. Despite the perception of anglophone enthusiasm and francophone lethargy, the condition of schooling in Prescott County, which was predominantly the responsibility of anglophone, was consistently poorer than the general Ontario norm.

Of course, any school development in these years might be considered remarkable, given the conditions which prevailed in the county. Since many settlements were relatively new, getting to local schools could involve long walks on poor roads and dirt paths. Parents were also concerned about the harsh climate, especially during winter, when young students use snowshoes to reach class. But environmental factors only partially explain the settlers' failure to give schooling a high priority during the mid-nineteenth century. A more important factor was that the family was the major social, as well as economic, institution for both anglophones and francophones. Townships such as Alfred and Caledonia operated with only a small amount of formal organization. Everyday life occurred within networks of kin and neighbours. The communal nature of existence in Prescott County cannot be overemphasized. Thomas Tweed Higginson's diary and other contemporary sources, both anglophone and francophone, provide a litany of borrowing and lending, of helping and being helped. This exchange of goods and services was an ongoing feature of the pursuit of survival and security, and it involved both kin and unrelated neighbours. "William borrowed Uncle Robert's oxen and drew out the beams and the sleepers." "William borrowed William McConnel's steers to draw up the girts and rafters from Mrs. Byer's field."[28]

The sense of mutual interdependence which characterized rural life in Prescott County became especially apparent in times of crisis. An outbreak of typhoid fever reached epidemic proportions in 1819; local communities survived by collective effort. Young women could be seen on horseback, "laden with dainties for distant sick acquaintances." Neighbours came together to harvest the wheat of those stricken by illness.[29] Similarly, kin and community rallied when fire struck. On 6 April, the "Emerald Hill house burned to the ground p.m. A burning chimney the cause. Great loss." The very next day, Thomas Tweed Higginson "went up to see Mother. She is pretty well but grieves about her loss." The community also responded immediately. On 8 April, "Neighbours helping to get timber to rebuild br. C.T.H.'s house. All turn out." Such work bees were approached with a sense of ambition and pride. The achievement of a collective effort for just a few hours could be substantial. "William and I went to Mrs. Whitcomb's chopping bee in the morning. Fourteen of us cut 23 cords of wood." Domestic chores also had a community dimension. "Mary Byers came up after dinner and helped Ellen to sew."[30]

The support of kin was similarly important in forming new families. By establishing a household within Prescott county, sons could continue to benefit from the wisdom and support of their parents. "Father came down to see us. He praises the farm and tries to make difficulties appear less." The presence of mothers in neighbouring communities could be just as advantageous. "Cousin John Walker here with his mother. They are both in very good spirits. She is going over to spend a few weeks with him in his backwoods home to help as a good angel, the little ones who watch for her coming with great eagerness."[31]

The attachment to family, kin, and community was reinforced by a social life based on home entertainment. Singing and dancing brought friends and relatives together and partly balanced the routine and drudgery of frontier existence.

John and Jane and Esther and I went to Richard's wedding. We arrived at Mr. Owen's at one o'clock, then the party went to Grenville Church where the marriage ceremony was performed by the Rev. Mr. Lewis. We then came back to Mr. Owen's and took dinner at five. The Duddridges entertained the company with some excellent songs and music until the fiddler came; then dancing commenced and was kept up until daylight.[32]

For such grand events, relatives and close friends came from all the surrounding area and contributed to large gatherings. Thomas Tweed Higginson held a "Jubilee party" for his mother in 1887 and invited 106 guests in addition to eleven members of the immediate family. For well-established families in Prescott County, even routine Sunday gatherings were large affairs, with thirty participants considered not very many.[33]

The experience of the Higginson family reflected a general acceptance that life in Prescott County involved informal collective effort. Other local writers, such as Mrs Ennid Christie, stressed that settlement was a communal activity; in 1860, she described how "the neighbours would all help one another" and added that "as a rule, as each house was done [they] would have a little party."[34]

For francophone immigrants, the proximity of Prescott County to the St Lawrence Valley particularly encouraged the maintenance of family ties. Slow periods during the winter were used to visit relatives in neighbouring Quebec counties, and throughout the nineteenth century, kinship ties connected both sides of the Ottawa River.[35] Like anglophones, francophones within Prescott County responded to misfortune informally but immediately. The death of a widow, Mme Ouimette, stranded her three small children but they moved in next door with Mme Ann Marquis, who not only cared for them but also sent them to school when they became of age.[36]

SCHOOLS IN A CHANGING WORLD: THE 1870s

The importance of family, kin, and neighbours to social organization helps explain why formal schooling had a low priority in Prescott County. Settlers simply did not feel a pressing need to build this type of institution with the ideal schoolhouses, maps, and teachers encouraged by school promoters. School reports from the 1840s to the early 1870s did not emphasize this fact in explaining the poor condition of schooling in the area; rather they focused on the negative influence of immigration from Quebec. This focus was justified in the sense that many francophone parents were not active in local school promotion and many francophone children did not attend class. However, the contrasting school-attendance patterns in Alfred and Caledonia townships show that the administrative structure of the fledgling school system effectively controlled the linguistic character of its clientele. Both anglophone and francophone children attended only when other obligations permitted and when appropriate schools were available. In these years, francophone children were at a relative educational disadvantage. However, it was not inherent attitudes but rather official policy, combined with the local demographic and economic setting, that was responsible for the significant difference in attendance between the language groups of Prescott County.

Not surprisingly, therefore, the changing demographic and economic structure of the period from the 1870s engendered a new educational context. Prescott County now included a substantial number of Ontario-born francophone children, as well as the offspring of new immigrants, and most of them lived in sizeable francophone communities that had been established for several decades. The opportunities available for family economies in the système agro-forestier of the 1850s and 1860s had allowed these francophone communities to gain some measure of temporary security in Prescott County and thus to build a foundation upon which to react to the changing material environment of the 1870s. This reaction intimately affected the persistent anglophone community, which itself was trying to come to grips with the failing economy.

The economic crisis resulting from the retreat of the forest frontier and the decline of land availability had two quite distinct implications for educational development. Obviously, the material difficulties of these years discouraged expenditure on schools. Although the quality of schoolhouses and the use of aids, such as maps, did show some improvement over time, the general quality of educational opportunity was hindered by the hard times of the later nineteenth century. In the same years, however, the changed Prescott County economy, by offering fewer productive opportunities for children, made school attendance more possible. As the county became an "old" agricultural area with few opportunities in the lumber industry, the demand for child labour within the family setting declined. Few other work alternatives for youth emerged. Some employment opportunities for young teenage boys increased at the sawmills in the Village of Hawkesbury, but townships such as Alfred and Caledonia offered few jobs. Despite various promotional schemes, Prescott County did not attract the kind of early factories and textile mills that depended heavily on the employment of youth and the piecework production

TABLE 33
French-Language Schools, Prescott County,
1870–83

	1870	1883
Alfred Township	4	10
Caledonia Township	0	3
Longueuil Township	2	3
Township of East Hawkesbury	6	5
Township of West Hawkesbury	0	0
North Plantagenet Township	0	7
South Plantagenet Township	1	4
Total	13	32

Source: Annual Reports of the local superintendents, 1870 (for
bibliographical information, see Chapter 1, note 39); and Minutes
of the Board of Examiners for the Counties of Prescott and
Russell, meeting of June 1883, RG2 H3 vol. 35, PAO.

of domestic economies. As a result, chidlren became more available
to attend school.

The decline of productive opportunities for children was paral-
lelled by continued establishment of schools, especially schools for
francophone youngsters. The shifting demographic balance and the
maturing of French-Canadian communities led to francophones' being
able to elect their own school trustees and thus to an increasing
number of French-language schools, despite the continuing obstacles
presented by the standardized administrative system. In 1870, Prcs-
cott County had thirteen French-language schools; by 1883, there
were thirty-two, with at least three in every township except West
Hawkesbury, home of Hamilton Brothers, where anglophone control had not yet been successfully challenged.[37] (See Table 33.)

Changes in Attendance Patterns

The increased availability of children combined with the school
building of the 1870s had an immediate impact on attendance patterns, especially of francophone children. Children were spending
less of their lives as producers and more as pupils. In the altered
environment of late-nineteeenth-century Prescott County, schooling
increasingly filled the space in children's lives that had earlier been
dominated by collective domestic activity.

TABLE 34
School-Age Population and School Enrolment, Alfred and Caledonia
Townships, 1881

| | Alfred Township | | | | | | Caledonia Township | | | | | |
| | Anglophones | | | Francophones | | | Anglophones | | | Francophones | | |
Age	Pop. Total	Pupils N	%	Pop. Total	Pupils N	%	Pop. Total	Pupils N	%	Pop. Total	Pupils N	%
5–6	26	9	35	199	77	39	41	13	32	67	24	36
7–12	85	72	85	464	351	76	119	87	73	158	115	73
13–16	41	21	51	242	57	24	72	34	47	101	25	25
17–21	40	0	0	287	4	1	95	1	1	83	1	1
All school ages (5–16)	152	102	67%	905	485	54%	232	134	58%	326	164	50%

Source: Manuscript census, 1881.

Nonetheless, there continued to be an important cultural dimension within the overall growth of schooling. Although French-language schools were increasingly available, francophone children still enrolled less frequently than anglophones. For Alfred Township, this pattern shows up clearly in the 1881 census, and it is quite surprising because earlier enumerations had shown little cultural distinction in school enrolment there. In 1871, for example, about half of both anglophone and francophone school-age children had attended class at some time during the year. (See Table 27.) One decade later, the anglophone proportion had jumped to 67 per cent while the francophone proportion held at 54 per cent (see Table 34). In Caledonia Township, the establishment of French-language schools doubled the proportion of francophone school-age children enrolled in class – from one-quarter in 1871 to one-half in 1881. At the same time, the proportion of anglophone pupils actually decreased from 72 per cent to 58 per cent as three schools switched to French-language instruction. (See Tables 27 and 34.)

The new similarity in Caledonia is particularly striking among the younger children and the oldest; the patterns of school enrolment rates were almost identical for anglophones and francophones. The only cultural difference was among thirteen- to sixteen-years-olds, for whom the anglophone rate of enrolment was twice that of the francophone. In contrast, the francophone children of Alfred – both the important seven-to-twelve years age group and the thirteen- to sixteen-year-olds – were less likely to be registered than their anglophone counterparts. The data also show for each age group the percentage of francophones enrolled in school was quite similar across the two townships. The proportions of anglophones also followed the same pattern in Alfred and in Caledonia, although the switch of three schools to French-language instruction clearly affected the registration of younger children.

Changes in Francophone Class Structure

Despite the presence of well-established French-language schools and a vast francophone superiority in population, the 1870s had changed the relative position of French Canadians with respect to schooling in Alfred Township. In order to understand this phenomenon, we must return to consideration of the economic crisis and its implications for Prescott county society. Two economic developments were especially relevant. The first was the emergence of local francophone merchants and skilled workers, who were now servicing the established francophone communities, such as those of Alfred Township. The second was the proletarianization of certain francophones; by 1881, some had little hope of making the transition from wage-labour to a family economy based on independent farming and the lumber industry.[38] The educational implications of these developments were striking. By 1881, there was wide variation within the overall school enrolment pattern of francophones.

For the purposes of analysis, the occupational structure of francophone parents with school-age children can be divided into three groups: merchants and skilled workers; farmers; and labourers. As would be expected in an agricultural township, the vast majority of potential school attenders were the children of farmers, but the other two categories were sufficiently well represented by 1881 to reveal several important patterns. First, the children of merchants, shoemakers, blacksmiths, and others with skilled occupations were far more likely to attend school than the offspring of farmers and labourers. The proportions shown in Table 35 make clear that children from farm-based families continued to be important to the domestic economy in 1881 and were not always able to receive schooling, even on a seasonal basis. Second, school enrolment among labourers' children was especially limited. For this group, the demands of the domestic economy were compounded by material insecurity. For labouring families, necessities such as shoes were still factors controlling formal educational experience. As a result, only about one-third of these children enrolled in school in 1881.

TABLE 35
Francophone School Enrolment by Parental
Occupation, Alfred Township, 1881

Parental Occupation	Total Francophone Children[a]	% Enrolled
Merchants, skilled workers, etc.	72	72
Farmers	644	55
Labourers	137	36

[a] Ages 5 to 16, residing with a parent for whom an occupation is listed in the manuscript census.

The emergence of a sizeable group of francophone proletarian families with very low school enrolment rates undoubtedly helps to explain the perceptions of anglophone educators and journalists about the cultural status of Prescott County in the 1880s. Reports of unschooled French Canadians living in "ramshackled apologies" for homes were based on an element of reality in this period.[39] At the same time, however, the emergence of a local leadership group of francophone merchants and skilled workers was an equally important development for the language-of-instruction issue. This development went unnoticed among visiting observers, but within Prescott County its significance was very clear to both anglophones and francophones. From the 1870s, francophone community leaders were frequently able to gain control of the administrative machinery of public schooling. As more and more of them gained positions as school trustees, new French-language schools appeared, and established schools switched their language of instruction. It was this phenomenon that was noticed by anglophone school officials in Caledonia Township, where they considered the transformation of several schools from English to French to have lowered the quality of education to "inferior" status.

THE SEARCH FOR TEACHERS AND ITS EFFECTS

At the heart of the issue of language and of the quality of schooling was the question of teachers. As factors converged to produce opportunities for French-language schools, Prescott County required an increasing number of francophone teachers. The implications of this need became the major preoccupation of Prescott County's Board of Examiners, which was responsible for testing candidates and awarding appropriate teaching certificates to successful applicants. The minutes of their meetings throughout the late nineteenth century reveal the conundrum presented by language diversity within a theoretically uniform school system.[40] This evidence further emphasizes the extent to which the simple policy of language toleration did not reflect the actual complexity of educational issues produced by francophone settlement in Ontario.

From its inception, in 1871, the Board of Examiners for Prescott County was prepared to examine candidates in either English or French. Examination papers for each language were prepared locally, and the board established parallel levels of teaching certification. In addition, the board resolved that "candidates who write in French and English be awarded their true merit in both languages."[41]

The examiners faced a series of substantial obstacles to implementing this system successfully. The most serious was the absence of any French-language teacher-training facility in Ontario. As a result, few francophone candidates came to the board. On the first examination day, in December 1871, only nine of twenty-seven candidates sought certification for teaching in French-language schools. Three years later, it was four out of twenty. Since the demand for French-language instruction was increasing at this time, these figures left the board with a real problem. How could it fulfil its responsibility to upgrade the quality of education and also respond to the local demand for appropriate teachers?[42]

The examiners' first answer to this question was to approve immediately francophone teachers already certified in Quebec. On 16 July 1872, the board passed a motion that "the Council of Public Instruction be requested to authorize the Inspectors to Endorse the Legal Certificates of Teachers in French coming from the Province of Quebec until the County Board of Examiners shall see fit to nullify such certificates."[43] The acceptance of teachers from Quebec was, however, only a very partial response to the demand for French-language instruction since Prescott County was not an attraction for such teachers. By the mid-1870s, the board formally adopted a more drastic strategy. The examiners resolved on 10 August 1876:

In order to supply a sufficient number of Teachers for all the schools in his district – the Inspector be hereby recommended to grant Interim Certificates (or eschew the time of former Interim Certs – as the case may be) in as many cases of those candidates who have not succeeded in obtaining regular certificates at the recent examination as he may think necessary –

it being understood that this resolution has special reference to French teachers and Schools.[44]

In other words, the Board of Examiners would now award teaching certificates to all francophones who presented themselves for examination, regardless of their eventual success or failure.

The results of this strategy exposed the fundamental contradiction of language diversity within the Ontario public school system. In August 1880, forty-three candidates, twelve of them francophone, came to write the examinations. Twenty candidates achieved at least a minimal pass; none were francophone. But because of growing demand for French-language instruction, all the failed francophone candidates were duly awarded interim certificates.[45] The process of examination simply had no effect on francophones who wished to teach in Prescott County.

The Board of Examiners recognized that this situation made a mockery of its role within the educational administration, and undoubtedly the examiners did not appreciate the constant criticism they received in the official school reports filed each year. The 1871 report for Prescott County accused them of being "criminally lenient." Two years later, the county inspector reported that the teachers in his domain had "no special training for the profession" even though most had at least third-class certificates.[46] The acceptance of certified teachers from Quebec was similarly criticized. Inspectors considered them far inferior to their Ontario-trained counterparts; "the standard of education there [Quebec] is so much lower than it is in Ontario that few of them [teachers] are able to pass our Third Class examination."[47]

The tremendous imbalance between the supply and demand for francophone teachers in Prescott County increasingly focused attention on the need for a teacher-training facility. At the 1878 meeting of the Board of Examiners, the awarding of interim certificates to failed francophone candidates was approved with the remark that "French is not taught in the Model School." At the same time, the board passed a resolution that "the Minister of Education be requested to make further special regulations to meet the cases of French teachers so as to facilitate their obtaining a legal standing as teachers in Ontario."[48] No response was forthcoming to this request.

When the minister of education, George Ross, finally decided to take the initiative, – with the regulations of 1885 described in Chapter 1 – his strategy ignored the very real problems faced at the local level and instead presented an additional array of challenges. The new regulations, which required some English-language instruction in all Ontario schools, exacerbated the already serious problems in Prescott County schools. Now it was the responsibility of the county examiners not only to provide teachers certified in the appropriate languages but also to ensure that francophone teachers could teach English. The board knew that this responsibility could not be fulfilled since a sufficient number of even unilingual francophone candidates could not pass the certification examinations. The official demand for bilingual teachers was completely unrealistic, and it is not surprising that Ross's 1885 regulations had no impact in the classroom.

The new Ministry of Education policy on language did, however, fuel discussion at the local level on the need for teacher training for francophones. At their 1885 meeting, the examiners noted again that there was "no suitable school where the French teachers could receive their professional training." This time, as described in Chapter 1, their complaint led to action. The County Council of Public Instruction appointed a committee to choose a location and to identify a "suitable staff" for a "French Model School."[49] Not surprisingly, the committee could find a location but not a staff for such a school, and the Board of Examiners had to continue granting interim certificates to failed francophone candidates.[50] This situation explains how newspapers such as the *Mail* were able to use investigative reports from Prescott County to argue that the standard of education was far below the provincial norm and that in many schools "no attempt or pretense whatever is made of teaching anything but the French language."[51] The Prescott County evidence confirms that George Ross was quite wrong in his claim that at least some English was taught in all Ontario schools in 1889.

In a sense, the rapid growth of French-language schooling in Prescott County during the 1870s and 1880s occurred outside effective administrative supervision by the provincial authorities. The schools were legally within the educational system, but they were not *of* the system. Ross and other observers outside Prescott County did not appreciate this distinction, and the debate that raged at the provincial level during the campaign for the 1890 election never probed the real issues engendered by francophone settlement in Ontario. Similarly, the three-man commission sent to report on the French-language schools in 1889 did not really understand what they observed in Prescott County. In fact, the commission's submission on the need to improve francophone teacher training was already a well-established ambition in Prescott County.

The provincial attention from the 1889 commission and from the electoral campaign did have a dramatic impact on French-language schooling in Prescott County, but the character of this impact was quite unintended and not recognized at the time. Two results were especially important. The first began with the finally successful establishment of a French-language model school in Prescott County. It immediately altered the success rate of francophone candidates who came before the Board of Examiners. Thirty-two francophones attended the examinations of December 1890; twenty-five of them were new graduates from the model school. In contrast to the traditional pattern of failure, twenty-three of the candidates passed, making this group of francophones by far the most successful in the history of the Board of Examiners. The pattern continued in the following years.[52] Thus, the establishment of the French-language model school meant that trustees now had less and less difficulty hiring teachers for their French-language schools. The francophone candidates for certification had to pass examinations in English grammar and composition as well as in other subjects written in French and, as a result, English became more widespread as an element of the curriculum in the French-language schools.[53] It was this phenomenon which the 1893 commission interpreted as evidence of the success of George Ross's language policy. At the same time, however, the availability of trained teachers made schooling more feasible and probably more attractive to francophones in Prescott County. In this sense, the establishment of the French-language model school certainly did not weaken the lynchpin of language within Prescott County. Rather, it contributed to the continued proliferation of French-language education.

The second unintended result of the provincial attention directed towards French-language schooling in the late 1880s was rapid conversion from public to separate schools. Although the Prescott County francophones were all Catholic, the language issue had not been significantly related to the establishment of separate schools. In fact, as we have seen, many French-language schools operated within the public system until 1889. The crucial event of that year was the arrival of the commissioners, whose mandate did not include separate schools. By inspecting only *public* French-language schools, they implicitly, if unintentionally, encouraged francophones to form separate schools as a way of shielding themselves from official investigation. This result had important consequences for the future of French-language schooling in Prescott County, but at the time provincial educators barely noticed. The 1893 commissioners' report simply mentioned in passing that a significant number of French-language schools had recently joined the separate system.

POLITICS, RELIGION, AND THE
LANGUAGE OF INSTRUCTION

The rapid spread of French-language schools and the dramatic increase of the separate system after 1889 occurred in a changing demographic and economic environment, but these developments also related directly to the institutions of politics and religion. Population patterns and the material structure of Prescott County framed the history of education during the nineteenth century, but the specific character of schooling in individual neighbourhoods also depended upon complex political and religious considerations. To some extent, these considerations reflected the provincial and national issues of the time, but, just as significantly, they were rooted in local circumstances. An analysis of politics in Prescott County reveals the dramatic implications of a "world turned upside down." Such an analysis also provides a background for understanding the role of the Catholic Church and specifically of separate schools within francophone society during the late nineteenth century. It was in these contexts that the language-of-instruction question had such great meaning for the people of Prescott County.

CHAPTER FIVE

Quatre fantômes et la foule: The Politics of Cultural Conflict

Political studies of minority-language education usually narrate the major electoral campaigns in which the school question has been a focus of debate. Historians have carefully reconstructed the chronology of discussion of, for example, the Ontario elections of 1890 and the federal election of 1896, in which the Manitoba school question attracted national attention.[1] These histories are valuable, but they limit our understanding of minority-language education in three ways. First, they assign an episodic quality to the language question, rather than portraying it as an ongoing issue in the evolution of certain communities. Political studies which emphasize particular elections deny a long-term perspective which situates periods of intense public debate within the appropriate context. Controversies about the language question in certain campaigns have histories of their own, a background which is not captured by a chronological focus on any specific election.

Second, established political histories emphasize the speeches of provincial or federal leaders; they rarely probe debate at the community level, which is assumed to have been engaged without a real life of its own. As a result, the main evidence of the established historiography includes the public statements of major political leaders and major newspapers and, to a lesser extent, private expressions offered in correspondence or diaries. Local leaders, even those from areas of serious conflict about minority-language education, are unknown in the historical literature on this topic.

Finally, established studies on the politics of the language question touch only lightly, if at all, on the social and economic context of electoral debate. Campaigning and voting are treated as aspects of intellectual history, understandable on their own terms. This approach divorces politics from other components of everyday life and ignores relationships between material and ideological considerations for both politicians and voters.

Exploring the politics of cultural conflict in Prescott County during the nineteenth century vividly illustrates the value of a longitudinal, local-level analysis to our understanding of minority-language education, partly because such analysis reveals significant agency in particular communities. The evidence suggests the existence of a dialectic between events in local areas and the great debate about language at the provincial and national levels. Moreover, the experience of Prescott County politicians emphasizes the importance of social and economic changes, as well as actual electoral decisions, to the nature of this debate. That demographic and material developments affected the political history of the language question is clearly evident in Prescott County, especially during the mid-1880s. By this time, politics emerged as a significant factor in the convergence of forces which produced the cultural conflict of the late nineteenth century.

The following discussion relies upon two general types of evidence: local newspapers (English-language and French-language) and election results for both provincial and federal seats. The newspapers permit a reconstruction of the chronology of events and provide journalistic perceptions of these political developments. Such literary evidence may, of course, represent the views and priorities of only certain community leaders (even though editors often spoke as if their thoughts were widely shared). That local newspapers cannot be treated as the voices of the people need not, however, be viewed as a limitation. In fact, the Prescott County newspapers provide a heretofore unexplored point of entry to the experience of those communities actually involved in the language controversy. An important weakness of the established historiography is its reliance on newspaper articles written by investigative reporters from Toronto. As will be shown, the journalism of Prescott County offers a quite different perspective on political events in the later nineteenth century.

In turn, local election results give an indication of how the voters of Prescott County reacted to the larger political debate. By analysing the voters' lists at the township level, electoral patterns for francophones and anglophones can be suggested for various elections. Moreover, the election data permit identification of candidates not only by party and language group but also by occupation and social position. This identification can then be related to voting patterns, as well as to the political debate of specific campaigns.

Taken together, the local newspaper accounts and the electoral evidence contribute to a general understanding of how the experience of communities interacted with developments beyond their borders.

THE STRUGGLE FOR CONTROL OF
THE CONSERVATIVE PARTY

The provincial election of February 1883 was a critical moment in the history of cultural relations in Prescott County. As the election approached, local observers recognized that the character of the campaign was unlike those of the past. In January, *The News and Ottawa Valley Advocate*, published in L'Orignal, said in an editorial:

[the] County of Prescott appears to be on the brink of a political struggle, and if the signs portray anything, we may prepare in the coming general election for the Assembly, for a pull between the French-Canadian and English-speaking electors of the County.[2]

Battles at the nominating conventions had contributed to the "signs" of an impending "national" confrontation. Francophone electors in Prescott County had traditionally supported the Conservative party, but, until the late 1870s, their vote had been considered "auxiliary to that of other nationalities."[3] As French-Canadian settlement grew, however, political considerations had to be adjusted accordingly.

The cultural shift in electoral influences most directly affected a sizeable group of anglophone Conservatives who had long controlled the local association through the machinery of party conventions. This group used language and the rules of procedure to minimize francophone participation in candidate selection and thus to maintain their position despite the changing constituency. As francophone settlement expanded, the increasing precariousness of the anglophone Conservatives inspired some imaginative schemes. John Hamilton, the Hawkesbury sawmill owner and an enthusiastic Conservative supporter, took initiative to limit francophone influence in the party from the time of Confederation. His most grandiose scheme involved an entente with Father Antoine Brunet of East Hawkesbury. The curé undertook to deliver the francophone vote to an anglophone provincial candidate in return for Hamilton's promise to direct the anglophone vote to a francophone federal candidate. In theory, this division would avoid any internecine political struggle that the changing cultural geography of Prescott County might engender within the Conservative Party. However, Hamilton's political manoeuvring was not sincere. He did not promote a francophone federal candidacy immediately after the entente and he actively opposed such representation in 1878, when a francophone was actually nominated. In dealing with Father Brunet, Hamilton was simply striving to stave off French-Canadian political leadership within the party and therefore within the county.[4]

Federal Elections

Nonetheless, the strategy of allotting the federal seat to a francophone and the provincial seat to an anglophone did have considerable merit for the position of the Prescott County anglophones, especially after 1874, when federal legislation abolished public nominations and balloting.[5] Hamilton's refusal to support the Conservative francophone candidate, Félix Routhier, in 1878 did not affect the election results; moreover, it revealed the weakening influence of anglophone voters in the county as French Canadians gained power within party politics. Although Hamilton and others had nominated a rival, English-speaking Conservative candidate, many anglophones maintained party loyalty; their ballots combined with the solid francophone vote to give Routhier victory. After this election, the major parties in Prescott County nominated no more anglophone candidates for federal contests. The 1878 results made clear to both parties that without francophone support, political victory was unlikely.[6] For the next federal election, the Liberals put all their support behind Simon Labrosse, who also attracted some support from renegade Conservative francophones. Félix Routhier ran again as the official Conservative candidate but lost to the Liberals as would that party's nominees in future elections (see Table 36).

The federal elections of the 1870s and 1882 clearly reveal to us the maturing of francophone communities in Prescott County. These years produced a new francophone group of local economic leaders and professionals, and some of them used their relatively secure economic positions to enter public life. Simon Labrosse, for example, was a local merchant and postmaster. He served as councillor and reeve before entering the federal arena; he sat in the House of Commons from 1882 to 1891, when he declined renomination. Félix Routhier, an immigrant from St-Plaçide, Quebec, was a small manufacturer in Vankleek Hill. Like Labrosse, he used his economic position as a basis of political activity at the federal level.[7]

Provincial Elections

Quite soon, the same trend appeared in provincial politics. The anglophone Conservatives of Prescott County had been able to main-

TABLE 36
Federal Election Results, Prescott County, 1867–96

Candidates	Party Affiliation	Votes
1867		
Albert Hagar	Liberal	1205
T. Higginson	Conservative	130
1872		
Albert Hagar	Liberal	Acclaimed
1874		
Albert Hagar	Liberal	665
Thomas White	Conservative	659
James Boyd	Liberal-Independent	292
1878		
Félix Routhier	Conservative	875
Albert Hagar	Liberal	870
Angus Urquhart	Conservative-Independent	661
1882		
Simon Labrosse	Liberal	1322
Félix Routhier	Conservative	1021
1887		
Simon Labrosse	Liberal	1414
Félix Routhier	Conservative	1223
1891		
Isidore Proulx	Liberal	1269
Félix Routhier	Conservative	608
E.A. Johnson	Independent	532
David D. Bertrand	Independent	335
1896		
Isidore Proulx	Liberal	1334
H. Cloran	Patrons-Liberal	996
D. Sabourin	Conservative	902

Source: Library of Parliament, Information and Reference Branch, *History of the Federal Electorial Ridings 1867–1980*, vol. 2 *Ontario* (Ottawa 1982–83), 628–9.

tain control of conventions while the party remained victorious during the 1870s. Under the leadership of this group, the linguistically mixed Conservatives defeated the predominantly anglophone Liberals in three consecutive provincial elections. In 1881, however, for a by-election following the death of William Harkin, the Liberal party employed a clever strategy to undermine the alliance of francophone and anglophone Conservatives. It ran two candidates: Simon Labrosse, who disrupted the Conservative francophone vote, and an anglophone, Albert Hagar, who attracted the usual majority of English-speaking voters. With the Conservative francophones thrown into chaos, the anglophone vote was sufficient to carry Hagar to an easy victory. Liberal strategies had successfully compensated for the changing cultural dimension of Prescott County politics, and they continued to do so throughout the rest of the century.

The voters' list prepared for the 1883 election confirmed that the cultural balance of power was indeed shifting in Prescott County. The editors of *The News and Ottawa Valley Advocate* informed readers that this list identified three townships in which francophone electors had assumed a clear majority. Moreover, French Canadians were only slightly in the minority elsewhere, leaving them with an overall county advantage of 125 voters. Anglophone electors still held a strong position only in the Township of West Hawkesbury.[8] (See Table 38.)

THE RISE OF FRANCOPHONE CONSCIOUSNESS

This electoral transition became particularly significant in the face of increasing evidence of francophone consciousness in Prescott County. During the spring of 1880, French Canadians began to direct energy and enthusiasm toward the establishment of cultural organizations. Félix Routhier, the federal member of Parliament for Prescott County, played an important role in cultivating and organizing this development. In early May, Routhier made an "eloquent speech" advocating the establishment of a local St Jean Baptiste Society to a large crowd of French Canadians who had congregated after mass on Ascension Day, an important Catholic holy day.[9] His suggestion gained immediate support, and later in the month Routhier presided over a larger, countywide meeting in L'Orignal to begin formation of the local organization.

The timing of this francophone assembly in L'Orignal was partly related to the announcement in Prescott County of a large-scale French-Canadian convention, planned for Quebec City, to access the "numerical strength" of the French-Canadian population in various regions of North America and to "take such means as can prevent or stop the very regrettable exodus" from Quebec to New England. Specifically, the convention would promote French-Canadian emigration to the "North West and to the three Great Canadian Valleys open to colonization – the Ottawa, the St. Maurice, and the Saguenay." The announcement fuelled the efforts of Prescott County's

TABLE 37
Provincial Election Results, Prescott County, 1867–98

Candidates	Party Affiliation	Votes
1867		
James P. Boyd	Liberal	838
T. McGee	Conservative	816
1871		
George Wellesley Hamilton	Conservative	853
James P. Boyd	Liberal	719
1875		
William Harkin	Conservative	988
R.P. Pattee	Liberal	591
1879		
William Harkin	Conservative	900
J. Ryan	Liberal	622
E. Johnson	Independent	232
J. Vanbridges	Independent	136
1881		
Albert Hagar	Liberal	1002
S. Labrosse	Liberal	950
T. Lee	Conservative	119
J. Butterfield	Independent	115
1883		
Albert Hagar	Liberal	1292
Alfred F.E. Evanturel	Conservative	1260
1886		
Alfred F.E. Evanturel	Liberal	1665
J.H. Molloy	Liberal	1522
1890		
Alfred F.E. Evanturel	Liberal	Acclaimed
1894		
Alfred F.E. Evanturel	Liberal	2038
J. Cross	Conservative	830
1898		
Alfred F.E. Evanturel	Liberal	Acclaimed

Sources: Roderick Lewis, *A Statistical History of All the Electoral Districts of the Province of Ontario since 1867* (Toronto: Baptist Johnson, n.d.): 217–18; Roderick Lewis, *Centennial Edition of A History of Electoral Districts, Legislatures and Ministries of the Province of Ontario 1867–1968* (Toronto: Queen's Printer 1969); Henry J. Morgan, ed., *The Canadian Parliamentary Companion* (Montreal: John Lovell 1974); and J.A. Gemmill, ed., *The Canadian Parliamentary Companion* (Ottawa: J. Durie 1891).

TABLE 38
Parliamentary Electors, Prescott County, for
the Election of 1883

Township / Village	Francophone Voters	Anglophone Voters
Alfred	436	97
Caledonia	164	207
Longueuil	142	62
East Hawkesbury	324	366
West Hawkesbury	30	327
North Plantagenet	342	218
South Plantagenet	212	221
L'Orignal	35	48
Hawkesbury Village	121	135
Total	1806	1681

Source: Voters' list as tabulated and presented in The News and
Ottawa Valley Advocate, 30 January 1883.

francophone leaders to establish their own cultural organizations.
The conference's agenda made clear to them that their position in
the lower Ottawa Valley now held an important place in the grand
design of the Quebec leadership.[10]

By early June, plans were in progress throughout the county for
parochial branches of the St Jean Baptiste Society. The official inaugural day of their establishment was set for Saturday, 21 June,
when a "grand celebration" of the society's patron saint enveloped
L'Orignal. This day witnessed a major development in the expression
of francophone affirmation in Prescott County.

Preparations have been going on for some time past for a fitting celebration
by our French people of their national day, and yesterday was appointed
as the time. On Saturday two beautiful arches were erected ... [and] nearly
every house in the village was decorated with flags and other adornments,
and a lively and pleasing effect was produced ... Early in the morning people
were astir making preparations for the coming display and many salutes
were fired in commemoration of the day. A brass band from Hull ... roused
many people from their sleep by its music. The procession formed at L'Ange
Gardien Corners and started on their march for the church, about half-past
ten. At this hour numbers of people had arrived from the country, and the
streets presented a most lively appearance. The procession proceeded, headed

by mounted marshals and prominent members of the Society toward the church ... Upon reaching the church the immense crowd thronged the doors and entered the capacious building. So intense was the crowd that nearly two hundred people could not gain admittance ... [After mass] the procession re-formed and proceeded in admirable order to Camerons' Grove where they separated and enjoyed a luncheon among the trees. After further music from the band, the people collected about a platform erected for the occasion and were addressed briefly by Mr. Routhier, M.P.[11]

At the conclusion of the celebration, the crowd cheered "lustily," and several organizers immediately left to participate in the Quebec City festivities.

According to the newspapers, anglophone residents in the county offered little negative comment on the initial francophone activities. Prescott County had historically included a complex array of English-speaking societies and organizations, which were usually affiliated with specific ethnoreligious subgroups of the anglophone population. *The News and Ottawa Valley Advocate* was generally supportive of French-Canadian cultural enthusiasm, describing the St Jean Baptiste Society branches as a "commendable suggestion."[12] Some of the anglophone population, however, immediately expressed uneasiness, and in the following year anxiety increased in intensity.

In May 1880, the *Plantagenet Plaindealer* concluded a report on French-Canadian organizational meetings with the hope that "there are no politics to be mixed up with the great national movement."[13]

By 1883, this hope was no longer realistic. The Conservative nominating convention for the February provincial election clearly evidenced a new level of francophone initiative and influence within the party. The convention was held in Alfred Township, the heart of French-Canadian settlement in the county, and Félix Routhier came to make a dramatic plea for a francophone candidate.

The Vision of Alfred Evanturel

That call was made especially appealing by the availability of Alfred F. E. Evanturel, a lawyer who appeared to possess all the qualifications for political success. Evanturel brought to the county a timely combination of legal training, bilingual fluency, and cultural consciousness.[14]

One disadvantage which Evanturel had to overcome was his opponents' claim that he was an outsider, a potent criticism in all local politics. Nonresident candidates, even high-profile politicians, usually met effective resistance in Prescott County. For example, Henry

J. Friel, owner of the Ottawa *Packet*, was defeated convincingly in 1863 by Thomas Higginson, the Hawkesbury merchant. In 1867, Thomas D'Arcy McGee attempted to combine his federal Montreal West seat with provincial representation of Prescott County, but he lost to James Boyd, a lumber dealer in West Hawkesbury. However, Evanturel's position differed somewhat from these precedents since he had moved to the county, from Ottawa, two years before seeking office and had gained a local reputation as an active public defender. Moreover, his rationale for coming to Prescott County was directly linked to the area's cultural identity. Evanturel explained that Prescott County represented "la plus française partie de l'Ontario" but lacked appropriate representation in basic sectors of social organization, such as the legal system. As a result, injustices had been done "aux pauvres justiciables français qui ne comprenaient ni la langue de la Province ni la manière de faire des tribunaux." Evanturel had, therefore, brought his law practice to the county for the sake of the francophone population and, in his first two years, he claimed great success:

Aucun Canadien Français n'a été depuis traîné devant une cour criminelle sans que je me sois fait un devoir de me placer entre le juge, le jury et lui; aucun homme n'a été condamné même dans une action civile, sans la satisfaction d'avoir fait comprendre à la cour ses raisons par un interprète qu'on ne pouvait ni intimider ni effrayer.[15]

Evanturel's legal activity was part of his larger belief in cultural protection and affirmation, which had led him to local involvement in Prescott County even when he was still living in Ottawa. Indeed, Evanturel had been a principal speaker at the momentous St Jean Baptiste celebration at L'Orignal in 1880. At that time, he concluded his address with an eloquent encouragement of cultural survival; the local newspaper translated it as:

Nationality keeping so religiously the faith and the sacred trust of its forefathers cannot be doomed for it was said that the grave shuts on those nations alone which intend to perish.[16]

By the early 1880s, a key element of Evanturel's view was that the French Canadians in Ontario had a common identity. Although quite distinct historical experiences had led to francophone settlement in various regions of Ontario, he perceived a basis of similarity among these groups. He was particularly struck by the sizeable community in Essex County, the western counterpart of Prescott County, where the French-Canadian population had also increased during the nineteenth century. Considering the growth of the two groups led him to a concept that was far-fetched for the time.

En présence de cet accroissement inattendu de Prescott et d'Essex, aux deux bouts de l'Ontario, je pensais involontairement aux grandes enterprises du jour, au percement des isthmes et à la construction d'un chemin de fer d'une mer à l'autre; – je me rappelais que dans ces travaux durables et gigantesques l'on débutait aux deux extrémités dans l'espoir de se rencontrer bientôt au milieu, en ne laissant rien d'incomplet en arrière.[17]

This statement from 1883 was the first public promotion in Prescott County of an integrated view of Ontario's various francophone settlements. There is no evidence that such a perspective was widely shared at the time. In fact, other contemporary reports of cultural affirmation indicate the strengthening of ties between Prescott County francophones and their counterparts in Quebec. The St Jean Baptiste celebration, for example, suggested that the extension of Quebec society into the eastern corner of Ontario, rather than an awareness of the actual meaning of the Ottawa River boundary. Nonetheless, Evanturel's perception of a francophone identity related to residence in Ontario is noteworthy, considering later developments. His judicial experience had given him an awareness which soon would be shared by many others in Prescott County.

The Election of 1883

Obviously, Evanturel's perspective severely tested the loyalty of anglophone Conservative party supporters in Prescott County. Their political calculations were complex. Without francophone support, the party would certainly lose to the Liberals, who attracted the majority of anglophone voters. But without at least some anglophone support, the Conservatives might also lose, since it was known that a small minority of francophones traditionally voted Liberal (reportedly, as a result of bribes or coercion, sometimes by employers). The Conservative nominating convention was obviously aware of these possibilities, and Routhier's promotion of Evanturel took into account the bilingual character of party support. Evanturel delivered speeches in both French and English, and he was formally nominated by both francophone and anglophone party members.[18] In accepting Evanturel, some anglophone Conservatives were responding to the changing political environment of Prescott County in order to salvage their own position. A reporter observed:

[The] English-speaking wing of the Conservative party in Prescott sought to obtain the cooperation of the French-Canadian wing but they were too weak – "the mountain would not go to Mahomet" so "Mahomet must go to the mountain."[19]

Evanturel's candidacy was also strengthened by the guilt some moderate anglophones felt over previous treatment of francophone voters, especially in party conventions. *The News*, which claimed an apolitical stance, concluded that the emergence of a francophone Conservative leader at the provincial level could be seen as justice finally done:

We cannot altogether blame our French Canadian friends now who wish to gratify a desire to retaliate upon their English-speaking friends who for so many years refused the Canadian people a voice in the representation of the County. While National prejudices exist it is human that such retaliation should be sought."[20]

Despite such sentiments, Evanturel's position as a promoter of francophone status was unacceptable to most anglophone Conservatives, and the party was severely split after the convention. As was early predicted, the 1883 campaign quickly took shape as a cultural confrontation: "It is evident the approaching struggle will be a national rather than a political one."[21]

For this struggle, the Liberals put forward Albert Hagar, the incumbent, who had won the 1881 election when their party split the Conservative vote by running an additional francophone candidate. Hagar, who had been born in Plantagenet in 1827, was quite successful as a local farmer, merchant and sawmill owner.[22] He began his political life in the federal arena, winning a seat in the House of Commons in 1867, 1872, and 1874. Hagar had lost to Routhier in 1878, but his earlier federal victories, as well as his provincial success in 1881, augured well for Liberal chances in 1883.

The Campaign. The campaign was short but intense. By 13 February, the "fight," as *The News* called it, was in progress. "The first shot has been fired. The campaign may be said now to be fully opened and the armies on both sides are gathering their forces for the battle."[23] As usual, the campaign centres were church steps, town halls, and taverns. Evanturel was a gifted orator, and his bilingual fluency gave him a great advantage over the unilingual Hagar, whose candidacy in this election fuelled the growing recognition of a cultural schism in the county. Hagar did make a half-hearted effort to attract francophone Liberal support by hiring French-language speakers to address audiences after his own orations, but these speakers were often shouted down by English-speaking Liberals, aware of their own opportunity to attract Conservatives who found Evanturel unacceptable.

The possible extent of such defection among anglophone Conservatives became the focus of speculation about the election's outcome. At the outset, Evanturel appeared to have the advantage. His prospects hinged on a solid francophone vote and at least some party loyalty among anglophone Conservatives. The convention had opened a deep division within the party, but as the campaign got under way, some evidence of reconciliation was reported. "The English-speaking Conservatives who at first charged Mr. Evanturel with raising the national cry are rapidly returning to Party allegiance and it is now evident that Mr. Hagar will not poll so many Conservatives as at first anticipated."[24]

The Election. By election day on 27 February, however, cultural ranks had closed completely, and early predictions that this election would be a national struggle were unequivocally confirmed. Hagar emerged victorious by thirty-two votes, a margin which reflected the close linguistic balance among Prescott County electors. English-speaking voters, "allowing national prejudices [to] get the better of them," consistently chose the Liberal Hagar, said *The News*, and francophone voters chose Evanturel.[25]

The consistency of this split is indicated in Table 39, which brings together data from the voters' list and the election results. This evidence reveals the electoral behaviour which determined Hagar's victory. In most communities, he had attracted a proportion of votes approximate to the proportion of anglophone electors. Small variations between these proportions might be explained by differences in voter participation between anglophone and francophone electors, although overall participation was high and there is no evidence of a linguistic distinction in this respect.[26] More certainly, anglophone strength was less than appears on the voters' list because of the multiple recording electors who held a sufficient amount of property in more than one township. This factor was especially evident in West Hawkesbury, where a variety of English-speaking electors were listed although they lived and actually voted elsewhere.[27]

In two areas of the county, however, Albert Hagar's proportion of votes differed markedly from the proportion of anglophone voters. In Hawkesbury Village, he polled only 37 per cent of the vote, although 53 per cent of the electors were English-speaking. This phenomenon resulted from Conservative party loyalty among a cer-

TABLE 39
Comparison of the Voters' List and the Provincial Election Results,
Prescott County, 1883

Township / Village	Voters			Votes		
	Total	Franco-phones	Anglo-phones	Total	For Evanturel	For Hagar
Alfred	533	82%	18%	391	83%	17%
Caledonia	371	44	56	254	40	60
Longueuil	204	70	30	142	67	33
East Hawkesbury	690	47	53	465	46	54
West Hawkesbury	357	8	92	250	19	81
North Plantagenet	560	61	39	467	40	60
South Plantagenet	433	49	51	339	44	56
L'Orignal	83	42	58	66	44	56
Hawkesbury Village	256	47	53	179	63	37
Total	3487	52	48	2553	49	51

Source: The News and Ottawa Valley Advocate, 30 January and 13 March 1883.

tain number of anglophone voters (such as those who had supported
Evanturel's nomination). The village had traditionally been the county
stronghold of the Conservative Association, and despite the general
anglophone defection, it maintained a degree of party allegiance.
This Liberal loss, however, was more than compensated by a surprising victory in the predominantly francophone township of North
Plantagenet. There the unilingual Hagar won 60 per cent of the
vote, although only 39 per cent of the electors were anglophones.
The Liberals' success in this township was the key to their victory in
the county and, not surprisingly, became the immediate focus of
public attention.

The Judicial Challenge. Foul play was quickly reported. A recount
followed, but the result remained unchanged.[28] The Conservative
party then mounted a legal petition against the return of Hagar,
launched for strategic reasons by an anglophone, Alexander Cun-
ningham, one of the party loyalists who had supported the nomination of Evanturel. The official hearing began on 24 July 1883 in
the county seat of L'Orignal. The testimony lasted four days and
clearly exposed the reasons for Hagar's success in his home township

of North Plantagenet. Witnesses testified that his friends there had employed two techniques to increase Liberal support: bribery, such as the offer of liquor on election day or free timber from Hagar's sawmill, and corruption. The latter involved the misuse of voter declaration forms, especially at Poll No. 3, where, the investigation revealed, almost one-half the voters "had voted openly and touched the pen to a declaration of some kind." Such declarations should have been limited to voters unable to read or physically incapacitated, as by blindness or loss of limbs. These documents were printed in English only and were thus easily misused, as they were by Hagar's long-time friend W.A. Chamberlain, who worked at Poll No. 3 in North Plantagenet. Under questioning, Chamberlain claimed incompetence rather than fraud, and Hagar dutifully denounced him as a "nuisance to the party and to his candidature."[29] Nonetheless, both Conservatives and Liberals knew that this kind of manipulation had provided the margin of Hagar's victory. In summarizing the evidence, the judges had to admit that corruption was apparent in North Plantagenet Township, but, given the Liberal control of Ontario, it is not surprising that they decided to uphold the election result.[30]

The Results. This decision added animosity to Prescott County's deteriorating cultural relations and made francophone leaders, such as Alfred Evanturel, more determined to mobilize the now-majority language group. The new voters' list compiled later in 1883 showed clearly that time was on Evanturel's side. The advantage of francophones over English-speaking electors increased from 125 to 331 on this list and continued to grow steadily as each year passed.[31]

Moreover, the rationale for French-Canadian cultural affirmation and group consciousness became increasingly strong in Prescott County. The election investigation which found corruption but upheld the result showed French Canadians that they still lacked real political influence at the county and provincial levels. This development exacerbated the split between francophone and anglophone electors within the Conservative party. The small group of English-speaking supporters in Hawkesbury Village was particularly chagrined by the turn of events. In ignoring their own cultural interests in order to remain loyal to the party, they had anticipated that a solid francophone vote, as promised by Evanturel and others, would carry the Conservatives to victory. The election results showed that this calculation was based on "too sanguine expectations of the French-Canadian strength."[32] Conservative leaders had not foreseen that bribery and skullduggery would weaken French-Canadian support just enough to alter the cultural balance. This development left English-speaking Conservatives in an awkward and powerless position.

EVENTS IN THE LARGER WORLD

Journalistic Attacks and Counterattacks

Within two years, they found themselves even more powerless, as the cultural pattern of Prescott County party politics changed suddenly and dramatically for reasons far beyond local circumstances. Francophone voters threw their allegiance to the Liberal Party, thereby ending decades of Conservative support. Alfred Evanturel himself ran as the *Liberal* candidate in the 1886 provincial election.

This dramatic turnabout began soon after the 1883 vote as the frustration and alienation of English-speaking Conservatives in Prescott County were fuelled by the vicious attack of major Toronto newspapers on the francophone population of eastern Ontario. This attack continued throughout the decade under the leadership of the Conservative party's mouthpiece, the Toronto *Mail*. Investigative reports from eastern Ontario described French Canadians as an "alien and unprogressive" people whose intellectual status was "deplorable" being "not far removed from the condition of the serfs of medieval Europe." Rampant illiteracy, blind obedience to the Catholic Church, and irrational patterns of reproduction were among the numerous traits said to separate the French-Candian mentality from the British standard. Unable to comprehend these perceived cultural traits, the *Mail* concluded that French Canadians were governed by "a power whose wires and springs are kept carefully concealed from ordinary observation."[33] Other Toronto newspapers added graphic details in describing the deplorable social element which French Canadians were believed to be introducing to Ontario. The *Evening Telegram* reported ghetto living conditions then probed the depths of journalistic slander:

The traveller who finds himself in this Providence-forsaken hole at evening may well pale with anxiety at the prospect of spending a night in any of the low-walled, ramshackled apologies for home which meet his gaze. If the houses themselves are not sufficiently repulsive, a glance at the inhabitants would certainly decide him in favour of taking to the woods for his lodgings. Dirty, greasy, bleary-eyed looking specimens, they no more approach the average country people to be found in Central Ontario than South African Hottentots approach the polished types of European Civilization.[34]

Toronto newspapers had subscribers in Prescott County; the *Mail*, for example, was received by local Conservative party leaders, such as Thomas Tweed Higginson.[35] Moreover, the journalistic attack from Toronto was particularly significant to Prescott County readers because the provincial attention converged with the deteriorating cultural relations of the local level, which were becoming evident in the local newspapers. *The News* attempted to maintain balanced reporting, but this objective became increasingly unpopular, especially after the 1883 election. One reader simply accused the newspaper of being too "Frenchy" and cancelled his subscription.[36] At the same time, the unabashedly Conservative organ, *The Advertiser*, seized the opportunity to attract new readers with editorials decrying the francophone takeover of local political positions.[37] By the mid-1880s, moderate journalism had only limited appeal in Prescott County; *The News* ended publication in 1888.[38]

Francophones in Prescott County responded quickly to the journalistic onslaught of the Conservative press. In September 1885, M. F.X. Boileau founded *La Nation*, the first French-language newspaper of the county. Its goal was the advancement of "notre religion, nos droits, la prospérité de notre pays, le bonheur de nos familles, la conservation de notre belle langue française." The newspaper began with an historical analysis of the French-Canadian identity in North America. The French-Canadian people were considered "une race homogène et tout-à-fait distincte des autres ... ni français, ni anglais, ni autrement européens"; rather, they were North Americans "pur sang" whose culture and tradition had developed through centuries of New World settlement. A French Canadian had a special historic attachment to the continent: "Depuis bientôt trois siècles il naît, vit et meurt sur le sol de ce continent, le labourant, le mettant à contribution pour sa subsistance, le fertilisant de ses sueurs et de son sang."[39]

In emphasizing French-Canadian heritage and tradition, *La Nation* was responding directly to the contemporary journalistic conclusion of *The Advertiser* and others that French Canadians did not have a legitimate position as an ongoing component of North American society. The Prescott County newspaper rejected the argument that "être canadien, et parler français, sont deux choses irréconciliables; que le soi-disant Canadien-français est ici un étranger; que sa langue et ses coutumes doivent au plus tôt disparaître de l'Amérique."[40] In the same spirit as François-Xavier Garneau had responded to Lord Durham, *La Nation* enthusiastically affirmed French-Canadian integrity.

It also emphasized, however, that francophones in Ontario were not just part of a general French-Canadian society in Canada. Rather, the editors perceived,

Une foule de questions regardent plus spécialement les Canadiens de l'Ontario, et mériteraient d'être traitées davantage. Nous sommes ici dans une position particulière et des intérêts particuliers nous touchent de près. Telles sont les affaires municipales, scolaires et provinciales; la question des interprètes français dans les districts judiciaires où domine l'élément français et bien d'autres encore.[41]

Thus *La Nation* promoted a twofold sense of francophone identity in Prescott County: francophones as descendants and members of the larger Quebec-based French-Canadian society, and francophones as minority residents of an English-language province. This twofold, integrated identity distinguished local francophones both from their anglophone neighbours and, to a far less but still noteworthy degree, from their Quebec counterparts. Revealingly, the editors argued that Quebec could no longer be considered the French-Canadian home; rather, "sa province est celle où il préfère élire domicile." The newspaper thus offered readers a clear description of Franco-Ontarian identity, although it did not use the term.[42]

La Nation's statement on the meaning of being francophone in Ontario was presented on 12 September 1885, two years after Alfred Evanturel offered his vision of a trans-Ontario francophone community. On 10 October 1885, one reader predicted to the editors that "votre excellent journal va devenir un puissant ressort pour enlever notre nationalité de sa position trop modeste et pour la pousser dans les voies du progrès et de la prospérité."[43]

This prediction was based on solid evidence. *La Nation* responded to a convergence of factors for the francophone population of Prescott County. The tone of the paper was proud and aggressive, with not a hint of defensiveness or apology. Indeed, the editors viewed with glee the anticipation that neighbouring Russell County would soon be almost completely francophone. *La Nation* announced that "L'anglosaxon ne peut vivre là où le français domine et commande."

The Hanging of Louis Riel

The optimism of the *La Nation*'s editors about francophone identity in Ontario had to come to grips, however, with more than local and provincial anglophone attitudes. During the autumn of 1885, politics and questions of identity had to be related to events as they unfolded on the distant prairies. Louis Riel's conviction in Regina was reported in the opening issue of the newspaper, and *La Nation* naturally became the major reporter and interpreter for Prescott County francophones.[44] The paper was not surprised by the outcome of the trial; "suivant toutes les apparences la condamnation à mort de Riel a été chose résolue d'avance."[45]

La Nation interpreted Riel's conviction as a cultural judgment and made no reference to any legal, political, or psychological considerations. He was simply presented as a French-Canadian protector facing anglophone power and prejudice, "un homme odieux, détesté, honni à cause de son origine, de son nom, de la religion professée par sa race." The real reason Riel was found guilty could be summarized simply: "Il ne s'appelle pas Rielson."[46]

In the weeks between Riel's trial and his hanging, *La Nation* followed closely and commented upon the political developments. Initially, the newspaper seemed resigned to the inevitability of Riel's approaching death. On 10 October 1885, it reported that effigies of Riel had been executed in the neighbouring communities of Kingston and Brockville. If the thirst for Riel's blood among certain anglophones in eastern Ontario could not wait for the stages of the judicial process, the journalists of *La Nation* saw little hope for the man who was not "Rielson."[47] A small glimmer of light then appeared through the thick gloom. The newspaper reported that an appeal of Riel's conviction had gone to the Privy Council in London, and on 22 October, readers were told of a rumour from London which suggested that Riel's death sentence would be commuted to life imprisonment.[48] This rumour soon proved false, but immediately another cause for hope was offered. Could it be that purely political considerations would prevent Riel's hanging?

Par exemple, est-il dans l'intérêt de tel ou tel parti politique qu'une commission médicale se prononce contre Riel? Sa mort va-t-elle faire du tort à certaines ambitions particulières, ou va-t-elle avancer les affaires de certains personnages à hautes prétentions?[49]

The hanging of Riel put a dramatic end to such speculation. *La Nation* grasped fully the importance of this traumatic moment in Canadian history. "Le 16 Novembre sera désormais une date lugubre, une souillure dans l'histoire du Canada; elle rappellera à nos descendants des jours mauvais, une époque de fanatisme, une ère de lâcheté et de trahisons."[50]

In the days following the hanging, memorial funeral services were held for Riel throughout Prescott County. But grief was not all that local francophones felt. Riel's conviction and death added a federal dimension to the local and provincial conflicts which had already emerged in Prescott County. In November 1885, the convergence of these dimensions of cultural conflict exposed clearly the true meaning of being not simply French Canadian but French Canadian outside Quebec. Anger and bitterness erupted almost immediately. Perhaps inspired by descriptions of public demonstrations elsewhere, francophones in Prescott County took to the streets.

Plantagenet – Le 27 novembre dernier, ce village a été témoin d'une démonstration politico-patriotique toute spontanée. C'était au sujet de la mort de Riel ... Un fil de feu fut tendu à la hauteur du toit des maisons, traversant la place publique. Vers les huit heures du soir, une foule de personnes, au milieu d'une profonde obscurité convergeaient des différentes rues vers notre forum local.

Soudain, des feux s'allument, alimentés par le bitume ou autres matières enflammables; à la faveur de la lumière blafarde et sinistre qu'ils répandent, quatre fantômes apparaissent suspendus à la broche de fer et portant de large inscriptions : c'était les noms de Sir Hector Langevin, Sir A. Caron, J.A. Chapleau, Sir John A.

La foule les condamna à être brûlés, et ils le furent bel et bien.[51]

The burning of effigies in the village of Plantagenet followed the format established at demonstrations in other francophone communities, both within and outside Quebec, but this similarity does not discount the importance of popular initiative in Prescott County. The demonstration was not the result of agents provocateurs. *The Advertiser*, an eastern Ontario newspaper, claimed that the effigy-burning was carried out by village troublemakers able to stir up a crowd from the area. *La Nation* immediately pointed out, however, that the organizers of the demonstration (including the founder of the newspaper) were "respectables," and the burning of effigies was definitely not the work of "certains rebelles."[52] In this sense, the demonstration can be seen as a socially diverse francophone response to the events of the preceeding weeks. The actions of 27 November were a response not only to Riel's actual hanging but also to the earlier execution of his effigy in anglophone strongholds of eastern Ontario.

Undoubtedly, the events in Regina engendered such anger and frustration in Prescott County because this national controversy had direct parallels in the local context. Cultural conflict was already well understood in the villages and townships. The political moment of 1883 and subsequent developments had prepared a framework for interpreting the national issue of Riel's conviction and hanging. The special vulnerability of being French Canadian outside Quebec had already been recognized in Prescott County. The gestation of francophone consciousness thus led to the birth of Franco-Ontarian identity in the autumn of 1885.

A CHANGED POLITICAL CONTEXT

What effect did these great events have on the party politics of Prescott County? In one sense, it drove the francophone voters to the arms of the Liberals. *La Nation* described with disgust the Conservative cabinet ministers from Quebec who had accepted Riel's hanging: "Le traître Langevin, le bourreau Chapleau et l'ignoble Caron."[53] From this time, francophones in Prescott County took over the Liberal party and, with leaders such as Alfred Evanturel, won all provincial and federal contests in Prescott County for two decades. The Conservatives did not even run candidates in the county for the provincial elections of 1886, 1890, or 1896, all of which returned Evanturel to Queen's Park.

In another sense, however, the events of 1885 made party politics beside the point for francophones in Prescott County. What evidence was there that any political party would represent their position in either Toronto or Ottawa? Riel's hanging convinced the editors of *La Nation* that the political struggles of the early 1880s were no longer relevant. On 26 November 1885, they concluded that "Aujourd'hui, il n'y a plus de conservateurs ni de libéraux; jamais peut-être depuis 1760 le sentiment populaire n'a été aussi unanime."[54] In this view, the rope of Regina had tied into solidarity the francophones of Prescott County. The result was that electoral politics had lost any great significance.

Indeed, in the provincial legislature over the next few years, Alfred Evanturel was almost silent during the heated debates on the language of instruction. On one occasion, he questioned a Conservative translation of a French text, and on another he suggested that the Opposition misunderstood the operation of French-language schools because anglophone Conservatives were not linguistically capable of assessing the classroom materials.[55] Otherwise, however, Evanturel was inconspicuous. He was not even in attendance on 11 March 1889 when the Conservatives launched their formal arguments to end French-language instruction.[56] In part, this reserve reflected Evanturel's position as a backbencher; more important, it demonstrated that the Liberal leadership was not prepared to allow a francophone to debate the language question on the Government's behalf.

Within Prescott County itself, Evanturel was more outspoken. In

1886, he became editor of a new French-language newspaper, *L'Interprète*, published in Alfred Township. For the next few years, it took over from *La Nation* the role of articulating a Franco-Ontarian perspective on local, provincial, and national issues, including the question of schooling. The newspaper promoted "notre langue et nos croyances" and specified, "l'amour de la patrie en un mot, c'est d'enseigner l'histoire nationale, dans tous les écoles, même les plus élémentaires."[57] In the legislature, however, Evanturel did not participate in any meaningful way.

The trauma of cultural conflict, local, provincial and national and the impotence of Prescott County's francophone politicians contributed to the changed context within which the question of identity and thus of schooling came to be linked to the position of the Catholic Church. Despite the fact that the decade of the 1880s was the time when francophones gained control of politics in Prescott County, these years also brought concerted political attack for which francophones had no effective defence. No party would represent their positions, especially on educational matters. By early December 1885, the political agenda was clear to the editors of *La Nation*: "Conservateurs et libéraux s'étaient réunis : ils se séparent nationaux [sic]."[58]

The logical conclusion for francophones in eastern Ontario was that another form of leadership was necessary. It was in this context that the Catholic Church became a major factor in the history of minority-language education in Prescott County.

The experience of the Catholic Church further illustrates the multidimensional character of these francophone communities. In the view from Toronto at the time and in the subsequent historiography, the communities appear as undifferentiated and passive. The question always concerned what should be done *to* them as a homogeneous group; no one suggested that they could, at least in part, determine their own destinies and that these destinies might not be identical. Analysis of the separate school issue exposes the ignorance of this view and indicates francophones' changing self-perceptions during the late nineteenth century.

CHAPTER SIX

Parishioners, the Catholic Church, and Separate Schools

In 1971, Jean-Pierre Wallot summarized the established conclusions of historical research on the relationship of the Catholic Church to French Canadians. Wallot perceived two quite contradictory interpretations in which French Canadians were treated as either

[a] devout, obedient, pastoral, and God-fearing people, entrenched behind parish and family life, endowed with the noble mission of permeating materialistic Anglo-Saxon America with spiritual values; or a traditional, semifeudal, ignorant, priest-ridden, and backward people, impervious to change and sealed to the outside world for two centuries until a grudging acceptance of industrialization unleashed the "Quiet Revolution."[1]

These interpretations presented different images of French Canadians, but they shared important assumptions about the timeless, dominant influence of the Catholic Church. Clerical control, as either a noble mission or oppressive semifeudism, was seen as an historical constant.

Since the early 1970s, a number of studies have redefined considerably the extent to which the Catholic Church can be considered a controlling force throughout the history of French Canada. These studies portray an ebb and flow of influence based on various convergences of factors, including the ambitions and resources of particular ecclesiastical officials, social and economic conditions, the political context, and popular perceptions. Church authority is now seen to operate in a larger social setting, involving both "top-down" and "bottom-up" agency.[2] For example, Jean-Pierre Wallot's own research has emphasized the weakness of the Catholic Church in the late eighteenth and early nineteenth centuries. During these decades, the ratio of priests to faithful fell dramatically; as early as 1790, seventy-five parishes lacked resident priests. In the context of contemporary social and economic restructuring, the result was that the clergy was "*not* very influential or dominant, except in strict matters of faith and dogma."[3]

By the later decades of the nineteenth century, when the language-of-instruction controversy emerged in Prescott County, the position of the Catholic Church in French Canada had changed dramatically. Recent research has shown that the ebb of clerical control by the early 1800s was followed by a flow of power, especially after 1850. Susan Mann Trofimenkoff analyses the third quarter of nineteenth-century Quebec in terms of "the Clerical Offensive," while Paul-André Linteau, René Durocher, and Jean-Claude Robert describe "the Catholic Church triumphant."[4] These scholars synthesize numerous studies which describe an institutional reorganization of the Church along with a rapid growth of both male and female religious orders in Quebec.[5] Church officials are seen to have achieved new understandings with political and economic leaders concerning social goals and the division of power. During the years after the mid-nineteenth century, the Catholic church occupied a "privileged position" in French Canada. Religious control became part of a broad social influence which especially involved schools.[6] After 1875, when the Ministry of Education was abolished in Quebec, the public school system came under the direct control of Catholic bishops, who could dominate within the new administrative structure.[7] The "triumph" of the Catholic church thus extended to Quebec classrooms. Schools became major elements of parish organization.

The resurgence of the Catholic Church from the mid-nineteenth century was not limited to French-Canadian society. Rather, this process was linked to similar developments elsewhere through the ideology of ultramontanism, which emphasized the hierarchical nature of the Catholic Church with authority flowing down to individual bishops from the pope (at the expense of national leaders) as well as the supremacy of religion over the state in all areas of life, very much including education. Historians of Ireland speak of the "devotional revolution" of this period, during which Paul Cullen returned from Rome to become the archbishop of Armagh in 1849 and then of Dublin in 1852.[8] Cullen spearheaded the ultramontanist reorganization of the Irish Catholic church in ways quite like those of his francophone counterparts in Quebec.[9] Such developments are noteworthy for two reasons. First, they undermine the traditional image of francophone religious uniqueness in Canada, especially at the end of the nineteenth century. Second, the Irish example is directly relevant to the Prescott County experience. After the 1850s, the county's anglophone Catholics, most of whom were of Irish ancestry, were rapidly declining in relative importance, but they were still a discernable minority, accounting for 12.3 per cent of all Catholics in the county in 1891.[10]

Unlike many other areas, Prescott County was not dominated by open conflict between anglophone and francophone Catholics over separate schools. Rather, local controversies reveal an array of divisions, often based on differences between community leaders and higher authorities. The general context of these controversies was an increasing formal religious influence among all Catholics in the late nineteenth century.

Developments outside Prescott County provided the framework within which local Catholic priests and parishioners came to grips with their changing circumstances. The question of schooling clearly exposed the ambitions of individuals both within the county and in hierarchies beyond. Located in Ontario but linked, by way of the Diocese of Ottawa, to the Catholic Church in Quebec, Prescott County residents had to face complicated decisions, especially by the 1880s. The reality of competing identities made these decisions quite difficult. The Catholic Church was clearly not in a position to nourish directly the infant of Franco-Ontarian identity. Church officials certainly recognized the importance of the French language but saw it mostly as a barrier to the Protestant world controlled by anglophones. Similarly, they acknowledged a distinct provincial context, but they understandably encouraged an identification which had no real geographic boundaries. Although parishes and dioceses were clearly delineated, they were seen as simply administrative units of a placeless, global community. This view was quite different from that of Ontario politicians and educators, who perceived the Ottawa River as a great divide, full of meaning. Catholic residents in Prescott County were thus torn by competing definitions and ambitions both within themselves and from authorities beyond.

The following examination of this phenomenon begins with an assessment of the overall structure and status of the Catholic Church at the parish level and then focuses on the question of schooling. The evidence of baptismal registers, parish reports, and correspondence suggests how the question of minority-language education interacted not only with circumstances in Prescott County but also with the changing position of the Catholic Church in the world beyond.

THE GROWTH OF THE CATHOLIC
CHURCH IN PRESCOTT COUNTY

The Early Days of Settlement

Until 1847, Prescott County was within the Church's administrative
domain of Kingston, and it was initially the responsibility of the priest
at Montebello on the north shore of the Ottawa River. The steady
inflow of Irish and French-Canadian Catholics, spreading as settlers
through eastern Ontario, led to the establishment of the Diocese of
Ottawa under Bishop Joseph-Eugène-Bruno Guigues.[11] The period
of Guigues's leadership, from 1848 to 1874, witnessed the steady
but slow establishment of the Catholic Church in the Ottawa Valley.
Guigues was a confirmed ultramontane, who had numerous ambitions for the new diocese. However, a variety of factors worked
against the establishment of a strong institutional presence during
his tenure. Among his problems was a constant struggle to keep pace
with the heavy Catholic immigration. One of his strategies was to
import from the Old World young men whom he ordained for
service in the Ottawa Valley. Of the thirty-nine new priests Bishop
Guigues ordained between 1848 and 1861, two-thirds had been born
in France or Ireland.[12]

These priests constantly faced environmental obstacles to maintaining contact with their numerous parishioners. The new clergy-
men encountered the same poor roads, bad weather, and hazards
of travelling through forests which challenged settling families. The
obstacles to land transportation usually inspired travellers to journey
by water whenever and wherever possible. Canoes were the fastest
and most accessible means of conveyance; they were also popular
because they could be used to navigate the many shallow streams
which feed the Ottawa River. But these streams include many rapids,
as does the Ottawa itself, and only the most skilled canoeist could
travel any significant distance without succumbing to the challenge
of jagged rocks and swirling waves. Therefore, even those priests
sufficiently fortunate to be able to travel by water between settlements were not guaranteed safety. In 1848, Bishop Guigues warned
his priests that the river "toutes les années, engloutit plusieurs d'entre
vous dans ses eaux."[13]

Many of the arriving priests faced an even greater challenge in
that they were not bilingual. Francophone religious leaders were
particularly concerned that anglophone Irish priests had almost no
success in parishes flooded by Quebec immigration. For example, in
1860, Father O'Malley, "sachant peu le français," lived in a Prescott

County community that was predominantly francophone; he was unable to obtain the financial support of his parishioners.[14] To overcome this kind of difficulty, it was decided to assign only recently ordained priests to linguistically mixed parishes "pour leur permettre d'apprendre ... pendant que leur mémoire avait encore de la souplesse."[15]

The newness of Catholic settlement in Prescott County did not help the financial position of the Church during the mid-nineteenth century. As immigrants focused on establishing themselves and participating in the farm and forest economy, only a small amount of support was available for the collection basket. Bishop Guigues attempted to facilitate settlement in the Ottawa Valley by forming, in 1849, a colonization society for Quebec immigrants which "frayait les voies en leur fournissant les renseignements nécessaires, en sollicitant du gouvernement l'ouverture des routes et l'arpentage du terrain."[16] But the society was small and ineffective at this time, and settlers depended upon their own resources. The collection basket at L'Orignal in the late 1840s was sufficient only for "cierges, vin de messe, et payer le lavage du linge de l'église." When a new priest arrived at L'Orignal in the spring of 1846, he found "rien ... dans le coffre-fort" and was immediately presented with several "comptes non payés."[17] After struggling for a few years, he asked to be reassigned, reporting that after having to "aller à pied, à travers bois" in order to visit various francophone settlements, he had received only "la somme dérisoire de cinq louis" during the previous nine months.[18]

The request for reassignment was not unusual. The conditions of life in Prescott County were reflected in a rapid turnover of resident priests. At L'Orignal, for example, Father McDonagh served just over two years while Father Cannon endured just six months. In the late 1840s, Father Alexander Macdonell resided four months before requesting transfer on the basis of untenable conditions. His replacement was equally dissatisfied.[19] Other parishes experienced an even more rapid change; the one in Plantagenet Township was served by eight different priests in less than ten years. Bishop Guigues remembered that during his tenure newly assigned priests usually "vinrent me faire connaître leur détermination bien arrêtée de m'abandonner" after only a few days of service.[20]

The Growing Ecclesiastical Presence

Over time, a convergence of factors contributed to a significant strengthening of the position of the Catholic Church in Prescott

County. In 1850, the county included only two clerical residences, but by 1896 it was divided into fourteen parishes. Similarly, the number of priests increased substantially after midcentury. In 1851, each Prescott priest was expected to serve an average of 2,714 Catholics; by 1891 it was half this number.[21] These figures compare unfavourably to the general pattern in Quebec, where a ratio of one priest to every five hundred Catholics was achieved by the 1880s.[22] Nonetheless, the rate of increasing clerical presence during the second half of the nineteenth century in Prescott County was similar to the rate in Quebec. In both settings, the overall ratio of priests to parishioners improved by approximately 100 per cent between 1851 and 1891. This similarity is striking given the late start of Church leadership in rural eastern Ontario plus the area's marginal location.

The position of the Catholic Church was also bolstered in Prescott County by the midcentury improvement in roads. By the 1870s, local priests could travel much better roads in sturdier carriages than they had used two or three decades earlier, and the laity could attend church more easily. As settlements matured, the actual church buildings even improved, despite the economic difficulties of the late nineteenth century. Parishes came to be organized around formidable stone constructions, rather than the modest wood chapels of midcentury. The parishioners of St Paul in Plantagenet replaced their wooden building with a stone one in 1878, and a stone priest's house was added in the following year. Similar occurrences followed in other townships. In the 1890s, Father Bérubé supervised the renovation and enlargement of the L'Orignal church at an expense of $11,000. A pontifical mass was celebrated in 1895 in St Thomas to bless the new "fine brick presbytère." At Vankleek Hill, the Catholic church was enlarged and renovated during the late 1890s so that it became "very imposing in appearance"; in addition, the parish was enhanced by a "commodious presbytère," which was "also of stone, and its architectural appearance, as well as the grounds around it, [were] objects of attraction."[23] Such developments were similar to those elsewhere, including the colonization areas of the Saguenay in Quebec. Prescott County was indeed part of the Irish historians' "devotional revolution" of the second half of the nineteenth century.

The Growth of Attachment to the Church

The institutional structure of the Catholic Church contributed to and reflected the level of importance which it held in the lives of Prescott County residents. For parishioners, the later nineteenth century was a time of steadily increasing contact with priests. Baptismal records, offer one way to assess this trend systematically. Such records can be used to measure the extent to which Catholic parents followed the Church's insistence that children be baptized as soon as possible after birth, preferably on the same day. This insistence was based on the belief that the gates of heaven would be eternally closed to those who died without having been cleansed of original sin through baptism. Immediate attention to this matter was necessary because of the high rates of infant mortality; even the shortest delay was considered an inexcusable risk for Catholic believers.[24] Research on specific parishes in Quebec has shown that baptisms did, in fact, immediately follow births where the Church was well established. In the rural area of Sorel, for example, almost one-half of all baptisms between 1740 and 1779 took place on the actual day of birth; 95.1 per cent occurred within three days.[25] Presumably, therefore, in nineteenth-century Prescott County, Catholic parents who practised their faith and who had access to a priest would have had their babies baptized as soon as possible. A comparison of the dates of births and of baptisms at various points in time should provide an indication of changing clerical contact with parishioners.

Figure 12 is based on the baptismal records of St-Paul in Plantagenet, which also served the southern part of Alfred Township until 1871, and on the records of the new parish, St-Victor-d'Alfred, from its establishment in 1871. Taken together, these records give longitudinal evidence reflecting different types of parish organization. The St-Paul records provide examples of clerical contact in an area without and then with a resident priest. The St-Victor evidence reveals the impact of the formation of an additional parish in a specific area. A longitudinal perspective is offered by taking evidence from five points in time, beginning in 1839 when the chapel at Plantagenet was established.[26]

During 1839 and 1840, the baptism at the chapel of St-Paul were performed by an itinerant priest, most often the resident at L'Orignal, who generally visited very three to four weeks. Not surprisingly, no infant baptisms occurred on day of birth, 2 per cent occurred within one day, and only 59 per cent took place within one month. The assignment of a resident priest in 1849 improved the situation. By 1851, the ideal of baptism on day of birth was still not obtained, but 20 per cent of the infant baptisms were performed within one day and 70 per cent occurred within one month.

The tremendous flood of immigration to Prescott County during the 1850s severely taxed the facilities of St-Paul, which continued to be responsible for Plantagenet and much of Alfred Township. Little

FIGURE 12

Interval between Birth and Baptism for Infants, St-Paul and St-Alfred-de-Victor, 1839−85

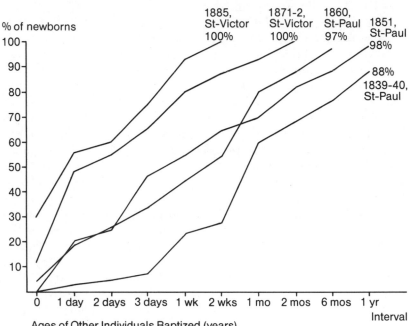

Ages of Other Individuals Baptized (years)
1839−40: 3, 6, 20, 26, 35, 45, 72, 90
1851: 2, 2, 20, 26
1860: 5, 21

improvement in the time lapse between birth and baptism was evident in 186o, but there was no major retroactive trend.

In 1871, the parish of St-Victor was established in Alfred Township, thereby giving the area its own resident priest. The increased clerical presence was immediately reflected in the intervals between birth and baptism. Twelve per cent of the infant baptisms in 1871 and 1872 were for newborns and a full 93 per cent were for children in their first month of life. In 1885, these proportions showed continued improvement. A substantial 3o percent of the baptisms in that year occurred on day of birth, and all were for children no more than two weeks old. Clearly, having a priest resident in Alfred Township brought the Church closer to Catholic settlers. By the

1880s, it was firmly established in the lives of these Prescott County residents.

The structural and quantitative aspects of the Catholic Church's presence in nineteenth-century Prescott County were the framework for the relationship between the Church and local adherents. But what was the quality of this relationship? What were the ways in which priests interacted with parishioners? And how did parishioners view ecclesiastical authorities outside the region? These questions are central to the issue of minority-language education in Prescott County. The quality of the relationship between the Catholic Church and its members contributed significantly to the character of schooling. The relatively weak institutional position of the Church at midcentury, followed by its increasing strength, especially from the 1870s, related directly to the county's educational history.

The key issue involved changing perceptions of separate schools. In the 1850s and 1860s, only a few Prescott County schools operated within the separate system. School officials generally reported that the separate school issue, which dominated educational debate among provincial leaders at this time, was not important in most of the county's townships. This fact is surprising since the official creation of school sections sometimes gathered different religious groups into the same catchment area. The Alfred Township report of 1861 commented, "Although five of the school sections are of mixed population, there is nothing ever said of separate schools." Similarly, the schools of the neighbouring township of Plantagenet North were all established on the "Free School non-sectarian principle" in the 1850s, and the contemporary residents of Caledonia Township were also considered "adverse to the Separate School System."²⁷ Although the vast majority of the county's public schools in this period were anglophone, some were francophone. Yet, somewhat remarkably, the questions of religion and the language of instruction were not joined locally at this time.

Why was the separate school question not of great importance in Prescott County at midcentury, when it was in other parts of Ontario? A series of factors enter the answer. The relative weakness of the Catholic Church as an institution and the generally low priority which schooling held for most residents produced little initiative for any educational development, much less the construction of separate schools that would require additional time, energy, and expense.

Moreover, the cultural geography of settlement meant that the extent of diversity within mixed populations was not great in the 1850s and 1860s. The character of local schools closely reflected the character of their student. The classrooms were quite homogeneous with respect to language and religion since influences such as the timing of settlement and considerations of soil type tended to separate cultural groups. Furthermore, in those school sections which forced together children of different languages and religions, whichever group achieved educational control usually operated the local school in its own image; children from other groups attended elsewhere or, more likely, not at all. Only in a few school sections did trustees hire two teachers to accommodate competing demands. Thus, as a result of settlement patterns, public schools in Prescott County varied considerably, but they varied in accord with their host communities. The manuscript school reports of the 1850s and 1860s show that the French-language schools, including those in the public system, offered religious instruction and used textbooks produced by the Catholic Church in Quebec.[28] In this context, the separate school question was not a focus of concern in Prescott County as it was among leaders of the Catholic Church and provincial educators.

The Initiative of Father Brunet

As the nineteenth century continued, however, Catholic Church officials in the Ottawa Valley pursued more and more aggressively the formation of separate schools as key elements of parish organization. Not surprisingly, local priests came to play important educational roles not only within denominationally Catholic schools but also within the public system itself. An early example of such involvement was the unusual circumstance of the Township of East Hawkesbury, where an exceedingly energetic curé, Father Antoine Brunet, was first stationed in 1855. His activity, which continued in Prescott County to the early 1870s, anticipated the developments of later decades and demonstrated the potential impact of educational leadership within Prescott County's francophone population. Under his initiative, East Hawkesbury came to include a decidedly disproportionate share of the county's French-language schools – six of a total of thirteen by 1870 – although it had only 27 per cent of the county's francophone population when the census was taken the next year. Even more significant, five of the six French-language schools in East Hawkesbury operated within the separate system by 1870.[29]

Clearly, Father Brunet's initiative contributed substantially to the establishment of French-language separate schools in the township, as well as to general educational developments in the county during his tenure as parish priest. In these years, he emerged as its major spokesman for French-language instruction, and he corresponded with Egerton Ryerson concerning the details of operating French-language schools within the new educational system.[30] Brunet was also able to gain positions of authority within the local school administration, which he then used to promote what he saw as the interests of francophones in Prescott County. By lobbying the County Council of Public Instruction, he succeeded in gaining the title of "special inspector of the separate schools." He then immediately refused to cooperate with higher administrative officials. On 15 March 1871, the local superintendent reported to Ryerson that the priest had collected the annual school trustees' reports and now "refused to give up" the reports for official review "although the matter was fully explained to him." The local superintendent lamented to Ryerson that "I waited until now expecting that after obtaining advice upon the subject – he would see the folly of his conduct, but waited in vain."[31]

Father Brunet also held a position on the board of examiners in the early 1870s, and he was an exceedingly active participant. The first meeting of the board involved six motions; he moved four of them and seconded another. At the next meeting, he was involved in all five motions, moving three and seconding two. Brunet used this forum to press the Toronto authorities for practical measures to facilitate French-language schooling in Prescott County as well as to ensure the preparation of teacher-examination papers for francophone candidates.[32] This activity encouraged the rapid increase of French-language schools, especially during the 1870s when a variety of factors were coming together to promote francophone educational participation.

The Language of Instruction

A particular crucial feature of Antoine Brunet's school promotion involved the link between the question of language and separate schools. Increasingly during the second half of the nineteenth century, local francophone leaders viewed the formation of separate schools as a way of resolving disputes over the question of language in some school sections. An early use of this strategy was in L'Orignal in 1867, when francophone residents established their own separate school "solely for the purpose of having their language taught."[33] The residents acted after the school trustees refused to hire a francophone teacher.

The formation of separate schools was, however, a complex process, involving families, parish priests, local school officials and, significantly, higher religious and political authorities. A detailed examination of this process in Alfred Township provides substantial insight into the complex considerations which governed attitudes and perceptions about minority language education. Most significantly, the character of the relationship between parishioners in Alfred Township and Church officials reveals the ways in which the changing demographic, economic, educational, and political context affected francophone thought and behaviour in the late nineteenth century.

The Horse Creek Controversy

The first establishment of a separate school in Alfred Township related to purely material considerations and, interestingly, resulted from a dispute solely among francophones. The Horse Creek controversy, which began in the early 1870s, involved Public School No. 7, located in the southern half of Alfred Township.[34] This region was a focus of francophone settlement during the mid-nineteenth century and, accordingly, the school employed French-language books in the classroom. Over time, however, francophone parents who lived some distance from the school began to push for the establishment of another school section to accommodate the spread of settlement. The plan called for an east-west division of Section No. 7 and the building of two new schoolhouses, each located near the centre of one of the proposed new sections. The existing schoolhouse would be closed. (See Figure 10.)

Not surprisingly, parents from the eastern and western corners of Section No. 7 heartily supported the plan, and they sent petitions to pressure school officials about the need for two schools. As one would expect, however, local opposition surfaced immediately from parents who lived at the centre of the section, in close proximity to the existing schoolhouse. These parents, who came from the earliest families of the area and were "plus riches et plus influents" than the petitioners, opposed the closing of their school. Under the proposed division of the section, their children would be required to travel east or west to one of the new schools, an imposition which "les gros casques du rang" considered unwarranted.[35] Their opposition prevented any new school establishment for several years, but the steady expansion of settlement eventually allowed the partisans of dividing the school section to gain official approval. As a result, Public School No. 14 was opened near the eastern border of the township.

The major supporters of School No. 7 did not greet this action with resignation. Rather, they quickly embarked on the formal procedure for transforming their school into a separate institution in order to maintain it in operation at its existing location. Their initiative was viewed with the acquiescence but without the leadership or enthusiasm of the parish priest. Father Lavoie, of St-Victor-d'Alfred, saw no practical advantage to having the school formally recognized as a separate school since it was already fully Catholic in terms of classroom activity. Moreover, he was justifiably concerned about the disunity of his parishioners.[36] The strategy of separate school establishment kept together the children of "les gros casques du rang" and ensured that their school remained financially solid. But in so doing, the opponents of the division undermined the attraction of School No. 14, whose originators had anticipated some participation by the major families of the area. When it did not materialize, some parents who had supported the new school at the outset returned to No. 7 "afin de payer moins cher." In this way, the division of the school section was substantially neutralized. The new public school continued operating but, lacking the full anticipated clientele, "cette école n'a fait que végéter."[37]

The coexistence of a public and a separate school at Horse Creek did present some advantages to financially disadvantaged parents as a result of a loophole in the official administration of the dual system. The loophole existed between clauses 40 and 47 of the Separate School Act. Clause 47 stipulated that a parent who wished to transfer support from a separate to a public school had to give official notice before the second Wednesday of January in any year. Clause 40 required that official notice be given before the first day of March by parents who wished to transfer their support from a public to a separate school.[38] Taken together, those two clauses produced a lag between the enumeration of public and of separate school supporters. Parents who sent their children to a separate school but also had access to a public school could take advantage of this situation. Timing was all. Before the second Wednesday in January, they could remove themselves from the separate-school rate list by giving official notice that they wished to be included on the public-school list. Then, before the first day of March, they could "change their minds" and retract their support from the public system to return to a separate school. As a result, their names might not appear on either the separate school or the public school enumerations for that year.

Given the economic crisis of the 1870s and later, material considerations of this kind were clearly important to some residents of Prescott County. Parents at Horse Creek who wished their children to attend school but were in economic difficulty thus began switching their official support periodically to avoid school taxation. As news of developments at Horse Creek spread, other separate schools were established to complement the public alternatives. This process confounded the collector for Alfred Township who lamented, "Tout est bouleversé ... Faire la carte des écoles du canton d'Alfred serait vraiment baroque. Jamais pareil gerrymander n'a été imaginé. C'est le chaos."[39]

ESTABLISHING SEPARATE SCHOOLS: LATER IN THE CENTURY

By the early 1880s, a variety of francophone leaders in Prescott County were building upon the foundation of separate school promotion begun by Father Antoine Brunet and enhanced by the grass roots initiative of parents, such as those at Horse Creek. Not surprisingly, the anglophone provincial educators looked with dismay upon the increasing number of separate schools. George Ross, minister of education, recognized that this pattern had significant negative implications for the larger ambitions of his ministry. Ross feared that separate schools would make more difficult the educational responsibility to assimilate disparate cultural groups. Once the francophone clergy exerted formal control on educational institutions, the French Canadians' integration into anglophone society in Ontario became even more unlikely. Ross believed that francophones had to be attracted to British norms through the mainstream educational system; they could not simply be conceded to the separate schools. In the late 1880s, this belief contributed to Ross's conviction, described in Chapter 1, that the general policy of language toleration had to be maintained in order to attract francophone participation in the public school system.[40]

At the same time, however, francophone leaders in Prescott County were increasingly promoting separate school establishment as a way of improving educational opportunities for francophones and thus maintaining and perhaps enhancing their own positions in the community. From their point of view, the separate-school issue related directly to the English-language regulations introduced in 1885. The promoters of separate schools in the late 1880s included lay leaders such as politician Alfred Evanturel and even Assistant School Inspector A. Dufort, who was called upon in his official position, to ensure conformity with the English-language regulations.[41] It was the Catholic Church, however, that provided the major leadership of the Prescott County separate-school movement. This leadership involved certain parish priests, but the changing context of cultural relations also led to the enthusiastic intervention into Prescott County of Archbishop Joseph-Thomas Duhamel of Ottawa.

Archbishop Joseph-Thomas Duhamel was a staunch ultramontanist who frequently visited Rome during his tenure at Ottawa, which began in 1874. He was exceedingly strict and uncompromising in his long administration, which followed Bishop Guigues' death and extended to his own death in 1909. For Archbishop Duhamel, Catholic children should only attend Catholic schools. This view had also been that of the more flexible Guigues, but Duhamel gave it a new sense of absolute necessity. From the mid-1870s, he constantly instructed his clergy to remind parents of "leur strict devoir d'établir, de soutenir les écoles catholiques et d'y envoyer ceux que Dieu leur a confié et qui sont plus les enfants de Dieu qu'ils ne sont les leurs."[42]

The Controversy in L'Orignal

The archbishop's specific involvement in Prescott County's school issues followed reception of a letter written in March 1890 by Father Octave Bérubé of St-Jean-Baptiste-de-L'Orignal[42] about the status of schools in his parish.[43] He began by reporting proudly that a language controversy involving a school in the village of L'Orignal had finally been resolved. This controversy had originated in 1886 when francophone ratepayers succeeded, for the first time, in gaining a controlling influence among the trustees for School No. 1 in L'Orignal. This school board had been responsible for constructing, in 1877, a major school building at a cost of $7,500. The building included a two-storey main structure, of containing a large hall and four classrooms, as well as a rear wing which was used by a high school that had its own board of trustees.[44] In the elementary school until 1886, a Protestant headmaster and an assistant instructed two classrooms of English-language students while a francophone assistant taught a French-language class. The new francophone trustees ended this arrangement. At its first meeting, the board announced that the anglophone teachers would be dismissed, and, despite protests and petitions from anglophone parents, it hired two francophone teachers to conduct the entire elementary school.

The transformation of L'Orignal Public School No. 1 from a dual-language school under the leadership of anglophones to a unilingual school controlled by francophones did more than reflect the changing cultural composition of the village. Adequate provision for the increasing number of francophone children did not necessitate the elimination of English-language classrooms. Forty-eight anglophone ratepayers detailed this argument in a letter to George Ross, requesting the minister's intervention on their behalf. They complained that the two new francophone teachers were only using half the space in the main structure of the schoolhouse and that the program "as now conducted is not kept in accordance with the rules and regulations, and the laws respecting Public Schools in this Province." The ratepayers reported that the Roman Catholic catechism as a regular part of the curriculum and that the pupils spent a great deal of time "with their observation of the forms and ceremonies of the Roman Catholic Church." These complaints, the letter emphasized, were, however, secondary to the question of which groups had rights to the schoolhouse. The anglophones explained to Ross that they had organized a private school immediately after their teachers had been discharged and planned to apply for establishment of a Protestant separate school. They had hoped that their temporary private school could operate in the two empty rooms of the elementary schoolhouse, but the francophone trustees "pre-emptorily refused" to allow this. In response, the anglophone parents turned to the high school board of trustees, where their cultural representatives were still in control, and they were able to gain permission to use one room for their school.

The success was short lived. When the anglophones formally applied to establish a Protestant separate school, the francophone trustees passed a resolution that it should not be allowed to occupy any part of the schoolhouse, including the high-school wing. The resolution made clear that the francophones were intent on gaining full control of the substantial schoolhouse, thereby forcing the anglophones to finance another building elsewhere. In an attempt to prevent this takeover, the anglophones implored Ross to investigate the "management and condition" of Public School No. 1 and to secure half of the elementary classrooms for the new Protestant separate school.

The letter from L'Orignal fuelled the minister's concern about the cultural status of schooling in Prescott County, but there was little he could do on behalf of the anglophone minority. The ratepayers' complaints were justified if religion were taught during regular school hours and if English were not part of the curriculum as required by the 1885 regulations;[45] however, Ross still had no effective way of enforcing these rules. In any event, the more important issue concerned the schoolhouse itself, and here Ross had no authority to intervene. Francophones had lawfully gained control of the public school board, and the trustees were within their rights to operate the schoolhouse and to hire any certified teachers of their choice. The anglophones of L'Orignal had thus discovered what francophones were familiar with in other areas of Prescott County; the elected trustees controlled the local schools, usually to the detriment of minority groups.

In his letter to Archbishop Duhamel in 1890, Father Bérubé reported that the L'Orignal anglophones had finally given up any claim to the main schoolhouse and had established their Protestant separate school in a different building. Bérubé expressed great satisfaction with this development, although he viewed it as only a temporary solution. Next, the school, now fully controlled by francophones, must be transformed from public to separate status. In his view, this strategy was related to purely material considerations. By remaining public until the anglophones withdrew to form their own school, the francophones had gained control of a newly built schoolhouse financed by both language groups. Bérubé's plan was to let the school continue within the public system until the construction debts were paid and then to establish a Catholic separate school "tout en conservant notre belle école." In this way, francophones could benefit from the financial resources of the anglophone ratepayers while promoting their own language and religion.[46]

The Controversy over School No. 4

In his letter, Father Bérubé was forced to admit that the resolution of the L'Orignal controversy coincided with the emergence of another conflict on the western border of the parish. At School No. 4, which included children from St-Victor-d'Alfred as well as St-Jean-Baptiste, the dominant francophone supporters were themselves divided over the question of whether it should be public or separate. In the late 1880s, a group of francophone families had decided to form a separate school, but they had been forced to relocate because No. 4 included a small number of Protestant anglophones who had the right to maintain the existing schoolhouse. The need to locate the separate school elsewhere had discouraged a significant minority of francophones from supporting its establishment; of twenty-four families residing in St-Jean-Baptiste parish, nine continued to send their children to the public school. Bérubé explained that these "récalcitrants" were encouraged by certain francophones in the neighbouring parish of St-Victor-d'Alfred, who already had a choice between No. 4 and a previously established separate school in the same section. Without united francophone participation, the new school was in trouble, struggling to pay the costs of operation. Bérubé knew that the answer was a single school, but he felt unable to resolve the dilemma: "Que faire, Monseigneur, je vous le demande."[47]

Archbishop Duhamel first responded to Father Bérubé's letter by asking for more information, especially about the legal method of creating separate schools in Prescott County. The curé replied in detail on 10 April 1890, outlining the procedure that had satisfied the provincial educational authorities in previous separate-school establishments in the county. He also made clear that his sentiments lay with the group which had formed a separate school at No. 4, although he felt incapable of persuading the other francophones to join them and thus secure the school's financial foundation. Bérubé emphasized again,

Ceux qui se sont mis en école séparée dans cette section sont trop faibles pour soutenir une école séparée catholique, cependant ils sont bien décidés à faire de grands sacrifices pour faire fonctionner leur école catholique pour jusqu'au mois de janvier prochain.

Having described the plight of this francophone group, Bérubé went beyond his initial request for guidance from Duhamel. He now suggested what he anticipated would be an easy solution – direct intervention by the archbishop. The curé had come to believe that a resolution was not possible "sans que vous, Monseigneur, y mettiez la main."[48]

The Archbishop's Intervention. Archbishop Duhamel responded immediately. In 1890, he toured the county and directly ordered all Catholic parents to send their children to separate schools when possible and to create such schools where necessary. This tour occurred at a timely moment, on the heels of the 1889 commission on French-language schools in the province. Since the commission had examined only schools operating in the public system, its investigation had engendered concern about the future of public, rather than separate, schools and had left francophones with "fear lest their privileges might be interfered with."[49] This anxiety was heartily nourished by the campaigns leading to the 1890 provincial election. The Conservatives' English-only demands and the ambiguous Liberal replies suggested an ominous future for French-language public schools in Prescott County. In this context, direct orders to form separate schools fell on sympathetic ears. The 1889 commission's focus on public schools implied that the provincial authorities had less interest in separate schools than in public ones, thereby unintentionally encouraging Prescott County francophones to view the separate system as a haven from provincial scrutiny and political attack.

This convergence of outside and local interests generated a powerful movement of separate school establishment. Thirteen French-language schools in Prescott County switched from the public to the separate system between 1889 and 1893. The most dramatic transition occurred in Alfred Township, where a total of seven French-language schools withdrew from public organization. (One of these schools was No. 14, thereby finally ending the protracted public-separate controversy at Horse Creek.[50])

Nonetheless, separate-school promotion was not effective in all sections of Prescott County. For various reasons, certain groups of francophone parents wanted to continue supporting public schools. For his part, Archbishop Duhamel made it clear that he would not tolerate differences of opinion: the sacraments would now be denied any francophone parent who did not support the separate system. This simple and decisive answer would have had promise if the widespread image of francophone passivity and subordination had actually represented reality. Father Bérubé had already learned that this might not be the case, but neither he nor the archbishop anticipated that local disputes would continue after "la main" had been placed.

The Responses of Local Residents. The initial response from local communities to the official directive supported this view. In the parish of St-Jean-Baptiste, the francophone trustees of School No. 4 immediately collapsed under the diocesan pressure. "Nous sommes près à abandonner tous [sic] les prétentions de notre école commune aux syndics de l'école séparée de notre section qu'il n'y ait qu'une seule école séparée centrale dans la section." In agreeing to join their separate school counterparts, the trustees emphasized that they were going against their financial self-interest since the separate school had a debt of several hundred dollars while they currently held a $100 surplus. Nonetheless, they were ready to support Archbishop Duhamel's policy.[51]

The parents from St-Victor-d'Alfred were less persuaded by the official directive on separate schools, although they were reluctant to confront Church authority personally. In an unsigned letter, they wrote to Archbishop Duhamel explaining their refusal to follow his orders. These anonymous parishioners who continued to support Public School No. 4 admitted that, under ideal conditions, conversion to a separate school would be desirable but said that in their present financial condition they were not "assez forts." Moreover, they explained, the public schoolhouse had recently been repaired, costing at least $250; if they withdrew to support the separate school, this expense would benefit only the remaining minority of anglophone Protestant children. The writers recognized the aging of the county's established population and the decline of immigration from Quebec, explaining to the archbishop:

Il y a moins besoin de deux écoles, à présent, que voilà dix ans passés parce que dans ce temps-là, il y avait beaucoup plus d'enfants qu'à présent; il y en a plusieurs qui ont fini d'élever leurs familles et qui n'ont plus d'enfants à envoyer à l'école.

The parents without school-age children were described as "les plus forts" in support of two schools since they did not care about the quality of the required teacher. To make the separate school financially feasible, these parents were prepared to hire a teacher "à bas prix qui menacerait l'éducation de nos enfants." Thus the financial argument took on educational implications. The anonymous writers stressed that the archbishop's simple policy did not reflect the complexity of these practical considerations. They declared their hope that they would be able to "faire nos Pâques comme par le passé," but they did not suggest that denial would change their position. Rather, they argued, "ça serait bien dur de se faire refuser les sacrements" just because they would not close a school in existence for fifty years in favour of one open for five years.[52]

This firm statement of opposition to diocesan policy was undoubtedly encouraged by the anticipated anonymity of unsigned correspondence. Archbishop Duhamel, however, quickly discovered the authors' identities. By writing to the parish priest, he obtained a "Liste des Dissidents" which identified ten heads of household in St-Victor who opposed the separate school in Section No. 4.[53] In addition, Duhamel inquired about the declining enrolment which the anonymous letter had emphasized in explaining local opposition. Father François Lombard of St-Victor responded that, given the position of the separate school between two parishes, there should be a sufficient number of children available for attendance.[54] (In fact, the parish reports of the early 1890s show that this separate school was the smallest in either St-Victor or St-Jean Baptiste, and its financial position remained precarious as the opposition held fast.[55])

On 22 February 1893, the position of the dissidents was reaffirmed in a letter to Archbishop Duhamel from Xavier Gauthier, a ratepayer and school trustee in Section No. 4. Gauthier again detailed the financial argument, but this time he made clear the legal distinction between public and separate schools. He explained that francophone Catholics totally dominated Public School No. 4, which was located in an area without resident Protestant families. The catchment area of the school did, however, include property owned by nonresident Protestants; as a result, the public school received about $60 per year beyond what the Catholic residents paid in rates. Gauthier saw no reason why this extra support should be surrendered simply to have a separate school. He argued that Public School No. 4 was traditionally "l'une des meilleures écoles catholiques du comté" and that, as parents, he and like-minded residents were not ready to sacrifice the education of their children for the sake of extending the separate system. Gauthier closed his letter by saying that the francophone public-school supporters deserved to receive the sacraments since they paid regularly to the parish funds through the church collections. In making this claim, however, Gauthier unconsciously informed Duhamel that, contrary to diocesan orders, the "Dissidents" had been given the sacraments during the previous Eastertide. He requested "la faveur d'être admis encore cette année au banquet eucharistique," thereby indicating that Father Lombard had succumbed to local opposition to the archbishop's policy.[56]

The Responses of Parish Priests. One week later, Father Lombard wrote to Archbishop Duhamel, abandoning any prospect of settling the separate-school issue himself. He contended that all possible paths of reconciliation had been explored and that the whole dispute now lay in the hands of "Votre Grandeur, le seul juge autorisé."[57] The question of separate schools was clearly exposing the underlying tension in the relationship between lay leaders and parish priests in Prescott County. By the late 1880s, this relationship involved a good deal of collaboration, and, as a result, the number of separate schools increased sharply. In some instances, however, the particular interests of lay leaders did not completely overlap the general diocesan perspective. Parish priests thus sometimes found themselves in uncomfortable positions despite their formal positions of authority. Father Lombard's admission of defeat and Gauthier's inadvertent disclosure that the francophone dissidents had continued to receive the sacraments combined to undermine the curé's position vis-à-vis the archbishop.

During the following months, Duhamel reaffirmed his policy of punishing public school supporters, but the implementation of this policy continued to be problematic. On 23 September 1893, he threatened to move Lombard to a new parish, accusing him of disobeying official orders. Immediately Lombard denied this accusation, claiming to have refused the sacraments to the francophone "chefs de famille" of Public School No. 4.[58] But the curé knew he was in trouble, caught between local and diocesan imperatives. In addition to protesting his innocence, he frantically wrote to neighbouring curés, asking for their support to save his position.[59] Yet Lombard knew there was only one solution: to convince the dissidents to join the separate school. But how could he do this without totally disrupting his parish?

Lombard's predicament was not made easier by Father Octave Bérubé of St-Jean-Baptiste, who attempted to profit at Lombard's expense by promoting himself to Archbishop Duhamel as an effective parish leader. Bérubé took pride in the early acceptance of a separate school by the francophone trustees in his parish, and he gloated somewhat as Lombard continued to be unable to gain control of the St-Victor residents. On 3 February 1894, Bérubé reported to the archbishop that Lombard was losing, rather than gaining, ground. The St-Jean-Baptiste curé gossiped that several separate school supporters were returning to the public school, thereby leaving the separate school "plus faible que jamais." Contending that his own promotion of diocesan policy was not always easy, Bérubé revealed his resentment toward Lombard's apparent reluctance to coerce parishioners; "On croit que le curé de L'Orignal est un peu trop ardent pour les écoles tandis que le curé d'Alfred ne tient pas du tout à s'en occuper."[60]

In writing to Duhamel, Bérubé was being mischievous at best. The parish reports show that Separate School No. 4 continued to be small, but they do not reveal any decline in enrolment.[61] Nor can Lombard be accused of inactivity. Throughout early 1894, feverish attempts were underway to integrate the public school into the separate system and thereby to unite all the francophone children. As the 1 March deadline neared for giving formal notice of separate school establishment, telegrams whisked back and forth between Lombard and Duhamel.[62] Were the supporters in line? Were the documents prepared? Would notice be given?

The 1894 deadline passed with Public School No. 4 still in operation. The dissident francophones had remained firm. Community strength proved irresistible in this instance. During the following years, the diocesan office subsidized Separate School No. 4 as its financial difficulties continued. In 1896, for example, the archbishop sent $141.26 to cover the school's debt.[63]

Conclusions about the Controversies

The steadfastness of the St-Victor francophones emphasizes that the power of the Catholic hierarchy was somewhat constrained by local interests. Official dictates were not always passively accepted. Despite the coercive strength of weapons such as the denial of the sacraments, Church leaders could not always ignore the perspectives of community leaders in Prescott County. The militant St-Victor francophones were certainly somewhat remarkable, but their opposition to the official promotion of separate schools was not an isolated phenomenon. The francophone leaders who gained control of the impressive schoolhouse in L'Orignal reacted in much the same way. Despite Father Bérubé's initial anticipation that the public school would be made separate once the anglophones had established a Protestant school elsewhere, these francophones continued to operate within the public system.[64] From their point of view, the incentive to establish a separate school was removed by the withdrawal of the Protestant anglophones. This development revealed a measure of strength within the francophone position, especially since George Ross had not directly intervened in response to the anglophone petition for arbitration.

In general, the potential insulation offered by the separate system was a powerful attraction for francophones after 1885. The examples of francophone resistance are noteworthy because they disprove the claims that Quebec immigration had brought a sheeplike population to eastern Ontario. They also show that a variety of factors determined the attitudes and actions of specific francophones in Prescott County. The French Canadians were not a monolithic group, especially after the 1870s. Differences in thought and behaviour reflected distinct individual and family circumstances. The attitudes and actions of "les gros casques du rang" at Horse Creek are entirely consistent with the patterns of Prescott County's social and economic history. The better-established families were more able and more ready than some other francophones to take on the added cost of a separate school. The former were not only somewhat more affluent but also able to exercise greater interest in schooling. Such families sent their children to school more regularly and for an additional number of years. Not surprisingly, therefore, the separate school question elicited differences of opinion among various francophone groups.

It is noteworthy that the complexity of francophones' thought and behaviour with respect to separate schools was quite similar to that of anglophone Catholics. An 1898 letter to Archbishop Duhamel from a group of the latter is remarkably like earlier francophone correspondence. These anglophones, ratepayers in sections No. 1 and No. 5, an area of Irish settlement in Alfred Township, wrote to oppose diocesan pressure to form a separate school. Material considerations were foremost in their minds. They explained that one-third of the public section's ratepayers were Protestant, but only one Protestant family sent children to the school. Moreover, "our separated brethren do not interfere in any wise with our school affairs and give us the full and entire liberty to act and manage the school to the full extent of Catholic interest in the school at all." The absence of cause to leave the public system was combined with powerful incentives to maintain the school as it was. The schoolhouse and surrounding property were valuable and, the ratepayers stressed, "immediate transformation into a separate school would involve serious losses and create innumerable difficulties."

Like the francophone supporters of Public School No. 4, these anglophone Catholics could see no reason to weaken the financial position of their school for the sake of formal separate status; they remained intransigent, and the school continued in the public system.[65]

The Church insistence that the Irish-origin Catholics of Section No. 1 and Section No. 5 form a separate school illustrates that ecclesiastical motives for promoting the system went beyond the growing menace to French-language instruction in the public system. In the view of religious leaders, the establishment of separate schools in Prescott County was part of general reorganization and strengthening of the Catholic Church in the later nineteenth century. This process was not specifically intended to nurture a sense of franco-Ontarian identity and, in fact, did not depend upon a perceived threat to language stability.[66] At the same time, the evidence from Prescott County shows that the language of instruction was directly connected to separate schools in the minds of francophone lay leaders. Community spokesmen did not emphasize the formation of separate schools as a necessary and desirable element of improved parish organization. For them, separate schools became primarily attractive as a refuge from provincial intervention by language-conscious educators.

In this sense, somewhat distinct motives led to the conversion of many schools from public to separate in Prescott County. Archbishop Duhamel sought most of all an improved and extended parish structure, while certain francophone lay leaders pursued continued French-language instruction in the schools as an end in itself. The symbiotic nature of these ambitions resulted in numerous French-language separate schools in late nineteenth-century Prescott County.

The ability of local lay leaders to maintain some of their own ambitions in the face of Catholic Church officials appears unusual in the general context of the time. Studies of Quebec parishes, including those in the northern colonization areas, reveal the broad social and economic power of many curés.[67] Historians emphasize that parishioners did not submit entirely to clerical control and that local conflict did occur. Ongoing popular resistance has not been found, however, especially in parishes where priests found ways to collaborate with community leaders. The difference between these findings and the Prescott County evidence involves the degree of clerical control. The Catholic Church was rapidly gaining strength in Prescott County, but it was not yet as firmly established as in Quebec parishes, such as Hébertville in the Saguenay.[68] Overall, the ratio of priests to faithful in Prescott County remained far behind the Quebec average in the late nineteenth century. Babies were baptized closer and closer to their dates of birth, but the delays remained long relative to those in Quebec, even in eighteenth-century rural Sorel. A possible conclusion is that Prescott County was more marginal in the minds of the francophone Catholic Church hierarchy than in the Torontonian view of anglophone educators. In any event, the result was that clerical control could not be completely arbitrary. Parish activity depended upon at least a partial convergence of local and diocesan interests.

SEPARATE SCHOOLS: LATE-NINETEENTH-CENTURY RESULTS

What were the educational results of separate school establishment? Were the francophones of Prescott County effectively shielded from the negative implications of minority-language education? Were they successfully rescued, even temporarily, from George Ross and the *Mail*? These questions focus on the actual conditions of the Prescott County separate schools. The most relevant historical sources are the inspectors' reports on the Roman Catholic separate schools.[69] The weakness of these sources is that the inspectors were anglophone representatives of the provincial school system. Despite the official status of separate schools in Ontario, a tendency toward undue criticism can be expected in their reports, especially in their interpretive comments. The strength of this evidence is that the inspectors' manuscript reports provide comprehensive information on individual schools. The data include enrolment, attendance, language taught, levels of proficiency, status of schoolhouses, quality of instructional material, and the inspector's general assessment of the school. The result is a wide-ranging description of separate schooling over time. If used cautiously, these reports can at least suggest the impact of separate school establishment in Prescott County.

The inspectors' reports for late-nineteenth-century Prescott County are unambiguous in describing the quality of separate schools as very poor throughout the 1880s and 1890s. The reports show that most of the schoolhouses in the 1880s were small log buildings equipped with outdated desks and few supplies. Separate School No. 2 at Chute-au-Blondeau in East Hawkesbury Township had a classroom "barely large enough for 25" despite an enrolment of eighty children. The school had "but 4 long desks" and only a "very small" blackboard. Other schools were similarly small, and although some did have aids such as maps, the characteristic "material equipment" was considered "defective."[70]

The inspectors generally praised the teachers for trying their best but recognized that they were not overcoming the obstacles to quality education in Prescott County. The separate schools were predominantly francophone, but the official pressure on all Catholics to support the separate system produced a few linguistically mixed classes, usually combining children of French Canadians and of Irish descent. Teachers were rarely prepared to reach effectively in such circumstances, especially given the usual large class sizes. The inspector reported sympathetically that at Separate School No. 7 in West Hawkesbury Township, "considering the large number of pupils and the dual nature of the work – English and French – this school does creditably well ... But the plain fact is that ... the school cannot bring out satisfactory results." At No. 4 in East Hawkesbury, the inspector remarked, "drill is needed as there are French and English children attending. Both languages are taught, but neither with great success." At No. 3 in Alfred Township, "too much has been attempted and too little done."[71]

The problems of teaching in linguistically mixed classrooms were not widespread, however, since the proportion of anglophones among Catholics in Prescott County was quite small, especially by the later nineteenth century. The more important pedagogical challenge after 1885 came from the official requirement that at least some English be taught in all Ontario schools. The inspectors' reports reveal that this requirement was often ignored and that even where francophone teachers made an effort to include English-language instruction, the results were not impressive. The 1890 report for Separate

School No. 7 in Longueuil Township noted that English teaching had only made a "beginning," while at No. 7 in the Township of South Plantagenet, the "general proficiency" of the school was considered "creditable except in English which is in a very backward state."[72] The difficulty of finding a sufficient number of even unilingual francophone teachers left little hope for hiring qualified bilingual instructors.

The evidence suggests that the overcrowded log school buildings, the inadequately equipped classrooms, the quality of teachers, and the problems posed by language combined to produce poor schooling for Prescott County francophones even within the separate system during the late nineteenth century. The anglophone inspectors may have overstated the case, but their reports provide no descriptive evidence that the separate schools were more than minimally viable. Moreover, these sources indicate that the poor conditions of elementary schooling not only affected francophone children when they were young but also undermined their chances of pursuing formal education as they grew older. The fact that English was not taught effectively to francophones in elementary school often precluded their participation in secondary schooling, which was still offered only in English in Prescott County. The economic climate of the times meant that few francophone parents could afford to send their children to French-language high schools elsewhere. In any event, the inferior quality of schooling could not have prepared many francophone students to pursue further education, even in their own language. The overall result was a situation not even approaching equality of educational experience for the francophones of Prescott County.

The school data reveal the narrow limits within which francophones could control their own educational destiny in Prescott County. The strategy of separate school formation could not overcome local conditions in a province in which dualism was simply not part of the dominant intellectual milieu.

CHAPTER SEVEN

Cultural Fission in Prescott County

Can official policies actually change attitudes and behaviour? Canadian policymakers, to say nothing of historians, have rarely even considered this question. Rather, they have assumed their own ability to control and change, sometimes through force but more often through argument and then legislation. This study of Prescott County documents the folly of this assumption, at least with respect to the language-of-instruction issue in the nineteenth century. The evidence emphasizes the importance of understanding the circumstances within which official educational policies can and cannot be effective. As N. Ray Hiner recently argued, "Any educator who assumes it is possible to gain complete command over a child's education understands neither children nor history."[1]

THE QUESTION OF LANGUAGE IN PRESCOTT COUNTRY

The 1901 census data are quite revealing about the effects of nine-teenth-century language policy. This enumeration was the first to include questions concerning English- and French-language ability. The special census commissioner gave two reasons for adding these questions:

In a country peopled with so many foreign elements as Canada, it is desirable to know if they are being absorbed and unified, as may appear by their acquirement of one or other of the official languages. And as English is now in a very large degree the language of commerce throughout the world, it is also desirable to ascertain to what extent citizens of French origin are able to speak it in addition to their own.

Specifically, the question asked was whether or not an individual could speak French and English. Enumerators were instructed to accept answers without regard to the "degree of proficiency" involved.[2] Thus, the results represent the upper bounds of the population's language abilities. In other words, the degree to which non-English speakers were being "absorbed and unified" would be revealed in the most "favourable" light possible.

The 1901 Census

In Prescott County, the 1901 enumerators documented what Toronto educators, politicians, and journalists all feared and what the people of townships such as Alfred and Caledonia all knew: the lynchpin of language had not been broken for many francophones. The enumerators found that in Prescott County only half the francophones five years of age and older were even minimally bilingual. A large proportion of the population still could not speak English, despite the early anticipation of voluntary assimilation and the coercive educational policies of 1885 and later. The 1901 evidence thus revealed that the 1893 commission on French-language schooling had been wrong in concluding that the breakdown of language attachment had finally begun in earnest.

What effect had the Ontario context had on the extent of francophone bilingualism in Prescott County? Very little, according to a comparison of its census data with that from Argenteuil, the Quebec county directly across the Ottawa River. In Prescott County, 55.9 per cent of the francophones had at least some ability in English. The figure for Argenteuil was almost identical: 50.3 per cent. Anglophones in both counties were considerably less likely to be bilingual. (See Table 40.) The Prescott-Argenteuil similarity suggests that educational policies and the Ontario environment per se did not determine linguistic patterns during the nineteenth century. Rather, the patterns appear to be related to the social context of the lower Ottawa Valley.

The Historical Context

In Prescott County, the language stability of many francophones was the product of a convergence of the demographic, economic, educational, and political factors which characterized the nineteenth century. Although contemporary observers focused on factors such as perceived newness of settlement or control by the Catholic Church, the actual history of Prescott County reveals the importance of understanding the social context of the language question. The central

TABLE 40

Language Ability (Without Regard to "Degree of Proficiency"), Prescott County and Argenteuil County, Quebec, 1901

	Prescott County		Argenteuil County	
	N	%	N	%
Francophones "Can speak French and English"	9,129	55.9	3,234	50.3
Unilingual	7,192	44.1	3,196	49.7
Total	16,321	100.0	6,430	100.0
Anglophones "Can speak English and French"	2,256	33.8	1,803	23.0
Unilingual	4,417	66.2	6,041	77.0
Total	6,673	100.0	7,844	100.0

Note: Data are for the population five years of age and older. The figures given for unilingual francophones and for total francophones are estimates that assume (1) proportional numbers of anglophones and francophones and (2) all individuals of French-Canadian origin spoke French and all those of non-French-Canadian origin spoke English.

Source: *Census of Canada*, 1901.

feature of this context was the establishment of quite distinct communities of anglophones and francophones before the time of conflict about minority-language education. For both groups, the family was at the heart of this process, from initial immigration to patterns of settlement and social organization. It is in this sense that the history of cultural conflict extends far beyond the perceptions, attitudes, and action of leadership groups.[3]

Settlers used family and kin in coming to Prescott County; thus they naturally maintained cultural attachment within the household setting. For many francophones, kinship ties to nearby areas in Quebec held fast. Relocation in Prescott County did not uproot them significantly. Moreover, family migration and kinship links prepared both anglophone and francophone immigrants for the family economy of lumbering and agriculture. During the mid-nineteenth century, many settlers functioned within family units based on economic interdependency and mutual support. In the absence of intermarriage between francophones and anglophones, this basis provided the material foundation for language continuity.[4]

Similarly, the family was the unrivalled social institution of Prescott County from the 1840s to the early 1870s. For the most part, communities functioned with little formal organization. For francophones, this characteristic is well illustrated by the weak role of the Catholic Church in these years, a fact which was not recognized by provincial leaders at the time. It was not ecclesiastical leadership that prevented the Quebec immigrants from being assimilated into "Canadian" life. The depiction of priest-ridden French Canadians cannot be applied to the settlers who changed the cultural geography of Prescott County or during the mid-nineteenth century. Rather, the family itself was the critical social and economic institution. As a result, cultural stability occurred naturally during the years when Egerton Ryerson anticipated the voluntary assimilation of Quebec immigrants.

Ironically, the availability of French-language schools in some areas of Prescott County further reinforced language attachment, despite the official assimilative goal of common schooling. Those French-language schools which could be established were part of the new common school system, but they closely reflected local rather than provincial imperatives. Children went to school only when attendance was in harmony with family responsibilities. Classes were taught in French by francophones who, if they were trained at all, were often trained in Quebec; textbooks were those used in Quebec. These patterns still obtained after 1885 when the policy of voluntary assimilation was partly abandoned in favour of new regulations requiring closer conformity to the Ontario ideal. Thus, the common schools were not, in practice, simply agents of assimilation or cultural standardization in the nineteenth century. For those who attended, schools in Prescott County reinforced family values and customs and contributed to cultural continuity for all ethnic groups.[5]

The patterns of land settlement in Prescott County also allowed Quebec immigrants to establish themselves in the 1840s and 1850s without significantly challenging settled anglophone communities. The timing of settlement and considerations of topography and soil type ensured that anglophones and francophones often lived in geographically distinct areas. As a result, there was little need for sustained, local interaction. The availability of land and a need to participate in the lumber industry initially meant that francophone families did not directly confront the larger anglophone world. In this sense, francophones were not fully forced, during the midcentury decades, to face all the negative aspects of their minority status. Differences of language did not seem very important when the family was the focus of most activity.[6]

The central importance of these factors in determining the nature of cultural relations during the mid-nineteenth century became clear by the 1870s, when the retreat of the forest frontier and the shortage of land forced francophones in Prescott County to confront the limits of their society's economic base. Many francophone families found it less possible to piece together a viable existence from the labour of various family members. Young francophone males could no longer plan to take up land in regions ignored by anglophone hegemony. Many, unlike their predecessors of the mid-nineteenth century, became proletarians in Prescott County. The new generation of francophones – now living in Ontario rather than the Province of Canada – had to recognize that security and even survival depended on coming to terms with the power of a different linguistic group. This fact may help to explain the absence in Prescott County of the trade union movement, which emerged so forcefully in other parts of Ontario, especially during the 1880s.[7] Poor economic conditions and the power of lumber merchants, such as the Hamiltons, contributed to this phenomenon, but the development of hostility between anglophones and francophones was also important. Under the leadership of journalists, politicians, and religious leaders, the material crisis of Prescott County was subsumed within the larger cultural crisis of late-nineteenth-century Canada, and cultural consciousness emerged as the dominant expression of local frustration and failure. A key aspect in this development was the emergence of a local francophone elite. From the 1870s, the predominantly Ontario-born francophone population included well-established farmers as well as local merchants and professionals. Some francophones now held the economic positions required to seek public leadership in Prescott County. Within the general environment of material anxiety, francophones were able to articulate their own ambitions.

By the 1880s, conditions were ripe for cultural conflict in Prescott County. The francophone settlement had become large and was still increasing, despite constant emigration. Both the increase and the emigration took on great significance as certain other parts of Ontario witnessed steady francophone colonization. Earlier in the century, the francophone presence in Ontario had been concentrated in the eastern and western corners of the province, but during the 1880s and 1890s, this presence spread, especially to the developing region of the north.[8] By itself, the growing francophone presence in Ontario was disturbing but not intrinsically worrisome to anglophones. The truly alarming aspect was the absence of any indication of substantial assimilation. The continued demand for French-language schooling reflected a degree of cultural stability that had not been anticipated and that was frightening to those who considered Ontario to be the bastion of English Canada and, indeed, of the new dominion. In this sense, there was an indirect causal link between immigration and the crisis over French-language schools. The issue was not simply that francophones were immigrating to Ontario. Rather, the perceived problem was that they did not appear to be assimilating quickly into the larger anglophone world.

THE DEVELOPMENT OF CULTURAL CONFLICT

The experience of Prescott County suggests that the cultural confrontation represented by the language controversy in Ontario was not simply another battle in the struggle of Canada's two founding peoples. Rather, the conclusions which have emerged in the preceding chapters suggest that the history of minority-language education in nineteenth-century Prescott County can be better explained by the changing interaction of land and family than by inherent intercultural attitudes. Social change engendered new mentalités. This process occurred in a context characterized by barriers to communication and general intercultural ignorance. Since only a small minority of the county's anglophones and about half its francophones were minimally bilingual even at the end of the century, language helped keep apart the two groups and encouraged rumour, suspicion, and stereotypes.[9] Moreover, the increasing articulation of francophone consciousness establshed new psychological barriers between the cultural groups of Prescott County and thus nourished cultural alienation. Even bilingual francophones in the county were viewing language in new ways by the late nineteenth century. In 1889, one observer noted that, as a result of the "St. Jean Baptiste celebrations, the Nationalist agitation, the Riel excitement, etc., many French Canadians, who can speak English perfectly, of late insist on being addressed in their own tongue."[10] In this context, intercultural ignorance could only have increased.

The identification of misperceptions and misunderstandings between anglophones and francophones does not imply, however, that accurate knowledge would have engendered acceptance and harmony. Rather, the evidence reveals a clear conflict of assumptions and expectations produced by distinct historical experiences. Even if the basis of the conflict had been properly understood by both anglophones and francophones, attitudes might have remained unchanged. It is clear that anglophone spokesmen tended to perceive inexplicable cultural differences. Our overview of Prescott County helps solve the mystery and negates the conclusion that French Canadians were simply governed by different wires and springs. Nevertheless, knowledge does not necessarily breed tolerance and understanding. In the context of the day, accurate perception might not have made much difference. The conflict did not result only from mutual ignorance but also from certain real differences, historically determined.[11]

Thus, the economic crisis of the 1870s and thereafter occurred among conditions which were, in themselves, contributing to the foundations of cultural conflict. The crisis challenged both the social structure and the social values which had been established during the mid-nineteenth century, and it produced a highly anomic society characterized by cultural anxiety. The realistic basis of this anxiety raised anglophone behaviour of the 1880s and later above the level of paranoic nativism. In the struggle for survival and security, francophones were indeed now challenging anglophone positions in almost every aspect of social and economic organization in Prescott County. Just as general economic opportunities were declining, francophones began rivalling anglophone farmers, merchants, journalists, school trustees, municipal officials, and political leaders. This rivalry was, strictly speaking, between individuals, but it became a clash of linguistic groups, each of which held intrinsically distinct visions of its own participation in the future of Prescott County and, indeed, of Ontario and all Canada. The different visions of uniformity and duality were mutually exclusive; the challenge was real.[12]

Cultural Fission in Prescott County

In the election of 1883, the situation attained a critical mass, and cultural fission exploded Prescott County. In the changing times, francophones were, in effect, bombarding the now unstable anglophone nucleus, and they set off a chain reaction of conflict which dramatically alienated the two groups. In the late nineteenth century, Prescott County disintegrated into redefined anglophone and francophone fragments.[13] Franco-Ontarian identity was born.

The metaphor of fission is not quite appropriate for describing these changed relations since Prescott County was not a closed system in any sense during the nineteenth century. Flows of migration, economic ties, and cultural attachments all connected it to the world beyond. But it was precisely these connections which gave tremendous power to the cultural disruption of the 1880s. During these years, Prescott County became part of the much larger disintegration of cultural relations at both the provincial and national level. The critical mass for this disintegration was attained nationally in 1885 with Riel's conviction and hanging and again provincially in the election of 1890. From the perspective of the people of Prescott County, Riel's hanging was thus not an isolated event; rather, it assumed great importance precisely because its implications reinforced trends already evident in their own villages and townships. Similarly, the language issue in the provincial election of 1890 was an old question in Prescott County; for local communities, the provincial campaigns were significant because they reinforced and injected an additional layer to a familiar cultural conflict. In these ways, the history of the longue durée in Prescott County intersected the larger Canadian histoire événementielle to produce the cultural discontinuity of the late nineteenth century.[14]

As this process occurred, the francophones' need for effective leadership became urgent, and, by more than coincidence, it was at this juncture that the Catholic Church began to assume great importance among them in Prescott County. The social psychology of this importance was based, at least in part, on the French Canadians' desire to escape the full impact of minority status in Ontario. The Church provided a variety of traditional reasons for attachment; in addition, it offered the francophones of Prescott County the chance to identify themselves not as minority Ontario residents but rather as members of the francophone section of the universal Catholic Church. This motivation became increasingly strong during the late 1880s, which brought a flood of anglophone political and journalistic attacks. Faced with them and with the fact that elected francophone politicians could not articulate their position in any effective way, many francophones in Prescott County found Church leadership appealing. It gave them a way of responding to the cultural challenge of anglophones. Through clerical leaders, generally educated and articulate, the francophones attempted to channel their feelings and to fight for their continued cultural existence. It is thus understandable that they attempted to offer the Church financial support despite the pressure of economic difficulties and, in certain cases, against their own better judgment. They did so to defend themselves at the local level and perhaps also to show the rest of Ontario that they intended to maintain the settlements established at midcentury.[15]

Francophone support for the Church was not, however, blind; as the history of Prescott County suggests, parishioners were not sheep to be herded in arbitrary directions. Rather, the Church's leadership resulted from at least a partial convergence of local and official interests at particular points in time. In the later nineteenth century, the specific strategy which often brought together the interests of Catholic Church officials and the francophone leaders of Prescott County was the transformation of French-language public schools into separate schools. However, this transformation reveals the noteworthy extent to which local leaders were willing and able to maintain their own integrity. The Catholic Church hierarchy discovered what education officials were also learning; policy was far easier to formulate than to enforce among the francophones of Prescott County.

In terms of the nuclear metpahor, the establishment of French-language separate schools diverted and thus weakened the francophone bombardment of the anglophone nucleus. After 1893, the mass of fissionable elements temporarily came below the critical point in Prescott County. Similarly, the 1890 election results and the misapprehension of a decided advance in assimilation in eastern Ontario relaxed cultural anxiety at the provincial level and allowed the outgoing minister of education to assume smugly in 1896 that the French-language problem in Ontario schools was solved.[16] This assumption was not immediately scrutinized since the eyes of anglophone Canada – and, indeed, the whole nation – had turned to Manitoba, where changing circumstances had engendered yet another cultural challenge to the future of Confederation.[17] In watching authorities attempt to answer the Manitoba Schools Question, Prescott County residents must have had a sense of déjà vu. They must also have been grateful that the national issue had combined with provincial misconceptions and local adjustments to retire, at least for a while, the French-language question as the central political and educational issue in their own lives. The reality of significant language stability ensured, however, that the question would not die.

CONCLUSION

A great deal remains to be learned about the history of francophones in Ontario. The experience of Prescott County shows how research on language, education, and identity reveals webs of relationships still poorly understood. A key question concerns the ways in which the infant of Franco-Ontarian identity eventually developed, finally to be fully acknowledged and named in the 1960s. The preceding study suggests that this process should not be analysed in terms of the "success" or "failure" of individuals to see themselves "accurately" and to act "properly." Rather, the Prescott County evidence emphasizes that ethnic identity emerges from specific historical processes in which individuals come to share common experiences in their efforts to shape the conditions of their lives. Decisions about language go beyond the interests and ambitions of those in authority. Such decisions are ultimately tied to the daily pursuit of material survival and security. Their consideration involves private conversations at home as well as public debates. In this sense, the history of Franco-Ontarian identity is part of the history of family strategies, of children and parents coming to grips with the world they face. This process is a central theme in the cultural drama of Canadian history.

Appendix

This study draws upon a series of computer files which I created from the information of the manuscript census for Alfred Township and Caledonia Township between 1851 and 1881. The personal schedules are available for the four enumerations during this period, but the agricultural schedules are extant for only 1861 and 1871.

I created eight files composed of an individual record for each resident of Alfred and Caledonia at the time of each enumeration. Each individual record includes nine personal variables and thirteen family and household variables:

1	Name	13	Origin of male head of household
2	Household status	14	Origin of female head of household
3	Sex	15	Religion of male head of household
4	Occupation	16	Religion of female head of household
5	Birthplace		
6	Religion	17	Total number of sons in family
7	Origin	18	Total number of daughters in family
8	Age		
9	Attending school?	19	Total number of children in family
10	Family category	20	Owner or tenant of land?
11	Household Category	21	Acres held
12	Occupation of head of household	22	Acres under cultivation

The personal variables (items 1 to 9) were coded as written by the enumerator, with the exception of origin in 1851 and 1861 (when this variable was not on the personal schedule) and household status (which was not one of the census variables in any of the enumerations). To assign an origin label for 1851 and 1861, I limited the possible values to British-Isles origin and French Canadian and considered last name, first name, religion, and place of birth for each resident and his or her family members, if present. I began by assigning the status of British-Isles origin to all residents who had at least one of the following characteristics:

1. Religion was not Catholic.
2. Birthplace was outside North America.
3. Birthplace of a parent, child, or sibling was outside North America.

Residents with none of these characteristics were categorized as British-Isles origin or French Canadian based on my own judgment of their first and last names and the first names of other family members. I tested the accuracy of my judgment and general strategy by performing the same assignment process in the 1871 census records. On a listing for Alfred and Caledonia that did not show the origin values coded from the manuscript census, I assigned a value for each resident based on the criteria described above. After completing this process, I compared the values I had assigned to those actually written by the enumerator. My assignment of origin differed from that of the enumerator's in only seven cases.

My designation of household status was facilitated by the nineteenth-century enumerators' usual practice of listing household members in the following order:

1	Head of house	4	Relatives
2	Spouse	5	Servants
3	Children	6	Boarders

Servants were distinguished from boarders by their occupational classification. Boarders could easily be distinguished from relatives in the 1851 and 1861 censuses by the "family member–non family member" designation. The 1871 and 1881 censuses did not, however, include this variable. To differentiate between relatives and boarders for those years, I followed the general reasoning suggested by Michael Doucet.[1] However, the designation "relative" was treated very conservatively, and I have no doubt that many individuals I listed as boarders were actually relatives, especially of married women in the household.

Record linkage of the Alfred Township enumerations was carried out manually with the aid of hard-copy listings of the computer files and, for 1861 and 1871, maps showing residences as listed in the agricultural census schedules. As always in this whole little science of its own, record linkage was made difficult by the inconsistent spelling of names.[2] The usual solution to this difficulty is to eliminate vowels and standardize consonants so that phonetically similar renditions of the same name can be treated as identical.[3]

This method is helpful, but it is not a complete answer to the problem of Alfred Township since the enumerations include French-Canadian names written by English-language enumerators whose comprehension of French often exceeded their ability to write names, especially in 1851 and 1861; for example, "François" was often written "Fraswa." The enumerators also took certain liberties with their cultural counterparts; one enumerator wrote the name "Noël" as "Christmas." Manual linkage and the use of the residence information from the 1861 and 1871 schedules helped me to overcome these difficulties and permitted linkage of French Canadians between these two enumerations. British-Isles-origin records were linked for the whole period.

In general, the most useful strategy involved attempting to link individuals by consistent reference to their family and household contexts. In the first stage, I attempted to link households and families, rather than individuals or even married couples. This approach added considerably to the number of variables which could be used to establish a link.[4] For example, a possible link between two sets of parents could often be strengthened or weakened by reference to the names and ages of their children. After such links had been decided on, the realm of possibilities for the remaining records was greatly reduced and, thus, the accuracy of the completed linkage was enhanced. Throughout the process, my own familiarity with the files was an enormous aid. Although very large files obviously cannot be dealt with in this way, I have no doubt that estimates of population turnover are always directly related to record-linkage strategies.

In addition to the census data, I also used the information from the extant Hamilton Brothers' employment records to create a file covering the 1856–7 period. Each record contains variables related to sawmill and shanty work, including wages and length of employment. This file could not be linked to other records, however, since names are the only identifying variables in the employment records.

I created the Hamilton Brothers file as well as the 1881 census files on an IBM mainframe at the University of Victoria. The 1851, 1861, and 1871 census files were created on a PDP-9 and PDP-10 at the Ontario Institute for Studies in Education. In all cases, data analysis was done using the Statistical Package for the Social Sciences.

Notes

PREFACE

1 This vast literature includes older works, such as C.B. Sissons, *Bilingual Schools in Canada* (London: J.M. Dent and Sons 1917), and newer studies, such as Paul Crunican, *Priests and Politicians: Manitoba Schools and the Election of 1896* (Toronto: University of Toronto Press 1974).

2 The text of Regulation 17 is included as Appendix VI in George M. Weir, *The Separate School Question in Canada* (Toronto: The Ryerson Press 1934), 286–9.

3 The historiography which discusses the French-language controversy in Ontario includes Franklin A. Walker, *Catholic Education and Politics in Upper Canada* (Toronto: J.M. Dent and Sons 1955), vol. 1; idem, *Catholic Education and Politics in Ontario* (Toronto: Thomas Nelson and Sons 1964); Lionel Groulx, *Les écoles des minorités*, vol. 2 of *L'enseignement français au Canada* (Montreal: Librairie Grarger Frères 1933); Marilyn Barber, "The Ontario Bilingual Schools Issue: Sources of Conflict," *Canadian Historical Review* 47, no. 3 (September 1966): 227–48; Margaret Prang, "Clerics, Politicians, and the Bilingual Schools Issue in Ontario, 1910–1917," *Canadian Historical Review* 41, no. 4 (December 1960): 281–307; Peter Oliver, "The Resolution of the Ontario Bilingual Schools Crisis, 1919–1929," *Journal of Canadian Studies* 7, no. 1 (February 1972); Robert Choquette, *Language and Religion: A History of English-French Conflict in Ontario* (Ottawa: Editions de l'Université d'Ottawa 1975); and Arthur Godbout, *Nos écoles franco-ontariennes: Histoire des écoles de langue française dans l'Ontario des origines du système scolaire (1841) jusqu'à nos jours* (Ottawa: Editions de l'Université d'Ottawa 1980).

4 Danielle Juteau-Lee, "The Franco-Ontarian Collectivity: Material and

Symbolic Dimensions of Its Minority Status," in R. Breton and P. Savard, eds., *The Quebec and Acadian Diaspora in North America* (Toronto: Multicultural History Society of Ontario 1982), 167–82; and Danielle Juteau-Lee and Jean Lapointe, "From French Canadians to Franco-Ontarians and Ontarois: New Boundaries, New Identities," in Jean Leonard Elliott, ed., *Two Nations, Many Cultures: Ethnic Groups in Canada*, 2nd ed. (Scarborough, Ont.: Prentice-Hall Canada 1983), 173–86.

5 A. Gordon Darroch and Michael D. Ornstein, "Ethnicity and Occupational Structures in Canada in 1871: The Vertical Mosaic in Historical Perspective," *Canadian Historical Review* 61, no. 3 (September 1980). Also see idem, "Ethnicity and Class, Transitions over a Decade: Ontario, 1861–1871," Canadian Historical Association, *Historical Papers* (1984), 111–37.

6 Frank Lewis and Marvin McInnis, "The Efficiency of the French-Canadian Farmer in the Nineteenth Century," *Journal of Economic History* 40, no. 3 (September 1980): 497–514. Also see R. Marvin McInnis, "A Reconsideration of the State of Agriculture in Lower Canada in the First Half of the Nineteenth Century," in Donald H. Akenson, ed., *Canadian Papers in Rural History* (Gananoque, Ont.: Langdale Press 1982), 3:9–49.

7 Paul-André Linteau, René Durocher, and Jean-Claude Robert, *Histoire du Québec contemporain : de la Confédération à la crise (1867–1929)* (Montreal: Boréal Express 1979).

8 For example, Lewis and McInnis's research has already been challenged in Robert Armstrong, "The Efficiency of Quebec Farmers in 1851," *Histoire sociale/Social History* 17, no. 33 (May 1984): 149–63.

9 During the past twenty years, intense debate has surrounded the applicability for historical data of statistics devised in other disciplines for nonhistorical data. Beyond agreement on the value of systematic analysis, a consensus has not yet been reached on this issue. The state of current discussion is reflected in *Statistics, Epistemology and History: Part I*, special issue of *Historical Methods* 17, no. 3 (Summer 1984), in particular, Ian Winchester, "History, Scientific History, and Physics," 95–106.

10 Thoughtful discussions include Howard Palmer, "Canadian Immigration and Ethnic History in the 1970s and 1980s," *Journal of Canadian Studies* 17, no. 1 (Spring 1982): 35–50; Roberto Perin, "Clio as an Ethnic: The Third Force in Canadian Historiography," *Canadian Historical Review* 64, no. 4 (December 1983): 441–67; John Higham, "Current Trends in the Study of Ethnicity in the United States," *Journal of American Ethnic History* 2, no. 1 (Fall 1982): 5–15; Olivier Zunz, "The Synthesis of Social Change: Reflections on American Social His-

tory," in Olivier Zunz, ed., *Reliving the Past: The Worlds of Social History* (Chapel Hill and London: University of North Carolina Press 1985), 53–114.

11 William Petersen, "Concepts of Ethnicity" in Stephan Thernstrom, ed., *Harvard Encyclopedia of American Ethnic Groups* (Cambridge, Mass., Harvard University Press 1980), 236.

CHAPTER ONE

1 Cities such as Toronto and Hamilton have been the object of a great deal of recent research. Major studies include Michael B. Katz, *The People of Hamilton, Canada West: Family and Class in a Mid-Nineteenth Century City* (Cambridge, Mass.: Harvard University Press 1975); and Michael B. Katz and Paul H. Mattingly, eds., *Education and Social Change: Themes from Ontario's Past* (New York: New York University Press 1975).

2 For example, see Alison Prentice, *The School Promoters: Education and Social Class in Mid-Nineteenth Century Upper Canada* (Toronto: McClelland and Stewart 1977); and Harvey J. Graff, *The Literacy Myth* (New York: Academic Press 1979).

3 The major studies are Robert Choquette, *Language and Religion: A History of English-French Conflict in Ontario* (Ottawa: Editions de l'Université d'Ottawa 1975); and Arthur Godbout, *Nos écoles franco-ontariennes : Histoire des écoles de langue française dans l'Ontario des origines du système scolaire (1841) jusqu'à nos jours* (Ottawa: Editions de l'Université d'Ottawa 1980).

4 For example, see Charles E. Phillips, *The Development of Education in Canada* (Toronto: Gage 1957).

5 For example, see Prentice, *The School Promoters*.

6 See D. Lawr and R.D. Gidney, "The Development of an Administrative System for the Public Schools: The First Stage, 1841–1850," in Neil McDonald and Alf Chaiton, eds., *Egerton Ryerson and His Times* (Toronto: Macmillan 1978): 160–83; idem, "Who Ran the Schools? Local Influence on Education Policy in Nineteenth Century Ontario," *Ontario History* 72, no. 3 (September 1980): 131–43; idem, "Bureaucracy vs. Community? The Origins of Bureaucratic Procedure in the Upper Canadian School System," *Journal of Social History* 13, no. 3 (Spring 1980):438–57; Bruce Curtis, "Preconditions of the Canadian State: Educational Reform and the Construction of a Public in Upper Canada, 1837–1846," *Studies in Political Economy* no. 10 (Winter 1983): 99–121; and, most recently, Donald Harman Akenson, *The Irish in Ontario: A Study in Rural History* (Kingston and Montreal: McGill-Queen's University Press 1984), especially 268–77.

7 A recent presentation of the traditional argument is James Love, "Cultural Survival and Social Control: The Development of a Curriculum for Upper Canada's Common Schools in 1846," *Histoire sociale/Social History* 15, no. 30 (November 1982): 357–82.

8 For example, see Prentice, *The School Promoters*.

9 Akenson, *The Irish in Ontario*, 268–77; and idem, "Mass Schooling in Ontario: The Irish and 'English Canadian' Popular Culture," in *Being Had: Historians, Evidence, and the Irish in North America* (Don Mills, Ont.: P.D. Meany 1985), 143–87.

10 See Lawr and Gidney, "The Development of an Administrative System."

11 For example, see Choquette, *Language and Religion*; and Marilyn Barber, "The Ontario Bilingual School Issue: Sources of Conflict," *Canadian Historical Review* 47, no. 3 (September 1966):827–48.

12 Meeting of the Council of Public Instruction, 25 April 1851, reported in *Regulations and Correspondence Relating to French and German Schools in the Province of Ontario* (Toronto: Warwick and Sons 1889), 3–7, 3. This volume is a compilation of letters, petitions, and official rulings.

13 Meeting of the Council of Public Instruction, 17 December 1858, reported in *Regulations and Correspondence*, 7.

14 Joseph Denie and Leonder Perout, trustees for the Township of East Hawkesbury, to James Gamble, local superintendent, 19 December 1859, typescript, The Thomas Fischer Rare Book Library, University of Toronto (hereafter, Thomas Fischer Library).

15 Gamble to Ryerson, 27 December 1859, and Ryerson to Gamble, 3 January 1860, typescripts, Thomas Fischer Library.

16 Denie and Perout to Gamble, 19 December 1859, and Ryerson to Gamble, 3 January 1860, typescripts, Thomas Fischer Library.

17 Meeting of the Council of Public Instruction, 9 February 1872, reported in *Regulations and Correspondence*, 12.

18 Donald McLean, John Cattenach, and Angus McDonnell, trustees for the Township of Charlottenburgh, to Ryerson, 16 April 1857, and Ryerson to McLean, Cattenach, and McDonnell, 24 April 1857, typescripts, Thomas Fischer Library.

19 D. Mills, local superintendent of Kent County, to Ryerson, 25 September 1856, and Ryerson to Mills, 8 October 1856, in *Regulations and Correspondence*, 22.

20 Edmund Harrison, local superintendent of Kent County, to Ryerson, 12 December 1865, and Ryerson to Harrison, 15 December 1865, typescripts, Thomas Fischer Library.

21 Ibid.

22 W.S. Lindsay, local superintendant of Essex County, to Ryerson, 24 July 1866; Ryerson to Lindsay, 13 October 1866; and J.M. Bruyère,

bishop of Sandwich, to J.G. Hodgins, Ryerson's assistant, 21 December 1866, in *Regulations and Correspondence*, 22–6.

23 Hodgins to Bruyère, 5 January 1867, ibid., 27.

24 Meeting of the Council of Public Instruction, 20 April 1868, reported in ibid., 27.

25 Hodgins to T.O. Steele, inspector for Prescott County, 26 November 1875, ibid., 27–8.

26 Ryerson to Higginson, private secretary of Sir Charles Metcalf, 8 March 1844, in J. George Hodgins, *Documentary History of Education in Upper Canada* (Toronto: Warwick Bros. and Ratter 1897), 5:108. See also Ryerson to Higginson, 30 April 1845, ibid., 240.

27 Egerton Ryerson, *The Nature and Advantages of an English and Liberal Education*, inaugural speech, Victoria College, Toronto 1846, pamphlet, Public Archives of Ontario (hereafter, PAO).

28 Ryerson to D. D'Everardo, Niagara District, 16 January 1847, R2, C1 Letterbook, PAO.

29 Ryerson, in Hodgins, *Documentary History* 5:108.

30 Prentice, *The School Promoters*, 56.

31 Ibid., 78.

32 Akenson, "Mass Schooling in Ontario," 145.

33 See Donald H. Akenson, *A Protestant in Purgatory: Richard Whately, Archbishop of Dublin* (Hamden, Conn.: Anchor Books 1981).

34 Akenson, *The Irish in Ontario*, 269.

35 *Report of the Speeches delivered by Hon. Mowat, Hon. Geo. W. Ross, and Mr. Evanturel, M.P.P. in the Legislative Assembly, 3 April 1980* (Toronto: Queen's Printer 1890), 5.

36 This sense was, however, used by certain nineteenth-century figures, including the often-quoted Dalton McCarthy, who asked an audience in Barrie, Ontario, in 1887 whether French Canadians "mix with us, assimilate with us, intermarry with us?" Quoted in Craig Brown, "Introduction," in Craig Brown ed., *Minorities, Schools, and Politics* (Toronto: University of Toronto Press 1969), ix.

37 E. Ryerson, "State of Education in Lower Canada," *Journal of Education for Upper Canada*, 1854 (July): 121.

38 Ryerson to John A. Macdonald, MPP., 2 April 1855, in *Copies of Correspondence Between the Chief Superintendent of Schools for Upper Canada and Other Persons on the Subject of Separate Schools* (Toronto, 1855), 54–5.

39 Extract from the report of Thomas Higginson, Ottawa District, in *Annual Report of the Normal, Model, and Common Schools, in Upper Canada for the Year 1848 ... by the Chief Superintendent of Schools* (Quebec 1849), 4. The precise title of the annual report changed frequently; hereafter

each is simply called Annual Report. The reports were published annually (for example, those for 1848 were published in 1849) in whatever city was the provincial capital that year. In most years, an appendix to the report presented extracts from the reports of district superintendents. Unless otherwise indicated, the citations to school reports herein are to these extracts. In addition, the manuscript annual reports of the local superintendents of common schools for the 1850–70 period are available for all the Prescott County Townships: see BG 2, F-3-B, PAO.

40 Upper Canada Annual Report for 1850, Table D, 98–113.

41 John Pattee, Prescott County, Annual Report for 1851, Appendix, 68

42 Thomas Steele, Prescott County, Annual Report for 1872, Appendix, 28; idem, Annual Report for 1873, Appendix, 17.

43 Pattee, Prescott County, Annual Report for 1851, Appendix, 68

44 John McMaster, Prescott County, Annual Report for 1857, Appendix, 149.

45 Humphrey Hughes, Alfred Township, Annual Report for 1858, Appendix, 6.

46 Higginson, Ottawa District, Annual Report for 1848, Appendix, 4; Pattee, Prescott County Annual Report for 1851, Appendix, 69; William Edwards, Clarence Township Annual Report for 1858, Appendix, 7.

47 Hughes, Alfred Township, Annual Report for 1861, Appendix, 159.

48 Steele, Prescott County, Annual Report for 1871, Appendix, 24–5.

49 Idem, Annual Report for 1872, Appendix, 29.

50 Idem, Annual Report for 1873, Appendix, 17.

51 Toronto *Mail*, 10, 11, and 25 December 1886. For a late nineteenth-century report on French Canadians in southwestern Ontario, see Télèsphore Sainte-Pierre, *Histoire des Canadiens du Michigan et du comté d'Essex, Ontario* (Montreal: La Gazette 1895).

52 See Brown, "Introduction," ix.

53 *History of the Bi-Lingual Schools in Ontario*, pamphlet for "distribution among Public School Supporters," (1910?), 9; and G.W. Ross, "Instructions to Teachers of French Schools, Public and Separate," September 1885, in *Regulations and Correspondence*, 39. As late as 1887, the inspector for Prescott and Russell counties was still totally confused about the implications of the 1885 regulations. He was forced to admit that even with bilingual teachers in place, he was "not quite certain whether it is intended that every child in school is to learn English during his whole school career, or whether he is first to learn the elements of French reading." These kinds of questions also stymied Ross, who, in turn, asked the inspector if he could envision a reason-

able solution to his own dilemma. W.J. Summerby, inspector for Prescott and Russell counties, to A. Marling, secretary of the Education Department, 25 June 1887, and Marling to Summerby, 29 June 1887, in *Regulations and Correspondence*, 4.

54 "Regulations Approved by the Education Department in August 1885," ibid., 13–14.

55 Toronto *Mail*, 21 December 1886 and 18 April 1887.

56 "Historical Sketch of Prescott and Russell," *The Prescott and Russell Supplement of the Illustrated Atlas of the Dominion of Canada* (Toronto: H. Belden 1881; Owen Sound, Ont.: Richardson, Bond and Wright 1972), 58.

57 Toronto *Mail*, 24 November 1886.

58 Marling to Summerby, 14 June 1886, and Summerby to Marling, 15 November 1886, in *Regulations and Correspondence*, 15.

59 Ross to Wm. Crockett, superintendent of education, Fredericton, New Brunswick, 10 January 1888, ibid., 47–8.

60 In one instance, however, the Prescott and Russell inspector did have some positive suggestions, although he wrongly implied that bilingual teachers were frequently available; see Summerby to Marling, 14 July 1887, ibid., 42.

61 Ibid., 39.

62 Ross to Summerby, 20 September 1887, ibid., 45.

63 Legislative Assembly of Ontario, *Newspaper Hansard*, 18 April 1887.

64 *Report of the Speeches ... 3 April 1890*, 5

65 *Speech delivered by Hon. Geo. W. Ross, Minister of Education, in the Legislative Assembly of Ontario*, 8 March 1889, 12.

66 Ibid., 6.

67 Ibid., 15.

68 Ibid.

69 Ross to Summerby and O. Dufort, 21 February 1889 and Dufort to Ross, 25 February 1889; in *Regulations and Correspondence*, 49–50: See also Toronto *Mail*, 19 March 1889.

70 Toronto *Mail*, 21 March 1889.

71 G.W. Ross, "Commission on French Schools," in *Regulations and Correspondence*, 51.

72 "Report of the Commission on French Language Public Schools in Ontario, 1889," ibid., 55, 63.

73 Ibid., 53, 55.

74 Ibid., 62.

75 G.W. Ross, "Instructions to Teachers and Trustees of French-English Schools," 17 October 1889. The approved bilingual readers were those used in Nova Scotia and New Brunswick. They were "accidentally"

discovered by Ross in the late 1880s and thereafter promoted for use in French-language schools. See Legislative Assembly of Ontario, *Newspaper Hansard*, 5 April 1889.

76 Dufort to Ross, 18 October 1889, and Summerby to Ross, 7 October 1889, in *Regulations and Correspondence*, 19–21.

77 P.J. Potts et al., North Plantagenet Trustees, to Summerby, 18 October 1889, ibid., 105–9.

78 *Report of Commissioners on Schools in the Counties of Prescott and Russell in Which the French Language Is Taught* (Toronto 1893), 5–19.

79 G.W. Ross, *The School System of Ontario* (New York: D. Appleton 1896), 67–9.

80 *Speech delivered by Hon. Geo. W. Ross*, 6.

81 *Report of the Speeches ... 3 April 1890*, 5.

82 See Toronto *Globe*, 1 December 1911.

83 Toronto *Daily Star*, 20 and 22 November 1911.

CHAPTER TWO

1 For example, Franklin A. Walker, *Catholic Education and Politics in Ontario: A Documentary Study* (Toronto: Thomas Nelson and Sons 1964); Marilyn Barber, "The Ontario Bilingual Schools Issue: Sources of Conflict," *Canadian Historical Review* 47, no. 3 (September 1966): 227–48; Robert Choquette, *Language and Religion: A History of English-French Conflict in Ontario* (Ottawa: Editions de l'Université d'Ottawa 1975); and Arthur Godbout, *Nos écoles franco-ontariennes: Histoire des écoles de langue française dans l'Ontario des origines du système scolaire (1841) jusqu'à nos jours* (Ottawa: Editions de l'Université d'Ottawa 1980).

2 Toronto *Mail*, 10, 11, and 14 December 1886.

3 Ibid., 15 and 25 December 1886.

4 The geographic dimensions of settlement are documented in Gaetan Vallières and Marcien Villemure, *Atlas de l'Ontario français* (Montreal and Paris: Editions Etudes Vivantes 1981).

5 The manuscript censuses are available in the Public Archives of Ontario (PAO). Hereafter, the manuscript censuses are identified by year but with no citation.

6 A. Gordon Darroch offers an insightful commentary on recent studies of migration in "Migrants in the Nineteenth Century: Fugitives or Families in Motion?" *Journal of Family History*, 6 no. 3 (Fall 1981): 257–77.

7 These and the following examples are drawn from local histories, which are helpful although not always accurate. The examples used are consistent with other sources. The local histories are Lucien Brault, *Histoire de comtés unis de Prescott et de Russell* (L'Orignal, Ont. 1965); C.

Thomas, *History of the Counties Argenteuil, Quebec and Prescott, Ontario* (Montreal: John Lovell and Son 1896; Belleville, Ont.: Mika Publishing 1981); Alan Douglas MacKinnon, *The Story of Vankleek Hill and the Surrounding Area*, vol. 1 (Belleville, Ont. Mika Publishing 1979); and William R. Byers, *The Church on the Hill* (Hawkesbury, Ont.: Holy Trinity Men's Club 1981).

8 The arrival of family units in Prescott County was part of a migratory phenomenon that has been noted in other local studies. John Mannion shows it, for example, in the Irish settlement of nearby Peterborough during the 1820s and 1830s; see *Irish Settlements in Eastern Canada: A Study of Cultural Transfer and Adaptation* (Toronto: University of Toronto Press 1974), 42–4. Peter Kenneth MacLeod emphasizes the importance of family and kin in the Scottish "shoulder to shoulder" settlement of Charlottenburg Township in Glengarry County, as well as in other Ontario communities, in "Gualainn Ri Gualainn: A Study of Concentrations of Scottish Settlement in Nineteenth Century Ontario" (MA thesis, University of Ottawa 1972). Valuable recent studies include Marianne McLean, "In the New Land a New Glengarry: Migration from the Scottish Highlands to Upper Canada, 1750–1820" (PH D thesis, University of Edinburgh 1982). The detailed work of Bruce S. Elliott traces Irish settlements, such as those discussed in "Migration and Stability amongst the Tipperary Protestants of the Ottawa Valley" (paper presented to the Canadian Historical Association, Ottawa 1982). Similarly, G. Lockwood shows the value of local history in "Irish Immigrants and the 'Critical Years' in Eastern Ontario: The Case of Montague Township, 1821–1881," in D.H. Akenson, ed., *Canadian Papers in Rural History* (Gananoque, Ont: Langdale Press 1984), 4: 153–78.

For a discussion of theoretical issues, see John Mogey, "Residence, Family, Kinship: Some Recent Research," *Journal of Family History* 1, no. 1 (Autumn 1976): 95–105. On the importance of kin in the initial settlement of an American frontier community in the nineteenth century, see Robert E. Bieder, "Kinship as a Factor in Migration," *Journal of Marriage and The Family* 35, no. 3 (August 1973): 429–39. The extent of family migration in North America is stressed by Darroch in "Migrants in the Nineteenth Century." The larger context of Scottish immigration is discussed in James M. Cameron, "Scottish Emigration to Upper Canada, 1815–1855: A Study of Process," in W. Peter Adams and Frederick Helleiner, eds., *International Geography* 1972 (Toronto: University of Toronto Press 1972), 1:404–6. Donald H. Akenson surveys the established literature and provides a revised framework for understanding Irish immigration and settlement in "Ontario: Whatever Happened to the Irish?" in Donald H. Akenson, ed., *Canadian*

Papers in Rural History (Gananoque, Ont.: Langdale Press, 1982), 3:204–56.

9 For brief histories of many of the communities in Prescott County, see Brault, *Histoire des comtés*, 189–277; and *The Prescott and Russell Supplement of the Illustrated Atlas of the Dominion of Canada* (Toronto: H. Belden 1881; Owen Sound, Ont.: Richardson, Bond and Wright 1972).

10 For biographical details on the Hamiltons and the Higginsons, see Byers, *The Church on The Hill*.

11 For more on the Highland migration to Glengarry County, see Marianne McLean, "Peopling Glengarry County: The Scottish Origins of a Canadian Community," Canadian Historical Association, *Historical Papers*, (1982), 156–71.

12 John S. Bigsby, *The Shoe and Canoe* (London 1850, New York: Paladin Press 1969), 66.

13 Certain features of French-Canadian settlement in Prescott County are carefully examined in Donald G. Cartwright, "French-Canadian Colonization in Eastern Ontario to 1910" (PHD thesis, University of Western Ontario 1973); see also idem, "Institutions on the Frontier: French Canadian Settlement in Eastern Ontario in the Nineteenth Century," *Canadian Geographer* 21, no. 1 (Spring 1977): 1–21. A comparative perspecitve on the importance of family within the migration process is offered by the historiography of Quebec emigration to New England, which shows that families learned of opportunities through kin as well as newspaper advertisements and consequently moved to specific towns such as Lowell, Massachusetts, and Manchester, New Hampshire. This historiography includes Ralph D. Viscero, "Immigration of French Canadians to New England, 1840–1900: A Geographical Analysis" (PHD thesis, University of Wisconsin 1968) and continues with such recent work as Frances H. Early, "French-Canadian Beginnings in an American Community: Lowell, Massachusetts, 1868–1886" (PHD thesis, Concordia University 1980). The most extensive research on kinship and the family among French Canadians in New England has been undertaken by Tamara K. Hareven, who has been a major force in establishing the family as a principal focus of historical investigation. The works include Tamara K. Hareven, *Family Time and Industrial Time: The Relationship between Family and Work in a New England Industrial Community* (Cambridge: Cambridge University Press 1982); and Tamara K. Hareven and Randolph Langenbach, *Amoskeag: Life and Work in an American Factory Town* (New York: Pantheon 1978).

14 The Alfred Township evidence closely resembles the findings of E.Z. Massicotte, who conducted a contemporary examination of French-

Canadian emigration from Quebec's Champlain County in the late nineteenth century. Most of these French-Canadian emigrants settled in New England. Although rarely utilized by historians, Massicotte's study is one of the few empirical investigations of the nature of French-Canadian migration in the nineteenth century. In studying Champlain County during the 1880–92 period, Massicotte found that the movement of established families accounted for the vast majority of French-Canadian emigration. A full 72 per cent of the 1,995 emigrants from Champlain during these years left in family groups that included children. The proportion of single male migrants reached only 10.1 per cent, while single females formed an insignificant 0.5 of the French-Canadian departure. Massicotte's findings are presented in "L'émigration aux Etats-Unis mais il y a quarante ans et plus," *Bulletin de recherches historiques*, vols. 39 and 40, cited in Yolande Lavoie, *L'émigration des Canadiens aux Etats-Unis avant 1930* (Montreal: Les Presses de l'Université de Montréal 1972), 59.

The Alfred Township data cannot be directly compared to Massicotte's evidence because we can garner from the census only estimates of family and individual migration.

15 The distinction between relatives and unrelated boarders is indicated in the 1851 and 1861 enumerations but not thereafter; for a discussion of this problem, see the appendix. The distinction is emphasized in Sheva Medjuck, "The Importance of Boarding for the Structure of the Household in the Nineteenth Century," *Histoire sociale/Social History* 13, no. 25 (May 1980):207–13.

Since the early 1970s, analysts have repeatedly emphasized the importance of family and household structure, particularly as a result of several provocative works: Peter Laslett and Richard Wall, eds., *Household and Family in Past Time* (Cambridge: Cambridge University Press 1972); Michael Anderson, *Family Structure in Nineteenth Century Lancashire* (Cambridge: Cambridge University Press 1971); and Lutz Berkner, "The Stem Family and the Development Cycle of the Peasant Household: An Eighteenth Century Austrian Example," *American Historical Review* 77, no. 2 (April 1972): 398–418. For a survey of developments during the 1970s, see Michael Anderson, *Approaches to the History of the Western Family 1500–1914* (London: Macmillan 1980), especially 17–38. Canadian evidence is presented in A. Gordon Darroch and Michael D. Ornstein, "The Regional Economy of Family and Household in Nineteenth Century Canada" (paper presented to the annual meeting of the American Sociological Association, 6 September 1982); David Gagan, *Hopeful Travellers: Families, Land and Social Change in Mid-Victorian Peel County, Canada West* (Toronto: University of Toronto Press 1981), chap. 4; and Sheva Medjuck, "Family and Household in the Nineteenth Century: The Case of Moncton, New Brunswick 1851–1871," *Canadian Journal of Sociology* 4, no. 3 (Summer 1979): 275–86.

16 Comparative perspectives are provided by Gordon Darroch and Michael D. Ornstein in "Family Coresidence in Canada in 1871: Family Life-Cycles, Occupations and Networks of Mutual Aid," Canadian Historical Associations, *Historical Papers* (1983), 30–55; and Bettina Bradbury, "The Family Economy and Work in an Industrializing City: Montreal in the 1870s," Canadian Historical Association, *Historical Papers* (1979), 71–96. It should be remembered that the actual migration of families into Prescott County undoubtedly often took forms other than the single movement of a united family. For example, the head of household may have preceded and prepared for the arrival of other family members.

Boarding has also been closely associated with economic and psychological transitions to adulthood. For example, for late nineteenth-century Boston, Modell and Hareven find that although the frequency of boarding in the city's South End was related to the area's function as a "depository for most newly-arrived immigrants," boarding also played a large role in the lives of native-born Americans. They conclude that "the practice of boarding" was a "function of the life-cycle" and suggest that a full one-third to one-half of all individuals represented in their data boarded in advance of formation of their own households. See John Modell and Tamara Hareven, "Urbanization and the Malleable Household: An Examination of Boarding and Lodging in American Families," *Journal of Marriage and the Family* 35, no. 30 (August 1973): 467–79, especially 471–3.

Similarly, Michael Katz does not explain boarding in mid-nineteenth-century Hamilton, Ontario, by reference to an influx of Irish immigrants but rather argues that a few years away from home served as a life-cycle stage for adolescents who were anticipating marriage. By boarding in an unfamiliar household, Katz believes that young men and women had the opportunity to experience some autonomy and thereby to prepare themselves psychologically for formation of their own homes. Katz considers the possibility that boarders were simply "young immigrants on their own" but rejects this explanation after estimating that most of the boarders' own families were also present in Hamilton; sons and daughters apparently left home after arrival in Canada with their families. Thus, in midcentury Hamilton, "most young people spent some time living in a semi-autonomous state in a household other than their parents'. This period intervened between leaving school and getting married." Michael Katz, *The People of Hamilton, Canada West: Family and Class in a Mid-Nineteenth Century*

City, (Cambridge, Mass.: Harvard University Press 1975), 264–5, 290.

In Alfred Township, boarding does not seem to have followed the same pattern as it did in either Boston or Hamilton since female boarding was consistently infrequent and male boarding rapidly diminished in importance after 1851.

17 Recent examples of studies of such data include Sune Akerman, "Swedish Migration and Social Mobility: The Tale of Three Cities," *Social Science History* 1, no. 2 (Winter 1977): 178–209; and L. Eriksson and J. Rogers, "Rural Labor and Population Change: Social and Demographic Developments in East-Central Sweden during the Nineteenth Century" (PHD thesis, University of Uppsala 1978). Darrell A. Norris analyses an unusual collection of annual census data in "Household and Transiency in a Loyalist Township: The People of Adolphustown, 1784–1822," *Histoire sociale/Social History*, 13, no. 26 (November 1980):399–415. Also see Bruce S. Elliott, "The Famous Township of Hull: Image and Aspirations of a Pioneer Quebec Community," *Histoire sociale/Social History*, 12, no. 24 (November 1979): 339–67. Important studies of geographic mobility as suggested by the decennial census include David Gagan, "Geographical and Social Mobility in Nineteenth Century Ontario: A Microstudy," *Canadian Review of Sociology and Anthropology* 13, no. 2 (May 1976): 152–64. Michael B. Katz, Michael J. Doucet, and Mark J. Stern, "Population Persistence and Early Industrialization in a Canadian City: Hamilton, Ontario, 1851–1871," *Social Science History* 2, no. 2 (Winter 1978): 208–29; and Christian Pouyez, Raymond Roy, and Gérard Bouchard, "La mobilité géographique en milieu rural: Le Saguenay, 1852–1861," *Histoire sociale/Social History* 14, no. 27 (May 1981): 123–55.

18 The agricultural schedules list lot and concession numbers, and although the evidence is not always complete, they provide valuable points of reference for record-linkage between 1861 and 1871. Unfortunately, neither the 1851 nor the 1881 agricultural schedules are extant. For a discussion of the record-linkage, used for this study, see the appendix.

19 For comparison, see David Gagan, "The Indivisibility of Land: A Microanalysis of the System of Inheritance in Nineteenth-Century Ontario," *Journal of Economic History* 36, no. 1 (March 1976): 126–41; and Gérard Bouchard, "Family Structures and Geographic Mobility at Laterrière, 1851–1935," *Journal of Family History* 2, no. 4 (Winter 1977): 350–69. The physical difficulty of family migration is reflected in the well-known "laws of migration" formulated by E.G. Ravenstein in the late nineteenth century. Ravenstein's seventh "law" states that "most migrants are adults: families rarely migrate out of their county of birth." See D.B. Grigg, "E.G. Ravenstein and The 'Laws of Migra-

tion'," *Journal of Historical Geography* 3, no. 1 (January 1977): 41–54, 42.

20 The distinction between demographic homeostasis based on balanced fertility and morality and constant population size based on both migration and vital rates is relevant to R.S. Schofield, "The Relationship between Demographic Structure and Environment in Pre-Industrial Western Europe," in W. Conze, ed., *Sozial Geschichte de Familie in der Europas* (Stuttgart: Klett 1977), 147–60: and D.S. Smith, "A Homeostatic Demographic Regime: Patterns in West European Family Reconstitution Studies," in R.D. Lee, *Population Patterns in the Past* (New York: Academic Press 1977), 19–51. For a comparative perspective on the relationship between population size and migration patterns, see David Gagan, "Land, Population, and Social Change: The 'Critical Years' in Rural Canada West," *Canadian Historical Review* 59, no. 3 (September 1978): 293–318. Calvin J. Veltman examines the way in which French-Canadian migration changed the cultural geography of a rural Quebec community in "Demographic Components of the Francisation of Rural Québec: The Case of Rawdon," *American Review of Canadian Studies* 6 no. 2 (Autumn 1976): 22–41.

21 *Census of Canada*, 1901.

22 The demography of migration from Quebec to the United States is examined in Yolande Lavoie, *L'émigration des Canadiens aux Etats-Unis avant 1930* (Montreal: Les Presses de l'Université de Montréal 1972). A bibliography of Franco-American studies is presented by Gérard J. Brault, "Etat présent des études sur les centres franco-américains de la Nouvelle-Angleterre," in C. Quintal and A. Vachon, eds., *Situation de la recherche sur la franco-américanie* (Quebec: Le Conseil de la vie française en Amérique 1980); 9–25. Brief discussions of French-Canadian settlement outside Quebec are included in Raymond Breton and Pierre Savard, eds., *The Quebec and Acadian Diaspora in North America* (Toronto: Multicultural History Society of Ontario 1982). For analysis of francophone settlement in western Canada in later years, see Robert Painchaud, "The Franco-Canadian Communities in Western Canada since 1945," in David Jay Bercuson and Phillip A. Buckner, eds., *Eastern and Western Perspectives* (Toronto: University of Toronto Press 1981), 3–18.

23 See A.N. Lalonde, "L'intelligensia au Québec et la migration des Canadiens français vers l'Ouest canadien, 1870–1930," *Revue d'histoire de l'Amerique française* 33, no. 2 (September 1979): 163–85; Robert Painchaud, "French-Canadian Historiography and Franco-Catholic Settlement in Western Canada, 1870–1915," *Canadian Historical Review* 59, no. 4 (December 1978: 447–66); and A.I. Silver, *The French-Ca-*

nadian Idea of Confederation, 1864–1900 (Toronto: University of Toronto Press 1982).

CHAPTER THREE

1 A detailed analysis of this type of economy is undertaken in Norman Séguin, *La Conquête du sol au 19e. siècle* (Sillery, Que: Boréal 1977); in it Séguin develops the approach taken earlier in Raoul Blanchard, *L'est du Canada français* (Montreal: Librairie Beauchemin Limitée 1935) 2 vols. A summary of Séguin's view is offered in "L'economie agroforestière: genèse du développement au Saguenay au 19e siècle," in Normand Séguin, ed., *Agriculture et colonisation au Québec* (Montreal: Boréal Express 1980), 159–64. Also see René Hardy and Normand Séguin, *Forêt et société en Mauricie* (Montreal: Boréal 1984); Gérard Bouchard, "Family Strategies and Geographic Mobility at Laterrière, 1851–1935," *Journal of Family History* 2, no. 4 (Winter 1977): 350–69; idem, "Démographie et société rurale au Saguenay 1851–1935," *Recherches Sociographiques* 19, no. 1 (January-April 1978): 7–31; John Willis, "Fraserville and Its Témiscouata Hinterland 1874–1914; Colonization and Urbanization in a Peripheral Region of the Province of Québec" (MA thesis, Université du Québec à Trois-Rivières 1981); and Graeme Wynn, *Timber Colony: A Historical Geography of Early Nineteenth Century New Brunswick* (Toronto: University of Toronto Press 1981). The Ottawa Valley lumber industry is examined in Michael S. Cross, "The Dark Druidical Groves: The Lumber Community and the Commercial Frontier in British North America to 1854" (PHD thesis, University of Toronto, 1968); and Sandra J. Gillis, *The Timber Trade in the Ottawa Valley, 1806–1854* (Ottawa: National Historic Parks and Sites Branch, Parks Canada 1975).

2 The standard general surveys of this period are A.R.M. Lower, *Settlement and the Forest Frontier in Eastern Canada* (Toronto: Macmillan 1936); and idem, *The North American Assault on the Canadian Forest* (Toronto: Ryerson 1938).

3 A variety of studies reveal an intricate interaction between cultural groups and their material environment in new rural areas. Scholars show that the frontier did not simply homogenize settlers from different backgrounds but rather was transformed by them in ways distinguished by what Rice terms "ethnic community"; see John G. Rice, "The Role of Culture and Community in Frontier Prairie Farming," *Journal of Historical Geography* 3, no. 2 (April 1977), 155–75. Also, see Frederick C. Luebke, ed., *Ethnicity on the Great Plains* (Lincoln, Neb.: University of Nebraska Press 1980); and Robert F. Berkhofer, "Space,

Time, Culture and the New Frontier," *Agriculture History* 38, no. 1 (January 1964): 21–30.

4 The importance of analysing the family in terms of the changing economy of the nineteenth century is demonstrated in recent research on both rural and urban areas. The most extensive rural study of the family in Ontario is David Gagan, *Hopeful Travellers: Families, Land, and Social Change in Mid-Victorian Peel County, Canada West* (Toronto: University of Toronto Press 1981).

5 A discussion of the enumerator's instructions for 1861 and 1852, as well as the original documents, are presented in David P. Gagan, "Enumerator's Instructions for the Census of Canada 1852 and 1861," *Histoire sociale/Social History* 7, no. 14 (November 1974): 355–65. The 1871 instructions were published as *Manual Containing "The Census Act" and the Instructions to Officers Employed in the Taking of the First Census of Canada*, 1871 and are now 98-1871 in the *Historical Catalogue of Statistics Canada Publications, 1918–1980* (Ottawa 1981).

After examining data for Peel County, David Gagan concludes that "whatever occupational mobility transpired in this community was primarily in one direction, towards the status of rural operator." He finds that "more than a quarter of the persistent heads of household in any vocational category in 1852 had become farmers nine years later." "Geographical and Social Mobility in Nineteenth Century Ontario: A Microstudy," *Canadian Review of Sociology and Anthropology* 13, no. 2 (May 1976): 152–64, 160.

Similarly, Gérard Bouchard suggests in his research on Saguenay that the cash income received by young French Canadians who worked in the forest during the winter facilitated accumulation of sufficient capital to establish their own farms. In his analysis, lumbering was in part a life-course experience which preceded marriage and formation of a separate household; see "Introduction à l'étude de la société saguenayenne aux xixe et xxe siècles," *Revue d'histoire de l'Amérique française* 31, no. 1 (June 1977): 3–27.

Tamara Hareven discusses recent American research on the interrelationships of individual and family life-cycles within the context of larger social patterns; see "Family Time and Historical Time," *Daedalus*, 106, no. 2 (Spring 1977): 57–70. See also John Modell, Frank Furstenburg, and Theodore Hershberg, "Social Change and Transitions to Adulthood in Historical Perspective," *Journal of Family History* 1, no. 1 (Autumn 1976): 7–32.

For a discussion of the interrelationships between origin and occupation throughout Canada, see A. Gordon Darroch and Michael D. Ornstein, "Ethnicity and Occupational Structure in Canada in 1871: The Vertical Mosaic in Historical Perspective," *Canadian Historical Review* 61, no. 3 (September 1980): 305–33.

6 There is no doubt that the actual number of employed women some-what exceeded the occupational listings of the census. For example, the 1861 census lists only three female teachers in Caledonia Town-ship, but the educational records suggest that six women taught school there that year. Such discrepancies resulted partly from the male enumerators' reluctance to attribute occupations to females but also partly from the "snapshot" quality of the census: only three women actually held teaching employment in Caledonia at the time of the census and thus only three received occupational titles.

Public recognition of the productive role of women in rural family economies is still very limited according to the National Farmers' Union Women's Advisory Committee, which has recently charged that the 1981 census enumeration grossly underestimated the female economic contribution; see "Farmers' Wives Dispute Census," *Toronto Globe and Mail*, 4 March 1983, p. 13.

7 The productive opportunities for children are discussed in more detail in Chad M. Gaffield, "Schooling, the Economy, and Rural Society in Nineteenth-Century Ontario," in Joy Parr, ed., *Childhood and Family in Canadian History* (Toronto: McClelland and Stewart 1982), 69–92. Valuable systematic analysis of the relationship of children to the concept of family economy in Canada West has been presented by R. Marvin McInnis in a series of papers, including "Childbearing and Land Availability: Some Evidence from Individual Household Data," in Ronald Dennis Lee, ed., *Population Patterns in the Past* (New York: Academic Press 1977): 201–27.

8 Thomas Tweed Higginson, *Diaries of Thomas Tweed Higginson*, ed. Thomas Boyd Higginson (London: The Research Publishing Com-pany 1960) 8.

9 Alexis de Barbezieux, *Histoire de la province ecclésiastique d'Ottawa* (Ottawa 1897), 1: 287.

10 Manuscript census, Prescott County, 1871. Also see William Greening, *The Ottawa* (Toronto: McClelland and Stewart 1961), 69. The very complex role of women within the family economy is well summarized for the case of France in Olwen Hufton, "Women and the Family Economy in Eighteenth-Century France," *French Historical Studies* 9, no. 1 (Spring 1975): 1–22. Also see Joan W. Scott and Louise A. Tilly, "Women's Work and the Family in Nineteenth-Century Europe," *Comparative Studies in Society and History* 17, no. 1 (January 1975): 36–64; and Louise A. Tilly, Joan W. Scott, and Miriam Cohen, "Women's Work and European Fertility Patterns," *Journal of Interdisciplinary History* 6, no. 3 (Winter 1976): 447–76. The changing nineteenth-century agricultural context of women's work is discussed provocatively in Michael Roberts, "Sickles and Scythes: Women's Work and Men's Work at Harvest Time," *History Workshop* no. 7 (Spring 1979): 3–28; and

Bengt Ankarloo, "Agriculture and Women's Work: Directions of Change in the West 1700–1900," *Journal of Family History* 4, no. 2 (Summer 1979): 111–20.

11 Local studies and general surveys consistently conclude that the native-born and the immigrant, the rich and the poor had at least one common ambition in mid-nineteenth-century North America: they all wanted to own land. See, for example, R. Cole Harris, Pauline Roulston, and Chris de Freitzs, "The Settlement of Mono Township," *Canadian Geographer* 19, no. 1 (Spring 1975): 1–17; Cole Harris, "Of Poverty and Helplessness in Petite Nation," *Canadian Historical Review* 52, no. 1 (March 1971): 23–50; and David Gagan, " 'The Prose of Life': Literary Reflections of the Family, Individual Experience and Social Structure in Nineteenth-Century Canada," *Journal of Social History* 9, no. 3 (January 1976): 367–81. The desire for land was based on the belief that it was the most trustworthy hedge against the vicissitudes of an uncertain economy; see David P. Gagan, "The Security of Land," in F. H. Armstrong, H.A. Stevenson, and J.D. Wilson, eds., *Aspects of Nineteenth Century Ontario* (Toronto: University of Toronto Press 1974); 135–53.

12 See L.S. Chapman and J.G. Putnam, "The Soils of Eastern Ontario," *Scientific Agriculture* 20, no. 7 (March 1940): 424–41; and R.E. Wicklund and N.R. Richards, *Soil Survey of Russell and Prescott Counties* (Guelph, Ont.: Canada Department of Agriculture 1962).

Settler evaluation of land was an initial step in the process of agricultural settlement; see Kenneth Kelly, "The Impact of Nineteenth Century Agricultural Settlement on the Land," in J. David Wood, ed., *Perspectives on Landscape and Settlement in Nineteenth Century Ontario* (Toronto: McClelland and Stewart, 1975), 64–77. For a general discussion of the importance of custom and tradition to the assessment of ecological characteristics, see A. Spoehr, "Cultural Differences in the Interpretation of Natural Resources," in W.L. Thomas, *Man's Role in Changing the Face of the Earth* (Chicago: University of Chicago Press 1956): 93–102. *Prescott and Russell Supplement of the Illustrated Atlas of the Dominion of Canada* (Toronto: H. Beldin 1881; Owen Sound, Ont.: Richardson, Bond and Wright 1972), 58.

14 Max Rosenthal, "Early Post Offices of Prescott County," *B.N.A. Topics* 24, no. 1:21.

15 See Edwin C. Guillet, *The Pioneer Farmer and Backwoodsman* (Toronto: Ontario Publishing Company 1963), 1:274; and Kelly, "The Impact of Agricultural Settlement," 64–5.

Contemporary writers were also concerned about the health implications of settlement in marshy areas. Ague, a malaria fever known to be fatal, was associated with regions of wet soil.

16 Joseph Tassé, *La vallée de l'Outaouais: sa condition géographique* (Montreal 1873), 7, 9; *Supplement of the Illustrated Atlas*, 58.

17 A. Labelle, *Projet d'une société de colonisation du diocèse de Montréal pour coloniser la vallée de l'Ottawa et le nord de ce diocèse* (Montreal 1879).

18 Donald G. Cartwright, "French Canadian Colonization in Eastern Ontario to 1910" (PHD thesis, University of Western Ontario 1973), 230–1. Systematic evidence on settlement patterns during the first half of the nineteenth century is presented for the eastern half of Prescott County in Jessie Turner Weldon, "The Salient Factors Contributing to the Earliest Settlement Patterns in East and West Hawkesbury Townships, Upper Canada, 1788–1846" (MA thesis, Carleton University 1980).

19 Local residents were well aware of the importance of the river road especially as a balance to north-shore development. In the early nineteenth century, Hawkesbury residents recognized that they had to improve road facilities along the river in response to similar activity on the opposite shore. As a result of a meeting in the tavern, they agreed that "without the road, their lands would be worthless – that trade and transport would fix on the opposite bank – and that they would be ruined." An assessment for the road was decided on, and the improvements were carried out. John J. Bigsby, *The Shoe and the Canoe* (London 1850; New York: Paladin Press 1969) 1: 67–8.

20 Weldon, *The Salient Factors*, 113.

21 T. P. French, *Information for Intending Settlers on the Ottawa and Opeongo Road and Its Vicinity* (Ottawa 1857), 26; A. Labelle, *Pamphlet sur la colonization dans la vallée d'Ottawa* (Montreal 1880), 3.

22 Duncan McDowell, deputy-surveyor to the Canada Company, "Report on the Townships in the Ottawa District," 21 September 1827, reprinted in Andrew Picken, *The Canadas, as They at Present Commend Themselves to the Enterprize of Emigrants, Colonists, and Capitalists* ... (London: E. Wilson 1832), 130–44, 137–80. Also see N.R. Crothall, "French Canadian Agriculture in Ontario, 1861–1871: A Study of Cultural Transfer" (MA thesis, University of Toronto 1968).

The most complete description of the soil of Quebec in the nineteenth century is contained in the work of J. Bouchette, the surveyor-general of Lower Canada in the early decades of the century; see *A Topographical Description of the Province of Lower Canada* (London 1815); *General Report of an Official Tour through the New Settlements of the Province of Lower Canada* ... (Quebec 1825); and *A Topographical Dictionary of the Province of Lower Canada* (London 1832).

23 Weldon, *The Salient Factors*, 123. Lord Durham had observed that the "English farmer carried with him the experience and habits of the most improved agriculture in the world ... He often took the very

farm which the [French] Canadian settlers had abandoned, and, by superior management, made that a source of profit which had only impoverished his predecessor." Quoted in Robert Leslie Jones, "French-Canadian Agriculture in the St. Lawrence Valley, 1815–1850," *Agricultural History* 16, no. 3 July 1942): 138. Even if Durham's observation was accurate, the reverse was also true, at least in Prescott County.

Marvin McInnis in collaboration with Frank Lewis challenges conventional assumptions about efficiency in Quebec agriculture in a series of articles: "The Efficiency of the French-Canadian Farmer in the Nineteenth Century," *Journal of Economic History* 40, no. 3 (September 1980): 497–514; and "Agricultural Output and Efficiency in Lower Canada, 1851," *Research in Economic History* 9, (1983): 45–87. McInnis responds to various criticisms in "A Further Look at French and Non-French Farming in Lower Canada" (paper prepared for a conference, "The Forgotten Majority," University of Victoria, 23–5 February 1984).

24 Manuscript census for Alfred Township, 1851.
25 Manuscript census for Caledonia Township, 1851.
26 *Supplement of the Illustrated Atlas*, 60.
27 The value of land in Alfred and Caledonia townships was given by the 1851 enumerators, who agreed that settled farms could be "estimated in value at from one to two pounds per acre," while unsettled land cost five to thirty shillings per acre. (British funds were readily accepted in Canada until 1853, when the Canadian dollar was made the legal currency; at midcentury, the pound was worth $4.86.)

In certain townships, land had to be bought from absentee landlords, many of whom were Montreal merchants. In the early nineteenth century, some observers considered these landlords a major cause of Prescott County's slow development; see, for example, the material quoted in W.H. Smith, *Canada: Past, Present and Future* (Toronto 1851), 2:376.

The interrelationships among economic opportunity, age-at-marriage, and family size are explored for England in David Levine, *Family Formation in an Age of Nascent Capitalism* (New York and London: Academic Press 1977); and David Levine and Keith Wrightson, *Poverty and Piety in an English Village: Terling, 1525–1700* (New York and London: Academic Press 1979). For mid-nineteenth-century Ontario, see Gagan, *Hopeful Travellers* chap. 4; Frank Denton and Peter George, "The Influence of Socio-Economic Variables on Family Size in Wentworth County, Ontario, 1871," *Canadian Review of Sociology and Anthropology* 10, no. 4 (1973): 334–45; and McInnis, "Childbearing and Land Availability." For a discussion of various historiographical issues, see Chad Gaffield, "Theory and Method in Canadian Historical Demography," *Archivaria* no. 14 (Summer 1982): 123–36: Maris A. Vinovskis, "Recent Trends in American Historical Demography: Some Methodological and Conceptual Considerations," *Annual Reviews in Sociology* 4 (1978): 603–27.

28 For example, see Kelly, "The Impact of Settlement"; and John J. Mannion, *Irish Settlements in Eastern Canada: A Study of Cultural Transfer and Adaptation* (Toronto: University of Toronto Press 1974), 104.

29 An overview of these developments is presented in Lower, *The North American Assault*. C. Grant Head offers a general discussion with specific examples in "An Introduction to Forest Exploitation in Nineteenth Century Ontario," in J. David Wood, ed., *Perspectives on Landscape and Settlement in Nineteenth Century Ontario* (Toronto: McClelland and Stewart 1975), 78–112. Also see Michael Cross, "The Lumber Community of Upper Canada, 1815–1867," *Ontario History* 52 (1960).

30 See Lower, *Settlement and the Forest Frontier*.

31 T.C. Keefer, Report, *Journal of the Legislative Assembly of Canada*, 1847, appendix 100, no. 5.

32 Tassé, *La vallée de l'Outaouais*, 7.

33 Manuscript census, Caledonia Township, 187

34 Manuscript census, Prescott County, 1851, 1861, 1871.

35 Higginson, *Diaries*, 9.

36 The manufacture of potash is described in W.H. Smith, *Canada: Past, Present and Future* (Montreal 1850); Edwin C. Guillet, *Early Life in Upper Canada* (Toronto: Ontario Publishing Company 1933); and Greening, *The Ottawa*.

37 de Barbezieux, *Histoire*, 1:285.

38 French, *Information for Intending Settlers*; Labelle, *Projet d'une société de colonisation*.

39 French, *Information for Intending Settlers*, 24–26; de Barbezieux, *Histoire*, 285.

40 *Census of Canada*, 1861, 1871.

41 The members of the Prescott County Historical Society have been very generous with their holdings, especially James Donaldson, who saved many Hamilton Brothers documents from thoughtless destruction. The following analysis is based on records lent to me by Mr Donaldson and now held by the Hawkesbury [Ont.] Public Library. Account books and other business records are held in the Provincial Archives of Ontario; see E.M. Titus, "Inventory of the Hamilton Brothers Records and Hawkesbury Lumber Company Records 1797–1939," 14 September 1971, PAO [no document locator number].

A.R.M. Lower includes a general description of Hamilton Brothers in *Great Britain's Woodyard: British America and the Timber Trade, 1763–1867* (Montreal: McGill-Queen's University Press 1973), 177–80. John Hamilton led the family business in the Ottawa Valley from the 1840s until his death in 1888. Robert Peter Gillis provides a biographical sketch in the *Dictionary of Canadian Biography* (Toronto: University of Toronto Press 1982), 9:379–81.

For a comparative profile of shantymen in the mid-nineteenth-century Saguenay, see Christian Pouyez, Raymond Roy, and Gérard Bouchard, "La mobilité géographique en milieu rural: Saguenay, 1852–1861," *Histoire sociale/Social History* 14, no. 27 (May 1981) especially figure 3, p. 129.

42 The importance of the shanty market is emphasized in Robert Leslie Jones, *History of Agriculture in Ontario, 1613–1880* (Toronto: University of Toronto Press 1946) 116; and by contemporary writers in volumes such as G.M. Grant, *Picturesque Canada* (Toronto 1882), 1: 216, 225.

Discussions of the changing agricultural context of nineteenth-century Ontario include J. Isbister, "Agriculture, Balanced Growth and Social Change in Central Canada since 1850: An Interpretation," *Economic Development and Cultural Change* 25, no. 4 (July 1977): 673–97; D.A. Lawr, "The Development of Ontario Farming, 1870–1919; Patterns of Growth and Change," *Ontario History* 64, no. 4 (December 1922): 239–51; Robert E. Ankli and Wendy Millar, "Ontario Agriculture in Transition: The Switch from Wheat to Cheese," *Journal of Economic History* 42, no. 1 (March 1982): 207–15; and Marvin McInnis, "The Changing Structure of Canadian Agriculture, 1867–1897," *Journal of Economic History* 42, no. 1 (March 1982): 191–98. For a recent emphasis on the wheat staple, see John McCallum, *Unequal Beginnings: Agriculture and Economic Development in Quebec and Ontario until 1870* (Toronto: University of Toronto Press 1980), chaps 2 and 4.

43 These figures were reported in *The Canadian Handbook and Tourist's Guide* (Montreal: M. Longmoore and Co. 1867; Toronto: Coles Publishing 1971), 95.

44 *Journal and Transactions of the Board of Agriculture of Upper Canada for 1856–1857*, 170, as quoted in Jones, *History of Agriculture*, 293.

45 *Journal of the House of Commons*, 1876, appendix 7, p. 26, as quoted in Jones, *History of Agriculture*, 302.

46 *Journal of the Legislative Assembly of Canada*, appendix 2, 1847, no. 1, 1 June 1847.

47 T.C. Keefer, *Montreal and the Ottawa* (Montreal 1854), 116.

48 John MacTaggart, *Three Years in Canada* (London 1828), no paging; Guigues, is quoted in Lucien Brault, *Histoire des comtés unis de Prescott et de Russell* (L'Orignal, Ont.: Conseil des Comtés Unis 1965), 298.

49 The negative impact of lumbering on agriculture is a major emphasis in Blanchard, *L'est du Canada français*; it is also discussed in Cross, "'The Dark Druidical Groves"; and Wynn, *Timber Colony*. A detailed

discussion of this view is offered by Graeme Wynn in " 'Deplorably Dark and Demoralized Lumberers'? Rhetoric and Reality in Early Nineteenth-Century New Brunswick," *Journal of Forest History* 24, no. 4 (October 1980), 168–87.

50 Higginson, *Diaries*, 8, 43.

51 Comparative examples are offered in Séguin, *La conquête du sol*; and Wynn, *Timber Colony*.

52 Hamilton Brothers employee records, 1856. The findings for contemporary logging in the Saguenay offer several points of comparison; see, for example, Pouyez, Roy, and Bouchard, "La mobilité géographique." Another comparison is provided by Anders Norberg and Sune Akerman, "Migration and the Building of Families: Studies on the Rise of the Lumber Industry in Sweden," in Kurt Agren et al., eds., *Aristocrats, Farmers, Proletarians: Essays in Swedish Demographic History* (Uppsala, Esselte/Studium 1973), 88–119.

53 The European context is surveyed in Lutz K. Berkner and Franklin F. Mendels, "Inheritance Systems, Family Structure, and Demographic Patterns in Western Europe, 1700–1900," in Charles Tilly, ed., *Historical Studies of Changing Fertility* (New Jersey: Princeton University Press 1978), 209–23.

54 The interrelationships of emigration and family strategies in Nova Scotia are discussed in Alan A. Brookes, "Family, Youth, and Leaving Home in Late-Nineteenth Century Rural Nova Scotia: Canning and the Exodus, 1868–1893," in Joy Parr, ed., *Childhood and Family in Canadian History* (Toronto: McClelland and Stewart 1982), 93–108.

55. On the lumber industry during the second half of the nineteenth century, see W.E. Greening, "The Lumber Industry in the Ottawa Valley and the American Market in the Nineteenth Century," *Ontario History* 62, no. 2 (June 1970): 134–6; Head, "An Introduction to Forest Exploitation" and Lower, *The North American Assault*.

56 *The News and Ottawa Valley Advocate*, 9 January 1877.

57 By the early 1880s, railways had reduced the cost of transportation from the lower Ottawa Valley to northern regions; see, for example, H.A. Innis and A.R.M. Lower, eds., *Select Documents in Canadian Economic History 1783– 1885* (Toronto 1933) 504–5. According to Richard L. Jones, the decline of the shanty market for Prescott County farmers began in the 1870s, when they were "reduced to supplying part of the requirements of the lumbermen operating up the Gatineau Valley and in other fairly accessible sections along the north shore of the Ottawa River." *History of Agriculture in Ontario*, 302.

58 *L'Interprète*, 30 July 1890.

59 The peak period for potash and pearl ash factories in Prescott County

was in 1861, when there were six establishments. There were three
asheries in 1871, four in 1881, and none by 1891. *Census of Canada,*
1851–91.

60 "Report of the Drainage Commission for the Province of Ontario,"
Sessional Papers, 1893, vol. 25, paper 32, p. 19.

61 Report of the Ontario Agricultural Commission, Vol. 5, appendix ʀ,
p. 14, as quoted in Jones, *History of Agriculture in Ontario,* 114. A
discussion of the region to the south of Prescott County (where the
economic crisis began a decade earlier) is provided in R. Marvin McInnis,
"Farms and Farm Families in the St. Lawrence Townships," *Historic
Kingston,* no. 24 (March 1976), 6–17.

62 *The News and Ottawa Valley Advocate,* 1 August 1876; and *L'Interprète,*
30 July 1890. The great debate about the extent of Quebec's agricultural difficulties in the early nineteenth century is continued in
R.M. McInnis, "A Reconsideration of the State of Agriculture in Lower
Canada in the First Half of the Nineteenth Century," in Donald H.
Akenson, ed., *Canadian Papers in Rural History* (Gananoque, Ont.:
Langdale Press 1983) 3: 9–49. For a description of agricultural difficulties in another système agro-forestier, see Séguin, *La conquète du
sol,* chap. 7.

63 C. Thomas, *History of the Counties of Argenteuil, Quebec and Prescott,
Ontario* (Montreal 1896; Belleville, Ont.: Mika Publishing 1982), pp.
475–6.

64 *L'Interprète,* 1 March 1894.

65 The emergence of cheese factories was part of a larger development
that is analysed in Ankli and Millar. Also see Earl Allan Haslett, "Factors in the Growth and Decline of the Cheese Industry in Ontario
1864–1924" (PHD thesis, University of Toronto 1969). The overall
Quebec experience is surveyed in Norman Perron, "Genèse des ac-
tivités laitières, 1850–1960," in Normand Séguin, ed., *Agriculture et
colonisation au Québec* (Montreal: Boréal Express 1980). The similar
experience of Quebec counties close to Prescott County, such as Soulanges and Vaudreuil, is documented in Jacques Letarte, *Atlas d'histoire
économique et sociale du Québec 1851–1901* (Montreal: Fides 1971). Jack
Little reports on a comparative study of anglophone and francophone
behaviour during the transition from wheat to dairy production in
"The Social and Economic Development of Settlers in Two Quebec
Townships, 1851–1870," in Donald H. Akenson, ed., *Canadian Papers
in Rural History* (Gananoque, Ont.: Langdale Press 1978), 1:89–113.

66 The special census commissioner explained, "No attempt has been
made to collect the production of home-made fabrics and cheese, for
as a result of the factory system these domestic industries have become

nearly extinct." See *Fourth Census of Canada, 1901* (Ottawa: S.E. Dawson 1902), 1:ix.

67 Evidence concerning the changing spatial pattern of Ottawa Valley lumbering during the 1870s is discussed in C. Grant Head, "Nineteenth Century Timbering and Sawlogging in the Ottawa Valley: Documentary Sources and Spatial Patterns," in Vrenia Ivonoffski and Sandra Campbell, eds., *Exploring Our Heritage: The Ottawa Valley Experience* (Toronto: Arnprior and District Historical Society 1980), 52–7.

The retreat of the forest frontier also inspired attempts to prevent complete resource depletion; see Robert Peter Gillis, "The Ottawa Lumber Barons and the Conservation Movement, 1880–1914," *Journal of Canadian Studies* 9, no. 1 (February 1974): 14–30; and H.V. Nelles, *The Politics of Development: Forests, Mines, and Hydro-Electric Power in Ontario, 1849–1941* (Toronto: Macmillan 1974).

68 Further discussion of employment in the Prescott County lumber industry during the late nineteenth century is included in Gaffield, "Schooling, The Economy and Rural Society"; and Harvey J. Graff, "Respected and Profitable Labour: Literacy, Jobs and the Working Class in the Nineteenth Century," in Gregory S. Kealey and Peter Warrian, eds., *Essays in Canadian Working Class History* (Toronto: McClelland and Stewart 1976), 58–82. The late nineteenth century is also the starting point for Donald MacKay, *The Lumberjacks* (Toronto: McGraw-Hill Ryerson 1978).

69 See Jean Hamelin and Yves Roby, *Histoire économique du Québec 1851–1896* (Montreal: Fides 1971).

70 This process is discussed as part of the larger context of rural child labour in Joy Parr, *Labouring Children: British Immigrant Apprentices to Canada, 1869–1924* (London: Croom Helm; Montreal: McGill-Queen's University Press 1980), chap. 5.

71 In the late nineteenth century, francophone migration to northern Ontario became quite important. The general context of this development is discussed in Morris Zaslow, *The Opening of the Canadian North, 1870–1914* (Toronto: McClelland and Stewart 1971); and Nelles, *The Politics of Development.* Aspects of the establishment of francophone communities in "new Ontario" are discussed in *Explorations et enracinements français en Ontario, 1610–1978,* Guide de ressources à l'usage des enseignants, Ministère de l'Education, Ontario (Toronto 1981), chap. 4. By the turn of the century, Quebec leaders envisioned northern Ontario as the most acceptable region for francophone emigrants. For an argument that this view did not influence actual migration patterns but rather reflected the trend already underway, see A.N.

Lalonde, "L'intelligentsia du Québec et la migration des Canadiens français vers l'Ouest Canadien, 1870–1930," *Revue d'histoire de l'Amerique française* 33, no. 2 (September 1979), 163–85.

72 Analysts also emphasize the importance of family connections, in both good and bad material circumstances, in contemporary urban areas; see Bettina Bradbury, "The Fragmented Family: Family Strategies in the Face of Death, Illness, and Poverty: Montreal 1860–1885," in Joy Parr, ed., *Childhood and Family in Canadian History* (Toronto: McClelland and Stewart 1982), 109–28; and Tamara K. Hareven, *Family Time and Industrial Time: The Relationship between Family and Work in a New England Industrial Community* (Cambridge: Cambridge University Press 1982).

73 *Eastern Ontario Review*, 15 December 1893.

74 *La Nation*, 26 September 1885, Public Archives of Canada (PAC).

75 *Eastern Ontario Review*, 15 December 1873. The importance of boosterism in the late nineteenth century has been particularly emphasized in urban areas; the most forceful argument is presented by Alan F.J. Artibise, *Winnipeg: A Social History of Urban Growth 1874–1914* (Montreal: McGill-Queen's University Press 1975). However, boosterism and an unrealistic anticipation of urban growth also characterized small towns including, for example, Orillia, Ontario, which was immortalized as Mariposa by Stephen Butler Leacock in *Sunshine Sketches of a Little Town* (London: J. Lane 1912). For a discussion of this phenomenon and related aspects of urban history, see Chad Gaffield, "Social Structure and the Urbanization Process: Perspectives on Nineteenth Century Research," in Gilbert A. Stelter and Alan F.J. Artibise, eds., *The Canadian City: Essays in Urban History*, 2nd ed. (Toronto: McClelland and Stewart 1984), 262–81.

76 *The News and Ottawa Valley Advocate*, 20 June 1876. The local francophone press also saw railway construction as a key to economic revitalization. In admitting that local residents were not even "aussi riches que ceux d'autres comtés relativement moins favorisés," *La Nation* asked "ne peut-on l'attribuer à leur manque de communications?" 10 December 1885, PAC. Similar promotion of railways is examined in E.J. Noble, "Entrepreneurship and Nineteenth Century Urban Growth: A Case Study of Orillia, Ontario, 1867–1898," *Urban History Review* 9, no. 1 (June 1980): 64–89.

77 *Prospectus Number, The News and Ottawa Valley Advocate*, February 1876.

78 *La Nation*, 4 June 1886, PAC.

79 *The News and Ottawa Valley Advocate*, 17 February 1880.

80 Ibid., 2 January and 12 December 1876.

81 *The Canadian Handbook and Tourist's Guide* reported in 1867 that the "medicinal qualities" of Caledonia Springs were especially appropriate

to those suffering from "rheumatic or curtaneous affections." The *Guide* also informed readers that "the 'season' here, which may be styled the Canadian Harrowgate, is during the heats of August; and to the invalid seeking a quiet locality, with agreeable society, this place will afford both." *The Canadian Handbook and Tourist's Guide* (Montreal: M. Longmoore 1867; Toronto: Coles 1971), 97. Local newspaper reports include *The News and Ottawa Valley Advocate*, 30 May 1876 and 3 February 1880.

82 *The News and Ottawa Valley Advocate*, 10 October 1876.

83 *La Nation*, 26 September 1885, PAC. The extent of the "campaign for industry" throughout late nineteenth century Canada is suggested by Artibise, *Winnipeg*, chap. 7.

84 *The News and Ottawa Valley Advocate*, 4 May 1880.

85 Ibid., 1 June 1880.

86 Ibid., 10 August 1880.

87 *Census of Canada*, 1891.

CHAPTER FOUR

1 A. Brunet, East Hawkesbury parish priest, to E. Ryerson, 29 November 1871, in *Regulations and Correspondence Relating to French and German Schools in the Province of Ontario* (Toronto: Warwick and Sons 1889), 38.

2 J. George Hodgins to Brunet, 4 December 1871, in *Regulations and Correspondence*, 38.

3 Annual reports of the local superintendents' of common schools, RG 2, F-3-B, Public Archives of Ontario (hereafter PAO).

4 The census question concerning school participation must be interpreted only as an indication of enrolment – that is, of a minimum level of attendance. Previous studies concerning aspects of the history of school attendance in Ontario which have used this variable include Ian E. Davey, "Educational Reform and the Working Class: School Attendance in Hamilton, Ontario, 1851–1891" (PHD thesis University of Toronto 1975); Frank Denton and Peter George, "Socio-Economic Influences on School Attendance: A Study of a Canadian County in 1871," *History of Education Quarterly* 14 (Fall 1974): 223–32; Haley P. Bamman, "Patterns of School Attendance in Toronto, 1844–1878: Some Spatial Considerations," *History of Education Quarterly* 12 (Fall 1972): 381–410; Chad Gaffield and David Levine, "Dependency and Adolescence on the Canadian Frontier: Orillia, Ontario in the Mid-Nineteenth Century," *History of Education Quarterly* 18, no. 1 (Spring 1978): 35–47; and Michael B. Katz and Ian E. Davey, "Youth and Early Industrialization in a Canadian City," in John Demos and Sarane

Spence Boocock, eds., *Turning Points: Historical and Sociological Essays on the Family* (Chicago and London: University of Chicago Press 1978), 81–119.

5 Alphonse Duhamel to Archbishop [Joseph] Duhamel, 27 February 1895, Alfred I.4B. (documents particuliers) (écoles: 1877 – 1949) Archives of the Archdiocese of Ottawa.

6 James McCaul, local superintendent, to Ryerson, 4 February 1861, typescript, Thomas Fischer Rare Book Library, University of Toronto.

7 Official views on schoolhouses were presented in J. George Hodgins, *The School House: Its Architecture, External and Internal Arrangements* (Toronto 1857). Specific discussion of this monograph is included in Alison Prentice, *The School Promoters: Education and Social Class in Mid-Nineteenth Century Upper Canada* (Toronto: McClelland and Stewart 1977) 97–104.

8 J. George Hodgins, *Hints and Suggestions on School Architecture and Hygiene with Plans and Illustrations* (Toronto 1886), 13–14; the regulations are included in the text. The established historiography has not paid much attention to the implications of school-site policy. The only study about Ontario is Bamman, "Patterns of School Attendance in Toronto"; it has an urban focus and obviously does not address considerations of soil composition and topography.

9 Many, many accounts from settlers across Canada speak of the oppressive boredom of house-bound winters, especially for children. For example, "Spent the day at home as quiet as possible considering the children; each with a new plan of making things lively. The confinement to the house has no charm for them, the longing for the green grass is quite the natural thing. More than the young would shorten the long winter of this Canada of ours." Thomas Tweed Higginson, *Diaries of Thomas Tweed Higginson*, ed. Thomas Boyd Higginson (London: The Research Publishing Company 1960), 32.

10 Additional analysis of school attendance in Prescott County is provided in Chad Gaffield, "Schooling, the Economy, and Rural Society in Nineteenth-Century Ontario," in Joy Parr, ed., *Childhood and Family in Canadian History* (Toronto: McClelland and Stewart 1982), 69–92. The social and economic context of school attendance is emphasized in Ian E. Davey, "The Rhythm of Work and the Rhythm of School," in Neil McDonald and Alf Chaiton, eds., *Egerton Ryerson and His Times* (Toronto: Macmillan 1978). The historiography of this issue is discussed in Chad Gaffield, "Demography, Social Structure, and the History of School," in David C. Jones et al., eds., *Approaches to Educational History* (Winnipeg: University of Manitoba 1981), 85–111.

11 Cyrus Thomas, *History of the Counties of Argenteuil, Quebec and Prescott, Ontario* (Montreal 1896; Belleville, Ont.: Mika Publishing 1981) 631.

12 Thomas Steele, Prescott County, Annual Report for 1873, Appendix,

19. See Chapter 1, note 39 for bibliographical details on the annual school reports.

13 Annual Report for 1855; Table F, 136. John Lawless, North Plantagenet Township, Annual Report for 1858, Appendix, 7.

14. Steele, Prescott County, Annual Report for 1873, Appendix, 19; idem, 1878, pamphlet, PAO.

15 W.J. Summerby, Counties of Prescott and Russell, Annual Report for 1882, Appendix, 117.

16 Steele, Prescott County, Annual Report for 1874, Appendix, 26; idem, 1878, pamphlet, PAO, 2–3.

17 Humphrey Hughes, Alfred Township, Annual Report for 1858, Appendix, 6.

18 Joseph Kyle to Hodgins, 27 April 1896, RG 2, E-2, Envelope 7, PAO.

19 Ibid.

20 Samuel Derby to Hodgins, 15 April 1896, RG 2, E-2, Envelope 7, PAO.

21 Peter Lindsay, Cumberland Township, Annual Report for 1861, Appendix, 160.

22 Summerby, Counties of Prescott and Russell, Annual Report for 1882, Appendix, 116. The reluctance of parents to pay the school tax was also discussed by Peter Eastman, local superintendent of schools in 1865; see file no. 1078, RG 2, C-6-C, PAO.

23 Lindsay, Cumberland Township, Annual Report for 1858, Appendix 8. The general evolution of hiring practices is discussed in Marta Danylewycz, Beth Light, and Alison Prentice, "The Evolution of the Sexual Division of Labour in Teaching: A Nineteenth-Century Ontario and Quebec Case Study," *Histoire sociale/Social History* 16, no. 31 (May 1983): 81–109.

24 James Gamble, Township of East Hawkesbury, Annual Report for 1851, Appendix, 69.

25 E.H. Jenkyns, Renfrew County, Annual Report for 1871, Appendix, 28. In some cases, trustees would hire a male teacher for part of the year and a female teacher for the remaining months. School superintendents considered this practice to be of no real advantage since "not infrequently" the female teacher "undoes what her predecessor was at great pains to do." Lawless, Plantagenet North Township, Annual Report for 1858, Appendix, 6–7.

Trustees often came under attack from local school officials for apathy as well as stinginess. If a school remained closed for want of a teacher, superintendents and inspectors inevitably blamed trustees for not finding an appropriate person. For example, see Steele, Prescott County, Annual Report for 1871, Appendix 23–5.

26 Lindsay, Cumberland Township, Annual Report for 1861, Appendix 160.

27 Ibid.

28 Higginson, *Diaries*, 7. The importance of kinship networks within nineteenth-century communities emphasizes that the household cannot be considered the only unit of analysis in the history of the family. For a general discussion of such networks in rural communities, see R. Cole Harris and John Warkentin, *Canada Before Confederation: A Study in Historical Geography* (New York: Oxford University Press 1974), 70–8. Similar evidence is provided in Herbert J. Mays, " 'A Place to Stand': Families, Land and Permanence in Toronto Gore Township, 1820–1890," Canadian Historical Association, *Historical Papers* (1980), 185–211.

29 John J. Bigsby, *The Shoe and Canoe* (London 1850; New York: Paladin Press 1969), 1:71.

30 Higginson, *Diaries*, 9–10, 64.

31 Ibid., 19, 31.

32 Ibid., 10.

33 Ibid., 25.

34 Ennid Christie, "A Narrative Account of Farm Life along the South Nation River," manuscript, 1860, p. 2, MU 2113, PAO.

35 This point is emphasized in Lucien Brault, *Histoire de comtés unis de Prescott et Russell* (L'Orignal, Ont.: Conseil des Comtés Unis 1965), 84.

36 This example occurred between 1861 and 1871 in the Village of Hawkesbury and was documented in the two census enumerations. For an exploration of the origins of institutional care for dependent children, see Patricia T. Rooke and R.L. Schnell, "Childhood and Charity in Nineteenth-Century British North America," *Histoire sociale/ Social History* 15, no. 29 (May 1982): 157–72.

37 A list of French-language schools in Prescott County was quite fortunately included in the minutes of the June 1883 meeting of the Board of Examiners, *Minutes of the Board of Examiners for the Counties of Prescott and Russell,* 1871–1897, RG 2, H 3, vol. 35, PAO. (The exact date is given for a meeting of the Board that lasted one day; only the month is given for a meeting that spanned several days – or even a week.)

38 The process of proletarization is examined in various historical contexts by the authors included in David C. Levine, ed., *Proletarianization and Family History* (New York: Academic Press 1984).

39 *The Evening Telegram*, 8 June 1889; this description was shortly thereafter quoted in G.W. Ross, "The Separate School Question and the French language in the Public Schools," *Report of the Speech delivered on the Occasion of the Annual Demonstration of the Toronto Reform Association, 29 June 1889* (Toronto 1889.) 14–15.

40 Minutes of the Board of Examiners, 1871–97.

41 Ibid., meeting of 16 December 1872.
42 Ibid., meetings of 18 December 1871 and 20 July 1874.
43 Ibid, meeting of 16 July 1872.
44 Ibid., meeting of 10 August 1876.
45 Ibid., meeting of August 1880.
46 Steele, Prescott County, Annual Report for 1871, Appendix, 23; idem, Annual Report for 1873, Appendix, 19.
47 Summerby, Counties of Prescott and Russell, Annual Report for 1881, Appendix, 117.
48 *Minutes of the Board of Examiners*, meeting of August 1878.
49 Ibid., meeting of July 1885.
50 Ibid., meeting of August 1886.
51 Toronto *Mail*, 21 March 1889.
52 *Minutes of the Board of Examiners*, December 1890 and July 1891.
53 Ibid., December 1890; and "Report of the Commission on French Language Public Schools in Ontario, 1889," in *Regulations and Correspondence*, 51–92.

CHAPTER FIVE

1 The 1890 Ontario election is emphasized in Franklin A. Walker, *Catholic Education and Politics in Ontario* (Toronto: Thomas Nelson and Sons 1964); and the 1896 federal election is examined in Paul Crunican, *Priests and Politicians: Manitoba Schools and the Election of 1896* (Toronto: University of Toronto Press 1974).
2 *The News and Ottawa Valley Advocate*, 30 January 1883.
3 Ibid. Conservative Party support among both anglophones and francophones in Prescott County during the 1870s was evident in the fall of 1877, when John A. Macdonald toured the county and met a warm reception of bands and processions. Large crowds assembled to hear him and other Conservative leaders address the audience in both French and English. For a contemporary account, see Thomas Tweed Higginson, *Diaries of Thomas Tweed Higginson*, ed. Thomas Boyd Higginson (London: The Research Publishing Company 1960), 37. For an examination of certain aspects of French-Canadian political activity in Ontario, see Victor Lapalme, "Les franco-Ontariens et la politique provinçiale" (MA thesis, University of Ottawa 1968).
4 Lucien Brault, *Histoire des comtés unis de Prescott et Russell* (L'Orignal, Ont.: Conseil de Comtés Unis 1965), 42–3.
5 The extent of the federal franchise is discussed in Norman Ward, *The Canadian House of Commons: Representation* (Toronto: University of Toronto Press 1950). The complexities of the franchise issue are briefly

addressed in Gregory S. Kealey, *Toronto Workers Respond to Industrial Capitalism 1867–1892* (Toronto: University of Toronto Press 1980), 367–8.

6 Some suspicion that the Conservative stronghold in Prescott County might be weakening was expressed in the late 1870s, specifically during the 1878 federal campaign. In response, committees were formed "to keep voters on the right track." See Higginson, *Diaries*, 44.

7 Brief biographies of Labrosse and Routhier are provided in J.K. Johnson, *The Canadian Directory of Parliament 1867–1967* (Ottawa: Queen's Printer 1968), 310–11 and 511.

8 *The News and Ottawa Valley Advocate*, 30 January 1803. In analysing the voters' list, the editors used names to attribute cultural affiliation, recognizing that this method was not always accurate. They explained, "Undoubtedly there were a few people with French-Canadian names who do not claim to belong to that nationality, and on the other hand there are a compensating number with English, Irish or Scotch names who are of French-Canadian birth and tendencies. Taking the one with the other it may be said that the calculation arrived at is a fair estimate of the numbers of each."

9 *The News and Ottawa Valley Advocate*, 11 May 1980.

10 A. Evanturel, letter to the editor, 13 May 1880, *The News and Ottawa Valley Advocate*, 18 May 1880.

11 *The News and Ottawa Valley Advocate*, 22 June 1880.

12 Ibid., 11 May 1880.

13 Reprinted from the *Plantagenet Plaindealer* in *The News and Ottawa Valley Advocate*, 8 June 1880.

14 Alfred Evanturel is rarely even mentioned in the established historiography. (A good indication of his undeserved obscurity is the fact that his name is sometimes inaccurately written as "Albert" Evanturel.) Evanturel was born in Quebec City on 31 August 1849. After studies at Laval University, he was called to the bar in 1871 and then moved to Ottawa, where he practised law until coming to Prescott County in 1881. For a summary of his career, see Henry James Morgan, ed., *The Canadian Men and Women of the Time: A Hand-book of Canadian Biography* (Toronto: William Briggs 1898), 315–16.

15 Alfred Evanturel, *Aux Canadiens français du comté de Prescott*, leaflet, November 1883, L'Orignal, I. 8(2), Archives of Archdiocese of Ottawa.

16 As translated in *The News and Ottawa Valley Advocate*, 22 June 1880.

17 Evanturel, "Aux Canadiens-français."

18 *The News and Ottawa Valley Advocate*, 27 February 1883.

19 Ibid., 13 February 1883.

20 Ibid., 30 January 1883.

21 Ibid., 9 January 1883.

22 Albert Hagar, whose parents were from the United States, was also a local school official. A brief biography is provided in Brault, *Histoire des comtés unis*, 63–4.

23 *The News and Ottawa Valley Advocate* 13 February 1883.

24 Ibid., 27 February 1883.

25 Ibid., 7 August 1883.

26 Voter participation ranged from a low of 67 per cent in the Township of East Hawkesbury to a high of 84 per cent in North Plantagenet. For all of Prescott County, 73 per cent of the listed electors actually voted in the 1883 election. (See Table 39.)

27 See, for example, the commentary in *The News and Ottawa Valley Advocate*, 30 January 1883.

28 Ibid., 13 March 1883.

29 Ibid., 31 July 1883.

30 Detailed evidence on the Ontario political context is offered in Margaret A. Evans, "Oliver Mowat and Ontario, 1872–1896: A Study in Political Success" (PHD thesis, University of Toronto 1967).

31 See *The News and Ottawa Valley Advocate*, 7 August 1883.

32 Ibid.

33 The Toronto *Mail*, 6 December 1882, 24 November 1886, and 14 and 15 December 1886. An extensive description of the journalistic attach is provided in Walker, *Catholic Education and Politics*.

34 The Toronto *Evening Telegram*, 8 June 1889. This passage was quoted by the minister of Education, G.W. Ross, in an 1889 speech; see G.W. Ross, "The Separate School Question and the French Language in the Public Schools," *Report of the Speech Delivered on the Occasion of the Annual Demonstration of the Toronto Reform Association, 29 June 1889* (Toronto 1889), 14–15.

35 See Higginson, *Diaries*, 32.

36 *The News and Ottawa Valley Advocate*, 9 October 1883.

37 The editor and owner of *The Advertiser* was Watson Little, who had earlier worked for the *Bytown Gazette* and then operated a newspaper in Cornwall. Little was a staunch supporter of John A. Macdonald, and *The Advertiser* consistently promoted the Conservative party position. Lucien Brault provides information about certain Prescott County newspapers in *Histoire des comtés*, 163–6.

38 The final cause of death for *The News* was the appearance of *The Prescott and Russell Advocate*, published in L'Orignal from May 1888. The new paper spoke for the Liberal cause from an anglophone perspective and succeeded in capturing former readers of *The News*, which was only published for a few more months.

39 *La Nation* 12 September 1885.

40 Ibid.

41 Ibid.

42 Notice that this description of Franco-Ontarian identity goes beyond the criteria of language and residence. In addition to these characteristics, *La Nation* emphasized the importance of membership by ancestry in the larger French-Canadian population. This sense of Franco-Ontarian identity has become controversial in the twentieth century as Ontario has come to include substantial numbers of francophones whose roots are outside Canada. Aspects of this subject are discussed in Danielle Juteau-Lee, "The Franco-Ontarian Collectivity: Material and Symbolic Dimensions of Its Minority Status," in R. Breton and P. Savard, eds., *The Quebec and Acadian Diaspora in North America* (Toronto: Multicultural History Society of Ontario 1982), 167–82; Danielle Juteau-Lee and Jean Lapointe, "From French Canadians to Franco-Ontarians and Ontarois: New Boundaries, New Identities," in Jean Leonard Elliott, ed., *Two Nations, Many Cultures: Ethnic Groups in Canada*, 2nd ed. (Scarborough, Ont.: Prentice-Hall Canada 1983), 173–86; and *The Canadian Encyclopedia*, s.v. "Franco-Ontarians."

43 *La Nation* 10 October 1885.

44 The now-enormous recent literature on Riel includes work by scholars from many disciplines. For example, see Thomas Flanagan, *Louis "David" Riel: "Prophet of the New World"* (Toronto: University of Toronto Press 1979).

45 *La Nation*, 12 September 1885.

46 Ibid., 30 October 1885.

47 Ibid., 10 October 1885.

48 Ibid., 22 October 1885.

49 Ibid., 29 October 1885.

50 Ibid., 19 November 1885.

51 Ibid., 3 December 1885.

52 Ibid., 15 December 1885.

53 Ibid., 19 November 1885. The political context of this development is described in Barbara Fraser, "The Political Career of Sir Hector Louis Langevin," *Canadian Historical Review* 42, no. 2 (June 1961): 93–132.

54 *La Nation*, 26 November 1885.

55 The principal days of debate in the legislature were 8 March, 11 March, and 4 April 1889. Evanturel's minor contributions are reported in the Legislative Assembly of Ontario, *Newspaper Hansard*, 9 March and 5 April 1889.

56 Ibid., 12 March 1889.

57 *L'Interprète*, 22 April 1887. Also see O. Mowat, *The Sectarian Issues and the History and Present Condition of the Public Schools in the French Districts of Ontario*, pamphlet of a speech delivered at Woodstock, Ont., 3 De-

cember 1889 (Toronto 1890), 13–14, 26–8; and *Report of the Speeches Delivered by Hon. Mr. Mowat, Hon. Geo. W. Ross, and Mr. Evanturel, M.P.P. in the Legislative Assembly, 3 April 1890* (Toronto: Queen's Printer 1890), 5.

58 *La Nation*, 3 December 1885.

CHAPTER SIX

1 Jean-Pierre Wallot, "Religion and French-Canadian Mores in the Early Nineteenth Century," *Canadian Historical Review* 52, no. 1 (March 1971): 51–93.

2 A valuable overview of the changing position of the Church is provided in Nive Voisine, *Histoire de l'Église catholique au Québec 1608–1970* (Montreal: Fides 1971). Also see Pierre Savard, *Aspects du catholicisme canadien-français au XIXe siècle* (Montreal: Fides 1980).

3 Wallot, "Religion and French-Canadian Mores," 90. In rewriting the history of Catholic Church influence among francophones, present-day scholars stress the "normal" aspects of this history, rather than the uniqueness often perceived in earlier studies. Wallot, for example, concludes that, for early-nineteenth-century francophones, "the quality of their religious life ... appears no more than normal (at best) in a society of farmers and labourers of some influence and little education in a time of economic restructuring and social change," p. 15.

4 Susan Mann Trofimenkoff, *The Dream of Nation: A Social and Intellectual History of Quebec* (Toronto: Gage 1983), chap. 8; and Paul-André Linteau, René Durocher, and Jean-Claude Robert, *Quebec: A History, 1867–1929*, trans. Robert Chodos (Toronto: James Lorimer 1983), 198–204.

5 Recent work includes Micheline Dumont-Johnson, "Les communautés religieuses et la condition féminine," *Recherches sociographiques* 19 (January-April 1978): 79–102; Marta Danylewycz, "Changing Relationships: Nuns and Feminists in Montreal, 1890–1925," *Histoire sociale/Social History* 14, no. 28 (November 1981): 413–34; and the essays in Bernard Denault and Benoit Lévesque, *Eléments pour une sociologie des communautés religieuses au Québec* (Montreal: Les Presses de l'université de Montréal 1975).

6 Examples of recent research include Serge Gagnon and René Hardy, eds., *L'Eglise et le village au Québec, 1850–1930* (Montreal: Leméac 1979); and Normand Séguin, *La conquête du sol au 19e siècle* (Sillery, Que.: Boréal Express 1977), chap. 9.

7 The standard work is Louis-Philippe Audet, *Histoire du conseil de l'instruction publique de la province de Québec, 1856–1964* (Montreal: Leméac 1964).

8 Donald H. Akenson relates Cullen to the Canadian context in "Mass Schooling in Ontario: The Irish and 'English Canadian' Popular Culture," in *Being Had: Historians, Evidence, and the Irish in North America* (Port Credit, Ont.: P.D. Meany 1985), 143–87.

9 For an example of the contact between Quebec and Ireland, see Robnerto Perin, "Troppo Ardenti Sacerdoti: The Conroy Mission Revisited," *Canadian Historical Review* 61, no. 3 (September 1980): 283–304. Additional comparative information is provided in Jay P. Dolan, *Catholic Revivalism: The American Experience (1830–1900)* (Notre Dame, Ind.: University of Notre Dame Press 1978).

10 In 1891, there were 2,284 nonfrancophones among 18,534 Roman Catholics in Prescott County, *Census of Canada*, 1891.

11 Valuable information on the Diocese of Ottawa is provided in Robert Choquette, *L'Eglise catholique dans l'Ontario français du dix-neuvième siècle* (Ottawa: Editions de l'Université d'Ottawa 1984); Donald G. Cartwright, "Institutions on the Frontier: French-Canadian Settlement in Eastern Ontario in the Nineteenth Century," *The Canadian Geographer* 21, no. 1 (Spring 1977); 1–21; and idem, "Ecclesiatical Territorial Organisation and Institutional Conflict in Eastern and Northern Ontario, 1840 to 1910," Canadian Historical Association, *Historical Papers* (1978), 176–99. Also see Nive Voisine and Jean Hamelin, *Les ultramontains canadiens-français* (Montreal: Boréal Express 1985).

12 Alexis de Barbezieux, *Histoire de la province ecclésiastique d'Ottawa et de colonisation dans la vallée de l'Ottawa* (Ottawa 1897), 1: 299–305. In the mid-nineteenth century, the Oblates of Mary Immaculate were a most important religious order in the Ottawa Valley. For a discussion of their activity, see Gaston Carrière, "Les Oblats dans la vallée de l'Outaouais 1841–1861," *La Société Canadienne d'Histoire de l'Eglise Catholique, Rapport* (1954–5), 25–58. More complete information is presented in idem, *Histoire documentaire de la Congrégation des Missionaires Oblats de Marie-Immaculée dans l'Est du Canada*, 12 vols (Ottawa: Editions de l'Universite d'Ottawa 1957–75).

13 Letter from Bishop Guigues, 24 August 1848, quoted in Barbezieux, *Histoire*, 1: 316.

14 Antonio Mandeville, *Historique de la paroisse de Saint-Jean-Baptiste de l'Orignal* (Ottawa 1936), 96.

15 Barbezieux, *Histoire*, 1: 298.

16 As quoted in G.S. Martineau, "La Survivance française dans les comtés de Prescott et Russell" (MA thesis, McGill University 1947), 60. The role of the curé is examined in Réné Hardy, "L'Activité de curé de Notre-Dame de Québec: aperçu de l'influence du clergé au milieu de XIXe siècle," *Histoire sociale/Social History* 3, no. 6 (November 1970): 5–32.

17 Mandeville, *Historique*, 77.

18 Barbezieux, *Histoire*, 1: 327–8.

19 Lucien Brault, *Histoire des comtés unis de Prescott et de Russell* (L'Orignal, Ont.: Conseil des Comtés, Unis, 1965), 173.

20 Barbezieux, *Histoire*, 1: 256–34.

21 *Census of Canada* 1851, 1891.

22 Louis-Edmond Hamelin, "Evolution numérique séculaire du clergé catholique dans le Québec," *Recherches sociographiques* 2, no. 2 April-June 1961): 189–242.

23 C. Thomas, *History of the Counties of Argenteuil, Quebec and Prescott, Ontario* (Montreal: John Lovell and Son 1896), 574, 632. See also Brault, *Histoire des comtés unis*, 273.

24 The attention of the clergy to this kind of concern is examined in Pierre Savard, "La vie du clergé québécois au XIXe siècle," *Recherches Sociographiques* 8, no. 3 (September-December 1967): 259–73.

25 Allan Greer, *Peasant, Lord, and Merchant: Rural Society in Three Quebec Parishes 1740–1840* (Toronto: University of Toronto Press 1985), 113.

26 The St-Victor records are still held in the presbytery in Alfred Village, and the St-Paul records are held in Curran.

27 Humphrey Hughes, Alfred Township, Annual Report for 1861, Appendix, 159; John Lawless, Township of Plantagenet North, Annual Report for 1858, Appendix, 6, Isaac Kendall, Caledonia Township, Annual Report for 1858, Appendix, 6. For bibliographical details of the annual school reports, see Chapter 1, note 39.

28 The textbooks of all the Prescott County schools were reported in the annual reports of the local superintendents of common schools, which are available for the 1850–70 period for all the county's townships in RG 2, F-3-B, PAO. James H. Love argues that the Department of Education for Canada West viewed standardized textbooks as important contributions to anti-American social and cultural stability in the mid-nineteenth century; see "Cultural Survival and Social Control: The Development of a Curriculum for Upper Canada's Common Schools in 1846," *Histoire sociale/Social History* 15, no. 30 (1982): 357–82. Bruce Curtis uses similar evidence (but more systematically) to challenge this argument, suggesting that books took on a quite new role under state control by 1850; see "School Books and the Myth of Curricular Republicanism: The State and the Curriculum in Canada West, 1820–1850," *Histoire sociale/Social History* 16, no. 32 (November 1983): 305–29.

For background on the recommended Irish National Readers, see D.H. Akenson, *The Irish Education Experiment* (Toronto: University of Toronto Press 1970). A traditional survey of educational developments in Quebec is provided in Louis-Phillippe Audet, "Education in Canada East and Quebec: 1840–1875," in J.D. Wilson, R.M. Stamp, and L.P. Audet, eds., *Canadian Education: A History* (Scarborough, Ont.: Prentice Hall 1970), 167–89.

29 Annual Report of the Local Superintendent of Common Schools, Township of East Hawkesbury, 1870, RG 2, F-3-B, PAO.

30 See, for example, Father A. Brunet, parish priest in East Hawkesbury Township, to E. Ryerson, 29 November 1871, in *Regulations and Correspondence Relating to French and German Schools in the Province of Ontario* (Toronto: Warwick and Sons 1889), 38.

31 Thomas O. Steele, inspector of schools, to Ryerson, 15 March 1871, RG 2, F-3-B, PAO.

32 *Minutes of the Board of Examiners for the Counties of Prescott and Russell, 1871–1897*, RG 2, H 3, vol. 35, PAO.

33 Brunet to Ryerson, 29 November 1871, in *Regulations and Correspondence*, 38.

34 The chronology of the Horse Creek controversy is summarized in "Mémoire sur les écoles séparées d'Alfred," a document prepared by Médéric Gareau for O. Routhier, Vicaire Général, Ottawa, Alfred, I.4B. 29, Archives of the Archdiocese of Ottawa (AAO).

35 Ibid.

36 L.A. Lavoie to Duhamel, 10 February 1877, I.4B (documents particuliers) (écoles: 1877–1949), AAO.

37 Gareau, "Mémoire."

38 *Revised Statutes of Ontario, 1887* (Toronto: Queen's Printer, Warwick and Sons 1887), 2: 2483–4.

39 Gareau, "Memoire."

40 See G.W. Ross, "The Separate School Question and the French Language in the Public Schools," *Report of the Speech delivered on the Occasion of the Annual Demonstration of the Toronto Reform Association*, 29 June 1889 (Toronto 1889). A relevant intellectual climate is described in J.R. Miller, "Anti-Catholic Thought in Victorian Canada," *Canadian Historical Review* 66, no. 4 (December 1985): 474–94.

41 On occasion, Evanturel acted as a representative for local groups in dealing with education officials. During the Horse Creek controversy, for example, he presented a petition to Ross asking that the establishment of a separate school in Section No. 7 be officially accepted even though the formal procedure had not been followed; see Gareau, "Mémoire." Dufort apparently used separate-school promotion as a way of reconciling his own French-Canadian consciousness with his official position as enforcer of provincial education rules and regulations; see, for example, the anonymous letter sent to Duhamel, 5 March 1879, I.4B (documents particuliers) (écoles: 1877–1949), AAO.

42 Mandements et Circulaires Duhamel, 2, 93–95, as quoted in Choquette, *L'église catholique*, 309.

43 Bérubé to Duhamel, 2 March 1980, L'Orignal: St-Jean-Baptiste, 1.4F. 1, AAO.

44 This description and the following narrative of the controversy are included in J. McMillan et al. to Geo. W. Ross, 1 December 1886, RG 2, Series o, Box 6, Education Records, PAO.

45 The evidence suggests that the school did conform to provincial guidelines. The 1889 commission on French-language schools reported that no religious instruction was provided and that English was taught daily for the obligatory time. The reports of the parish priest indicate that the school provided the allowable half-hour of religious instruction after regular class hours. See "Report of the Commission on French Language Public Schools in Ontario, 1889," in *Regulations and Correspondence;* and "Rapport sur les écoles de la Paroisse St. Jean-Baptiste, L'Orignal, Ontario, 13 July 1891," L'Orignal, 1.4F, (documents particuliers) (écoles: 1890–1921) AAO.

46 Bérubé to Duhamel, 2 March 1890; L'Orignal: St-Jean-Baptiste, 1.4F.1, AAO.

47 Ibid.

48 Bérubé to Duhamel, 10 April 1890, L'Orignal: St-Jean-Baptiste, 1.4F.Z, AAO.

49 *Report of Commissioners on Schools in the Counties of Prescott and Russell in Which the French Language Is Taught* (Toronto: Warwick and Sons 1893), 17.

50 Ibid. 22–3.

51 Syndics of Section No. 4, Longueuil to Duhamel, 1892, Alfred, 1.4B (documents particuliers) (école: 1877–1949), AAO.

52 Unsigned letter from certain French Canadians of the parish of St-Victor-d'Alfred to Duhamel, 5 March 1892, Ibid.

53 "Liste des Dissidents;" L'Orignal, 1.4F (documents particuliers) (écoles: 1890–1921), AAO.

54 François Lombard to Duhamel, 13 March 1892, Alfred:, 1.4B (documents particuliers) (écoles: 1877–1949), AAO.

55 These reports are filed as Alfred, 1.4B (documents particuliers) (écoles: 1877–1949), AAO; and L'Orignal 1.4F (documents particuliers) (écoles: 1890–1921), AAO.

56 Xavier Gauthier to Duhamel, 22 February 1893, Alfred, 1.4B (documents particuliers) (écoles: 1877–1949) AAO.

57 François Lombard to Duhamel, 3 March 1893, ibid.

58 Lombard to Duhamel, 25 September 1893, ibid.

59 For example, Lombard to Alexis Huitouburgh, 26 September, 1893, ibid.

60 Bérubé to Duhamel, 3 February 1894, L'Orignal, 1.4F (documents particuliers) (écoles; 1890–1921), AAO.

61 Alfred, I.4B (documents particuliers) (écoles: 1877–1949), AAO.
62 Telegrams between Lombard and Duhamel, February 1894, Alfred, I.4B (documents particuliers) (écoles: 1877–1949), AAO.
63 Receipts for $51.26 (28 December 1896) and $90 (30 December 1896) for funds from Duhamel to pay debt of separate school at No. 4, ibid.
64 *Report of Commissioners (*1893), 32; and, for later in the century, "Rapport des écoles de la Paroisse St. Jean-Baptiste, L'Orignal, pour 1898," L'Orignal, I.4F (documents particuliers) (écoles: 1890–1921), AAO.
65 Alfred, I.4B (documents particuliers) (écoles: 1877–1949), AAO. The writers of this letter represented the core of anglophone settlement which had originated in Alfred Township during the 1830s and 1840s; John McCusker et al. to the Archbishop of Ottawa, 1898.
66 A comparative historical perspective on this issue is suggested by the experience of Roman Catholic schooling in the United States. By the late nineteenth century, French-language parochial schools were rapidly increasing in New England. At the same time, parochial schools were also growing dramatically in Irish and German neighbourhoods; while some bilingual programs were established in German-speaking areas, the language of instruction was not an issue in many of these schools. Thus, the formation of Catholic schools did not depend only on perceived threats to minority-language groups.

An overview of the United States experience is provided in *Harvard Encyclopedia of American Ethnic Groups* (Cambridge, Mass.: Harvard University Press 1980), s.v. "education." For a revealing case study, see David A. Gerber, "Language Maintenance, Ethnic Group Formation, and Public Schools: Changing Patterns of German Concern, Buffalo, 1837–1874," *Journal of American Ethnic History* 4, no. 1 (Fall 1984): 31–61. Also see Murray W. Nicolson, "Irish Catholic Education in Victorian Toronto: An Ethnic Response to Urban Conformity," *Histoire sociale/Social History* 17, no. 34 (November 1984): 287–306.
67 See Séguin, *La conquête du sol,* chap. 9. Also see René Hardy and Jean Roy, "Encadrement social et mutation de la culture religieuse en Mauricie," *Questions de Culture* 5 (1983): 61–78; and Benoît Lacroix and Jean Simard, eds., *Religion populaire: religion de clercs?* (Quebec: Institut Québécois de recherche sur la culture 1984).
68 Séguin, *La conquête du sol,* chap. 9; and Gagnon and Hardy, eds., *L'église et le village.*
69 Inspectors' reports, Roman Catholic Separate Schools, Education Department Ontario, RG 2, F-3-F, PAO.
70 East Hawkesbury, No. 2 and Alfred, No. 3, December 1883, ibid.
71 East Hawkesbury, No. 7, June 1890; and No. 4, December 1883, ibid; and Alfred, No. 3, December 1883, ibid.
72 Longueuil, No. 7, June 1890, and South Plantagenet, June 1890, ibid.

CHAPTER SEVEN

1 N. Ray Hiner, "Domestic Cycles: History of Childhood and Family," in John Hardin Best, ed., *Historical Inquiry in Education: A Research Agenda* (Washington, D.C.: American Educational Research Association 1983), 272.

2 *Census of Canada, 1901* (Ottawa: S. E. Dawson 1902), viii, xx. Criticism of this vague instruction led to different questions in the next enumeration. The wording has changed with almost every census, but the problem still remains unsolved.

3 Only in recent years have scholars turned attention to the study of rural ethnic communities. Kathleen Neils Conzen's work has been especially important in this regard. See her "Historical Approaches to the Study of Rural Ethnic Communities," in Frederik C. Luebke, ed., *Ethnicity on the Great Plains* (Lincoln, Neb. and London: University of Nebraska Press 1980), 1–18.

4 Although Canadian historians have traditionally emphasized the importance of family and kinship among French Canadians, they have only recently given similar attention to these factors among English Canadians. However, many studies now emphasize that ethnic stability has been substantial in both Canada and the United States and that family and kinship have been instrumental in maintaining this stability. The traditional Canadian historiography is addressed directly by way of Prescott County experience in Chad M. Gaffield, "Canadian Families in Cultural Context: Hypotheses from the Mid-Nineteenth Century," Canadian Historical Association, *Historical Papers* (1979), 48–70. The emergence and vitality of the journal *Canadian Ethnic Studies* testifies to the increasing acceptance of cultural continuity in Canadian history. Also see *Polyphony*, published by the Multicultural History Society of Ontario under the direction of Robert F. Harney. It was in this journal, for example, that Pierre Loranger discussed L'Union du Canada, the first French-Canadian mutual-aid society in Ontario, which strongly emphasized the connection between material security and cultural security; see "La revue de l'Union du Canada 1895–1941; défenseur de la langue française," *Polyphony* 2 (Winter 1979).

5 The role of the common schools in maintaining non-British-Isles-origin cultures in Ontario was certainly not appreciated in the nineteenth century and is still not fully recognized by historians. The thrust of the revisionist studies of the 1970s concerned the assimilative ambitions of people like Egerton Ryerson, rather than the extent to which these ambitions were fulfilled; in this sense, only half of the story was told. The importance of considering both intentions and achievements is suggested in R. D. Gidney and D. A. Lawr, "Bureaucracy vs. Com-

munity? The Origins of Bureaucratic Procedure in the Upper Canadian Schools," *Journal of Social History* 13, no. 3 (Spring 1980): 438–57; and idem, "Who Ran the Schools? Local Influence on Education Policy in Nineteenth-Century Ontario," *Ontario History* 72, no. 3 (September 1980): 131–43.

6 Language was, of course, very important in the lumber industry, where teamwork was essential both to production and individual safety. For this reason, workers tended to be grouped by language. Sometimes this grouping did not occur. For example, one francophone in Quebec in the 1930s vividly remembered his own experience decades earlier: "At nineteen I went to the *chantier* with my brother. We had never been out before. At the first camp we were with a lot of English. We could not understand them, and they could not understand us ... If I had ever had any experience in the *chantier*, it would not have been so hard to understand the directions they gave me in English ... The second year we understood a little and it was better. It was not the wood which was difficult but the language." "The Autobiography of an *Habitant*," in Horace Miner, *St. Denis: A French-Canadian Parish* (Chicago: University of Chicago Press 1939; Phoenix edition 1963), 279–80. F. W. Remiggi pursues the connection between historical geography and cultural relations in his "Quelques origines spatiales du présent conflit francophone-anglophone au Québec: exemple de la Basse-Côte-Nord," *Cahiers de Géographie du Québec* 24, no. 61 (April 1980): 157–66.

7 The absence of labour organization is striking particularly, during the 1880s when the Knights of Labor attracted widespread support; see Gregory Kealey and Bryan Palmer, *Dreaming of What Might Be: The Knights of Labor in Ontario* (New York: Cambridge University Press 1982); and Fernand Harvey, "Les Chevaliers du Travail, les Etats-Unis et la société québécoise, 1882–1902," in Fernand Harvey, ed., *Aspects historiques du mouvement ouvrier au Québec* (Montreal: Boréal Express 1979). An analysis of a lumber industry strike up the Ottawa River is provided in Edward McKenna, "Unorganized Labour versus Management: The Strike at the Chaudière Lumber Mills, 1891," *Histoire sociale/Social History* 5, no. 10 (November 1972): 186–211.

8 In 1901, the Ontario census district with the heaviest concentration of French-Canadian settlement was Nipissing, where 15,384 French Canadians made up 42 per cent of the district's population. Research on northern French-Canadian settlement is often reported in the *Revue du Nouvel Ontario*.

9 Social psychologists have long emphasized that the presence of barriers to communication is an important condition in encouraging prejudice and cultural alienation. A classic work on the interrelationships of

cultural patterns and social structure is Gordon W. Allport, *The Nature of Prejudice* (Reading, Mass.: Addison-Wesley 1954), especially chap. 14. The social psychology of cultural identities in Canada is largely unexplored, although a provocative approach is suggested in W. Peter Archibald, *Social Psychology as Political Economy* (Toronto: McGraw-Hill 1978), 229–47. Also see Robert C. Gardner and Rudolf Kolin, eds., *A Canadian Social Psychology of Ethnic Relations* (Toronto: Methuen 1981); and Alan B. Anderson and James S. Frideres, *Ethnicity in Canada: Theoretical Perspectives* (Toronto: Butterworth 1981).

10 John J. MacLaren, letter to the editor, Toronto *Globe*, 15 March 1889. This Prescott County evidence particularly emphasizes the extent to which the pursuit of self-respect and self-esteem is a crucial dynamic of the experience of minority groups. With specific reference to the worth of French as a language in Ontario, see Loranger, "La revue de l'Union du Canada."

The potential parallels between Franco-Ontarians' changing attitudes toward language during the late nineteenth century and developments in Quebec from the 1960s on can be explored by implication in books such as Denis Monière, *Le développement des idéologies au Québec: des origines à nos jours*, (Montreal: Editions Québec/Amérique 1977); Dale C. Thomson, ed., *Quebec Society and Politics: Views from the Inside* (Toronto: McClelland and Stewart 1973); Dale Posgate and Kenneth McRoberts, eds., *Quebec: Social Change and Political Crisis* (Toronto: McClelland and Stewart 1976); and Calvin Veltman, ed., *Contemporary Quebec* (Montreal: Les Presses de l'université du Québec à Montréal 1982).

11 The relationship between knowledge and intercultural attitudes has not been systematically explored in historical contexts, but Robert Choquette makes clear that, in late-nineteenth-century Ontario, mutual ignorance cannot be held fully responsible for the high-level political and ecclesiastical struggles between English and French Canadians; see *Language and Religion: A History of English-French Conflict in Ontario* (Ottawa: University of Ottawa Press 1975).

12 For a similar emphasis on the importance of realistic preceptions of conflict in explaining cultural attitudes, see Patricia Roy, "British Columbia's Fear of Asians 1900–1950," *Histoire sociale/Social History* 13, no. 25 (May 1980): 161–72. Roy argues that the extent of fear about the "Oriental Menace" may have been "irrational" but "Asians provided sufficient, effective competition in the fishing grounds, in the fields, in the market place, in the classrooms, and on the battlefield to warrant deep fears about the ability of white British Columbians to maintain their dominant position in the province," p. 161.

13 Of course it would be wrong to conclude that the cultural challenge

of the late nineteenth century severed all amiable relations between English and French Canadians in Prescott County. In fact, routine exchanges of goods and services continued as part of everyday life. For example, François Deslauriers cut Thomas Tweed Higginson's hair, "making a nice job" in preparation for the Christmas season of 1900. Thomas Tweed Higginson, *Diaries of Thomas Tweed Higginson*, ed. Thomas Boyd Higginson (London: The Research Publishing Company 1960), 85.

14 The nature of cultural discontinuity and its relationship to social structure has become a central focus of historical research. For a discussion of certain aspects of this development, see Patrick H. Hutton, "The History of Mentalities: The New Map of Cultural History," *History and Theory* 20, no. 3 (Summer 1981): 237–59. Examples of cultural conflict in Canada are numerous during the late nineteenth and early twentieth centuries. The political histories of such conflict have been well studied in books such as J.R. Miller, *Equal Rights: The Jesuits' Estates Act Controversy* (Montreal: McGill-Queen's University Press 1979), 297. The extent of cultural conflict is suggested in the articles collected in Craig Brown, ed., *Minorities, Schools, and Politics* (Toronto: University of Toronto Press 1969).

15 Comparative perspectives on this phenomenon are offered in D.R. Louder and Eric Waddell, eds., *Du continent perdu à l'archipel retrouvé* (Québec : Les Presses de l'université Laval 1983).

16 G.W. Ross, *The School System of Ontario* (New York: D. Appleton 1896) 67–9.

17 The ecclesiastical and political aspects of this conflict are examined by Paul Crunican, *Priests and Politicians: Manitoba Schools and the Election of 1896* (Toronto: University of Toronto Press 1974).

APPENDIX

1 Michael J. Doucet, "Discriminant Analysis and the Delineation of Household Structure: Towards a Solution to the Boarder/Relative Problem in the 1871 Canadian Census," *Historical Methods Newsletter* 10, no. 4 (Fall 1977): 149–57.

2 The literature on record linkage is extensive including E.A. Wrigley, ed., *Identifying People in the Past* (London: Edward Arnold 1973); Ian Winchester, "The Linkage of Historical Records by Man and Computer: Techniques and Problems," *Journal of Interdisciplinary History* 1, no. 1 (Autumn 1970); 107–24; idem, "Priorities for Record Linkage: A Theoretical and Practical Checklist," in Jerome M. Clubb and Erwin K. Scheuch, eds., *Historical Social Research: The Use of Historical and Process-Produced Data* (Stuttgart: Klett-Cotta 1980), 414–30; Jacques

Légaré, André LaRose, and Raymond Roy, "Reconstitution de la population canadienne au XVIIe: méthodes et bilan d'une recherche," *Recherches sociographiques* 14, no. 3 (September-December 1973): 383–400; and Gérard Bouchard and Patrick Brard, "Le programme de reconstitution automatique des familles saguenayennes: données de base et résultats provisoires," *Histoire sociale/Social History* 12, no. 23 (May 1979): 170–85.

3 For an example of this strategy, see Michael B. Katz, *The People of Hamilton, Canada West: Family and Class in a Mid-Nineteenth Century City* (Cambridge, Mass.: Harvard 1975), appendix 3. David Gagan, who used the same system, which Ian Winchester devised for the Hamilton project, reported special problems with Scottish surnames which were rendered in "bewildering variations" in Peel County; see *Hopeful Travellers: Families, Land, and Social Change in Mid-Victorian Peel County, Canada West* (Toronto: University of Toronto Press 1981), 178–9, no. 39. Record linkage problems are also discussed in Douglas Sprague and Ronald Frye, "Manitoba's Red River Settlement: Manuscript Sources for Economic and Demographic History," *Archivaria* no. 9 (Winter 1979–80): 179–93.

4 Gérard Bouchard's project on the Saguenay has been especially important in advancing the literature on record linkage; see Raymond Roy, Christian Pouyez, and François Martin, "Le jumelage des donnés nominatives dans les recensements: problèmes et méthodes," *Histoire sociale/Social History* 13, no. 25 (May 1980): 173–93; and Gérard Bouchard and Christian Pouyez, "Name Variations and Computerized Record Linkage," *Historical Methods* 13, no. 2 (Spring 1980): 119–25. Also see the problems raised in Myron P. Gutmann, "The Future of Record Linkage in History," *Journal of Family History* 21, no. 2 (Summer 1977): 151–58.

Index

Adolescents. *See* Children

Advertiser, The, 147, 150

Age distribution: in marriage patterns, 48, 56; of child-bearing, 49, 57; of home-leaving, 50; of farmers and labourers, 64, 92; of shantymen, 80; of school enrolment, 103, 108, 123; and infant baptisms, 160

Agriculture: work, 66–7; production, 79–82; farm size, 82; markets, 79–82, 83–7; dairy production, 90

Agricultural societies, 90

Agricultural traditions, 70–2

Akenson, Donald Harman, 14–15

Alfred Township: school quality in, 17–20; British-Isles-origin settlement of, 34–9; ethnic identity of British-Isles-origin residents of, 40; francophone settlement of, 40–4; persistence of residence in, 45–6, 51; marriage patterns in, 47–8, 56; family size in, 49, 57; home-leaving in, 50; farmers and labourers in, 64, 92; lot sizes in, 77; agricultural production in, 81; improved land in, 82; school enrolment in, 103, 108, 123, 125; school location in, 106; turnover of teachers in, 118; French-language schools in, 122; elections in, 138; 144. *See also* St-Victor-d'Alfred

Allen Settlement, 36

American immigrants, 36

Anglican Church. *See* Church of England

Anglophones. *See* British-Isles-origin population

Argenteuil County, 181–2

Artisans, 65–6, 124–5

Associations, voluntary, 139. *See also* St Jean Baptiste Society

Atlantic Canada: birthplace in, 36